# HOW TO OPEN AND OPERATE
## A HOME-BASED
## WRITING BUSINESS

# HOW TO OPEN AND OPERATE
# A HOME-BASED
# WRITING BUSINESS

by Lucy V. Parker

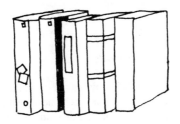

OLD SAYBROOK, CONNECTICUT

Copyright © 1994 by Lucy V. Parker

All rights reserved. No part of this book may be reproduced or transmitted in any form by any means, electronic or mechanical, including photocopying and recording, or by any information storage and retrieval system, except as may be expressly permitted by the 1976 Copyright Act or by the publisher. Requests for permission should be made in writing to The Globe Pequot Press, P.O. Box 833, Old Saybrook, Connecticut 06475.

Cover and text illustrations by Kathy Michalove

**Library of Congress Cataloging-in-Publication Data**
Parker, Lucy V.
    How to open and operate a home-based writing business / by Lucy V. Parker. — 1st ed.
        p.   cm.
    Includes bibliographical references.
    ISBN 1-56440-396-3
    1. Authorship—Marketing. 2. Desktop publishing. 3. Home-based businesses. I. Title.
    PN153.P37 1994
    808'.02—dc20                                   93-48966
                                                        CIP

Manufactured in the United States of America
First Edition/First Printing

*For Mike*

# Contents

*This book's purpose is to provide accurate and authoritative information on the topics covered. It is sold with the understanding that neither the author nor the publisher is engaged in rendering legal, financial, accounting, or other professional services. Neither the Globe Pequot Press nor the author assumes any liability resulting from action taken based on the information included herein. Mention of a company name does not constitute endorsement.*

# Acknowledgments

My thanks to Betsy Amster, of Betsy Amster Literary Enterprises, Los Angeles, for suggesting this book and having faith in me as its author, and to my editor, Mace Lewis, at The Globe Pequot Press. Thanks also to the ten professionals who gave generously of their time and experience to provide profiles for this book and to the many other writers and desktop publishers I talked with in doing my research. Newsletter design consultant Polly Pattison of Westminster, CA, provided much-appreciated advice and resources. Thanks to sales trainer John Klymshyn of Palmdale, CA, and creative services consultant Maria Piscopo of Costa Mesa, CA, for permission to draw on their material. Special thanks for reviewing sections of this book go to Derek Anderson, Sports Information Director, Chapman University, Orange, CA; Wayne Kaplan of CompTutor Desktop Publishing Services, Huntington Beach, CA (one of the professionals profiled); and my son, Michael B. Parker of Parker Consulting, Menlo Park, CA. Any errors that may remain are mine, not theirs.

# Introduction

## Three Ways to Use This Book

1. **Leaf through the pages.**

   You'll see that writing and desktop publishing from a home office can be a viable and profitable venture—and you will be encouraged to start your own home business.

2. **Skim for specific information.**

   Study the "hidden market" for writing and desktop publishing jobs listed in chapter three, along with the list of potential clients; the marketing techniques described in chapter seven; the sales techniques discussed in chapter eight; and the pricing strategies explained in chapter nine. You'll get new ideas about services to sell and proven, effective ways to market and price them.

3. **If you are really serious about starting your own home business as a writer or desktop publisher, read chapter one this week.**

   Then line up one or more mentors—friends or associates *who have been successful at running a creative home business for several years.* If you don't know an appropriate mentor, see if you can get an introduction to one. Most people enjoy helping others by sharing their experiences.

   Over the next two months or so, read chapters two through ten—one chapter each week. Dip into the source directory and make notes on the worksheets. Then meet on a designated day for an hour with one of your mentors to discuss that week's topic and your own plans. If weekly meetings seem too frequent, try meeting every other week or once a month. It's not unusual to spend a year or more planning a new home business.

Do you know any other writers or desktop publishers who are thinking about starting their own business? If so, consider inviting them to join your meetings. In my experience, "making it seem real" is one of the biggest hurdles to clear in starting a business. These discussions will help you leap that hurdle, while providing useful information and personal feedback. Remember that you must *always* take feedback with a grain of salt, comparing several opinions and measuring them against your own judgment.

After you have completed the reading, research, and planning involved in chapters one through ten, sit down and write your strategic business plan. Share it with everyone involved, including your spouse or significant other. If appropriate, use it to obtain loans and leases. Then follow the directions for keeping your strategic business plan up-to-date as your business gets under way.

While your plans are taking shape, treat your mentors to a good meal or some other favor. Good businesspeople always acknowledge favors and pay professional debts promptly—although the best repayment you can make for this help will be to advise some fledgling writer or desktop publisher years from now, when you are well established.

# 1

# Getting Started as a Home-Based Writer and Desktop Publisher

"Until you make it, fake it."
That's what they say.
"Until you make it, fake it."
There is no other way.

I don't mean "buy a new Mercedes"
If the payments would come hard.
I don't mean "put three-hundred-dollar dresses
On your MasterCard."

But fake a little confidence—
Just fake the way you feel.
'Cause fakin' now will teach you how
And soon it will be real.

# "Until You Make It, Fake It"

No, these lyrics never made it to the "top 40." But composing it and other topical ditties kept me in touch with writing as I drove the southern California freeways, tape recorder in hand, calling on my printing sales clients during the early 1980s. Supporting myself as an outside sales rep was part of my plan to make the transition from higher education public relations to freelance writing and graphic designing. And it worked.

This particular selection from my heretofore unpublished and unproduced "Sales Success Song Cycle" may help you, too, as you step off the diving board into your own home-based writing and desktop publishing business.

Let me share a secret: At first, it doesn't seem real. You may even feel as though you are pretending to be in business—an imposter "playing office" with a toy telephone and a kiddie computer. That's OK. Don't worry about it. *"Until you make it, fake it."*

Acting like a professional will set you apart from equally talented writers and graphic designers who, in reality, are between jobs—who don't have a compelling vision of themselves as self-employed and won't be there in two years when a client wants them to rewrite or redesign an early project.

You *will* be there to handle such an assignment! By that time, you will have become a real entrepreneur—part of the vast small-business backbone of every free economy. You will be a real businessperson with real clients, real jobs to do, real cash flow, real equipment that probably needs upgrading, and dreams that are really coming true.

I did it—and so can you!

# How I got Started as a Home-based Entrepreneur

No one in my immediate family had ever worked for anything but large employers—the Chicago school system, United States Steel, the U.S. Department of Agriculture, the Navy—that kind of employer, that size. It was my former husband's Naval career that brought us to California from the Midwest, and I went to work for the state university system. It was all I knew—benefits, a monthly paycheck, security in numbers.

If you have a relative who is self-employed, count yourself lucky, and start soaking up small business ambiance in Cousin Harry's restaurant or Aunt Betty's beauty salon. Virtually my entire career after graduating from Northwestern University's Medill School of Journalism had been spent in public relations, publications, and grant writing for public and private colleges and universities. Not only did I know nothing about self-employment, I knew nothing about business itself.

In 1975 my experience as the public relations representative and journalism instructor on a semester-long study voyage to Europe, the Middle East, Africa, South America, and the Caribbean forever changed my typically academic, out-of-touch view of business. Until that mind-blowing three months at sea, I had irrationally (but conveniently) conceived of the business world as being overwhelming on the one hand and unworthy of my efforts on the other. Seeing street vendors in every culture we visited—so like the swap meet culture then emerging in the United States—demolished my ivory tower perspective. It made me understand that business—*the exchange of goods and services*—is a basic endeavor that sustains and will always be part of human life.

As my new understanding evolved, I began to dream of freelancing and controlling my own schedule. In 1978, I sold an op-ed piece to the *Los Angeles Times* about a liberated single mom (me) taking a part-time vacation to see how staying home would feel (heavenly).

"Perhaps our work-crazy American system, even with its incredible wealth, just can't allow institutional time to become human time," I concluded. "We single mothers, juggling the demands on us, may be only the tip of an iceberg of discontent— the frenzied fringe of an entire generation that is frantic to earn more and more money looking for Mr. Goodlife. . . . In my own case, it's taken me [years] to catch on, but finally I stopped racing long enough to smell my rosebush this morning."

Leaving my college job in 1980, I made a 180-degree turn to outside commissioned sales. As a printing buyer in higher education, I had watched scores of sales reps make their pitch and thought: "I could do that." I knew the move was transitional, but I decided that outside sales would teach me about the business world and force me to structure my time.

Well, I still struggle with structuring my time (Charles Hobbs's *Time Power* tapes and my Day-Timer have helped). But I did learn to feel at home in both large and small corporations, and I did achieve an understanding of what business is about. I built a printing clientele largely through networking in professional organizations, and I helped my clients by designing and editing for them on the side. When I made the leap to full-time freelancing in 1986, my printing clients provided a base.

While sadly many of my corporate friends have learned that in a downsizing economy, their professional loyalty does not guarantee them job security, I'm glad I have learned to scramble and survive. In addition to providing me with a financial cushion during a recession, my home-based business has also improved my sense of physical well-being. For years, in high-pressure public relations work and occasionally during a printing sales crisis, I got terrible headaches. I couldn't help noticing that periods of extra stress were often followed by periods of pain. In the eight years I have been self-employed, I've experienced lots of stressful deadlines, but almost no headaches. I'm not sure why. I guess I just feel more comfortable with stress I can control.

# Why Work at Home?

Why *not* work at home? Especially if you can earn a good living, be your own boss, and work on projects you enjoy. Today, in the words of management expert Tom Peters, "We're in the midst of an earthshaking change in the way business gets done." In 1900,

Peters reports, 50 percent of U.S. workers were self-employed. With the rise of giant corporations, that number had shrunk to 7 percent by 1977. You are part of the small business revival which is slowly reversing that trend. By 1993, Peters states, 13 percent of our work force was self-employed.

And the number of people working at home is rising, too. According to Link Resources, which tracks home workers, 33 million people (both self-employed and those working for others) were working at home in 1990, up 22 percent from the year before.

Computers, faxes, modems, and E-mail have made home-based communications services not only feasible for writers and graphic designers but very convenient. Today a well-run home office is every bit as professional as a cubicle in some high-rise business center—and a lot handier for *you*. But there's still another reason to work at home. If you can avoid the pitfalls of home business (see "Tips for Managing Your Business and Yourself" in Chapter Ten), your costs will be significantly less than those of your competitors, who must add office rent, utilities, and employee benefits to the basic expenses of equipment, supplies, and marketing. That makes you an economical alternative— exactly what clients are looking for.

The layoffs and downsizing of the early nineties have caused both pain and pleasure for creative workers. Companies and organizations everywhere are seeking to meet their writing and design needs without maintaining a staff of writers and graphic designers who draw salaries whether they're busy or not, and whose skills may not be well suited for every project.

The down side of this situation is well summarized by the following example. One successful writer I interviewed for this book told me about a friend who had been working full-time for a national publishing firm, producing a newsletter. The company abruptly laid the editor off, and, in less than a week, hired the dazed woman back to continue putting out the newsletter—for less money and with no benefits. She accepted, thinking it might be the start of a freelance career, but with no preparation for freelancing and a near full-time job producing the newsletter, she was not finding time to organize or market her business.

With the help of this book and your own research and planning, you can avoid such a trap and tap into what I call "the hidden market" for writing and desktop publishing: businesses, government agencies, retailers, restaurants, hotels, hospitals, professional groups, universities, and many other local clients who buy services like yours in every community.

Of course, these clients could and often do meet their needs by hiring an advertising, public relations, marketing, or design agency—but they can't do it at the prices *you* can charge working out of your home!

The result? With effective marketing and a professional approach, you can gain important and lucrative jobs from very large clients—sometimes snatching them away from well-established agencies and sometimes serving as an agency subcontractor. I've done both—and so can you!

# What Kinds of Writing and Desktop Publishing Jobs Are We Talking About?

Throughout this book, we are talking about assignments you can realistically expect to receive as a new freelance writer or desktop designer—assignments that are available to you in most communities and can add up to a full-time income.

We're talking about such meat-and-potatoes jobs as producing newsletters, product sheets, brochures, and letterhead or logo designs; and creating press releases and press kits, ad copy, speeches, and trade journal and company magazine articles. We're talking about developing instructional and technical manuals, creating audiovisual and video scripts, editing and ghost-writing, even writing resumés.

In other words, this book will teach you how to be your own boss while doing what other writers and graphic designers do in salaried positions. Being your own boss is a big achievement—the goal of a lifetime for many people. But if your dreams go further, *keep those dreams!* One of the benefits of being a home-based freelancer is the opportunity to do personal creative projects— and as a businessperson, you'll make every creative project profitable if you can.

It's true that some writers support themselves at home writing novels, movie scripts, or articles for national magazines, and some home-based graphic designers make a living designing record jackets and gorgeous posters. Aim high, and while you grow, let meat-and-potatoes jobs pay the bills.

Perhaps your dreams are more entrepreneurial: You'd like a high-profit home business writing and producing your own products for sale to retailers, business buyers, or consumers. Examples might be a line of greeting cards, a subscription newsletter, a series of independently published books. Such ventures require additional capital but can significantly increase your return on money and time invested. Many of the business practices you'll learn in this book will help you if you decide to go in that direction.

# What this Book Offers— and Assumes

In addition to describing the kinds of jobs that are available, this book explains how to set up your business and your office, how to market and sell, and what to charge—with worksheets to help you develop and evaluate your plans. I started my freelance career when the home-based business was less recognized as a significant entrepreneurial option. But because of the current business trend toward downsizing and hiring freelancers, you're starting at a very good time—with more credibility and many more resources.

I am assuming that you already know your craft—how to write and do desktop publishing. But what if you only know one skill or the other?

In that case, I invite you to *consider* doing both, if you have the talent and interest. But even more important, I urge you to *offer* both services to your clients from the start by building relationships with other freelancers.

## How to use the business success worksheets

When you have completed the Business Success Worksheets, which accompany each chapter, pull your notes together for the final section of Chapter 10, "Writing Your Strategic Business Plan." With the exception of specific financial data about your individual costs and resources, you will have everything you need to write your business plan.

# I Understand "Writing," but Just What *Is* "Desktop Publishing"?

Desktop publishing is an inspired marketing term, but something of a misnomer. It's not really publishing in the sense that a book, magazine, or software publisher produces and markets a product. For the purposes of this book, I define desktop publishing as *the process of combining text and graphics into page layouts on a computer screen and outputting the pages on a laser printer or other imaging system so that they are ready for reproduction.*

In my opinion, the new access that we have to affordable professional typesetting and page layout tools through the use of a microcomputer qualifies as one of the most important developments in the history of the printed word. Many of us in the communications field have practiced this new technology, learned the rules, and can now fly with unprecedented freedom and creativity.

Unfortunately, desktop publishing has been oversold. "Just buy our products," say the ads, "and you can produce your own instant newsletters and brochures!" Like good writing, good design takes talent, skill, and experience—not just good hardware and software. That's why we are in business!

# The Case for Combining Writing and Desktop Publishing

Since its introduction in the mid-eighties, desktop publishing software has revolutionized prepress print production. More recently, software for producing slides and overhead transparencies and multi-media software, which combines video and sound with text and graphics, have launched similar revolutions in the areas of spoken and audiovisual presentations. Thus, for virtually every graphic product, the creation of content and appearance has become a nearly seamless process. Using today's software, it's just another program on the computer to move from text to finished graphics—whether the final product will be printed material or an audiovisual presentation.

As a result of this new technology, more and more clients expect to make a one-stop purchase—and if you can offer a one-stop service, you will get more business. It's as simple as that. By dealing with only one vendor—you—your buyer can save time and money.

Being able to handle all phases of the writing and production process is also helpful when clients want to share their files with you. For example, many clients give me text files, using either disk or modem, and my task is to turn the text into a newsletter or brochure. Usually, writing headlines and captions is part of the job, which sometimes involves editing as well.

For one major corporation, I write short articles and send them via modem to their staff designer. This way the firm avoids paying a secretary to rekeyboard what I have written.

In other words, both writers and graphic designers *must* be computer literate. But that doesn't mean you should try to sell both writing and desktop design unless you can do both well. Today the business world is bandying about a new buzzword: "virtual corporations." Virtual corporations are temporary networks of companies brought together for a specific project. These entities reflect a key business trend of the nineties: partnering. When market opportunities appear, companies are finding it faster and less costly to partner with other businesses than to develop additional expertise in-house.

This is what home-based creative professionals have been doing all along. When we have a project that requires special skills, we draw on a group of trusted colleagues.

It's kind of neat to be in the vanguard of American business practice. Maybe some home-based writers and designers should be lecturing to Harvard M.B.A. candidates.

# Resources for Gaining Skills You Don't Now Have

If you want to become a professional writer or desktop publisher but are not at that level now, accept the fact that gaining these new skills will take serious effort and time. We are not talking about going back to college to earn a new degree or spending years learning on the job, but we *are* talking about steady concentration, practice, evaluation, and revision—a solid learning process.

There are ways to short-circuit traditional methods of mastering a craft and build the sense of authority you need in order to offer your services to the public. One is to focus very specifically on learning how to design or write only the type of thing you most want to sell—or that is most often called for by the clients you serve. As you scan the many types of writing or desktop publishing discussed in Chapter Three, ask yourself which of these you might learn to do. Once your skills in that area reach a professional level, you can concentrate on adding others.

I have a degree in journalism, I've taken endless workshops and seminars, and I've racked up some thirty years of experience as a writer, but there are still areas of writing—profitable ones— that I pass up when they are offered to me because I don't feel I do them well. Offering for sale only what you do well is professional. Offering to write or design "anything" and charging your clients for it is amateur behavior at best.

## Classes and workshops

Looking for classes in writing or graphic design? Try community colleges and evening adult schools first. Costs are minimal and over a semester's time you will become familiar with the material, even if the instructor is not commercially oriented. You can also take a class to brush up on basics, such as grammar or computer techniques.

Your computer instructor—as well as any desktop publishers you meet—will be happy to advise you on what equipment to buy or where you can rent desktop publishing equipment. Ask them. Also read computer catalogs and magazines. The only thing you must never do as a desktop publishing novice is show up at a computer store with your checkbook open, relying on the salesperson to equip you—unless, of course, you want to get rid of excess cash.

Once you've mastered the basics, advanced courses at a local professional school or university might be your next step. In the meantime, watch for short-term workshops and seminars. Some are priced in the Fortune 500 stratosphere, but others are more affordable. If you are not on mailing lists for such offerings, check with your library or computer store. And don't be too shy to ask professionals in the field—advertisers, public relations practitioners, corporate communicators, graphic designers. These worthy souls get seminar mailings by the bushel and should be only too glad to pass them on to you.

## Personal coaching and observation

Personal coaching and observation are like a self-administered internship. A local, non-competing professional may let you observe for free and might even let you help in her office or studio if you are willing to commit serious time to the project. This can be a good way to get feedback from a professional on your early efforts.

For an ongoing coaching arrangement, however, expect to pay a reasonable consulting fee. It's an uncommon, but totally natural way for someone in your situation to learn—by spending time, one-on-one, with someone who knows a lot about what you are studying. Approach people who are active in their professional associations—a good indication of their desire to help others.

A variant on this idea, in the graphics area, is to visit places where the work you are interested in is being done. List the kinds of vendors you may be using—such as desktop publishing service bureaus, commercial typesetters, graphic film shops, lettershops, commercial printers—and arrange to tour typical establishments. Some firms will give you a tour just because you ask for it. If that doesn't work, perhaps a regular customer could arrange for you to visit. To help understand the process, ask to be shown the steps a job takes as it goes through the shop. Ask to be shown examples of good and bad work and have the differences between the two explained. Ask what you, as a graphic designer, can do to make it easier for the vendor to serve you and to save money.

## Volunteer projects

Get your feet wet as soon as possible by doing volunteer writing or design projects. You can learn much more from planning and completing a real project than from doing a made up one—and you don't need professional level skills to volunteer as a writer or desktop publisher. Your church, club, or fraternal organization will be grateful for whatever you come up with. Then call on the network of professionals you are establishing to critique your work and find out how you could have made it better. Save your best volunteer efforts to start your personal sample file.

## Reading and sample collecting

Read. Read. Read. The bibliography in this book will start you off. Rely on periodicals to give you the "feel" of the specialty you want to master, reveal current trends, and point out major players. Rely on books to give you solid historical and technical grounding. Ask the writers or desktop publishers you respect what books and periodicals they find useful.

From the moment you decide to master your new skill, start collecting samples of work you like. As you gain more theory and experience, ask yourself why a particular piece works. Sometimes it's a good idea to collect samples of work you don't like, too. You can't help but develop a better sense of design if you keep your eyes open.

# What's Your Next Step? Ways to Get Started

The sooner you start making concrete plans for your new business, the sooner you will be a full-time home-based writer or desktop publisher. If you are already or have at one time been self-employed, you must still make the transition to a new type of business. But you are far ahead of the game! For most of us who are accustomed to working for a monthly paycheck, the transition is long and complex, often as wrenching as it is exhilarating. But careful planning can help. And that includes a written schedule projecting what steps you will take and when you will take them.

## Starting part-time vs. full-time

Some writers and desktop publishers have started out by combining part-time regular employment and part-time freelancing. Others have established an "outsource" relationship with their present employers, continuing to do the same work, but as an independent contractor. I used commissioned sales to nudge me toward freelancing, and I was emboldened to leave selling when one of my printing clients offered me the equivalent of a half-time salary to carry out a specific writing project. That was the "nut" I knew I must have to pay the bills for the next few months.

Dividing your time between freelancing and regular employment probably takes its biggest toll on your marketing efforts. It's hard (but possible) to push into new market areas and follow up every lead, when four or more hours a day are committed elsewhere. For this reason, some writers and desktop publishers take the instant full-time plunge, relying on savings or a loan or another family member's income to survive.

## Financing

Desktop publishers, who require a much larger investment in equipment than writers, sometimes obtain a formal business loan to finance their start-up efforts. But more typically, both writers and desktop publishers finance their initial costs from current income or savings or through help from a family member. The talented director Spike Lee is reported to have financed his early films on credit cards. That takes guts or maybe desperation, but I don't recommend it for commercial writers or desktop publishers. A more conventional option is to borrow on your home or to liquidate or borrow on other assets—but consider this option carefully and use it as a last resort.

## Getting some money coming in

I believe it is far better to get some small amount of real business income trickling in as soon as possible—income you can (and probably must) use to pay the light bill or the dentist—than to draw on a savings account temporarily fattened by a mortgage loan. That borrowed money isn't real. You didn't scramble and sweat for it, and it's more likely than earned money to go for an elegant oak desk or an elaborate capability brochure. Wait to buy those refinements with income from your new career. Your business will be a lot healthier for it!

## Health insurance (and peace of mind)

If you are in reasonably good health, giving up your employee benefits is nothing like the big deal many salaried people fear when they consider self-employment. You can replace all your necessary benefits at relatively affordable rates. It may be a jolt to your budget at first, but I've done it and so have millions of others.

Health insurance policies, including traditional fee-for-service plans with an annual deductible, preferred provider plans, and health maintenance organizations, are widely available to individuals. Typically, these plans provide basic care, but not the bells and whistles of a top-drawer corporate plan. A major medical plan, covering only catastrophic costs, is another option. You may get better rates or better coverage by joining a professional organization that offers group insurance. In addition, some alumni and fraternal groups offer major medical plans. Individual vision-care and dental plans are also available. Be aware that insurance companies are rated by standard industry ratings and by consumer advocates such as *Consumer Reports,* and check before you buy.

Unfortunately, as this book goes to press, if you or your spouse or child have a serious health problem, you may still be denied health insurance—the most vital benefit to most of us—through the channels I have just described. This, hopefully, will change soon.

The situation currently varies, state by state, and many do provide an assigned risk health insurance pool for those who are hard to insure. Keep researching, and don't give up!

## Disability insurance

You probably have life insurance or own some assets that would at least partially provide for your family if you should die suddenly. But what about the far more likely possibility that you may be injured or ill and unable to maintain your customary income? Disability insurance will help you through such a period and, depending on the coverage you select, it will also help retrain you for a new career, should that become necessary—or even help care for you if you are totally disabled.

A very wide range of options is available, including credit card or mortgage loan insurance, so do some research and talk to several agents before you decide. While you don't want to be "insurance poor," and you can't protect yourself against everything, a reasonable amount of disability coverage will give you and your family protection and peace of mind.

## Working Toward a Business Plan

### BUSINESS SUCCESS WORKSHEET ONE

**Concept:** *Expand your capabilities and have a transition plan.*

*Providing both writing and desktop publishing services will increase your business. A carefully planned transition to your full-time home business will give you a good start.*

- Do you plan to be a home-based writer, desktop publisher, or both?

- Do you currently have professional-level skills in both areas?

- If you lack professional-level skills in one of the two areas, do you eventually intend to develop those skills?

- How? Learning options include classes, individual study, private consultant training, and practicing on volunteer projects. Can you think of other methods?

- If you do not want to develop additional skills, do you know, or can you locate, trustworthy writers or desktop publishers with whom you can work?

- How will you make the transition from employment to a full-time home-based business?

  —Part-time employment, part-time freelancing?

  —"Outsourcing" for your present employer?

  —Living on savings or a loan as you build up your business?

  —Living on someone else's income as you build up your business?

  —Other options?

- How will you replace such employee benefits as health and disability insurance?

# Life as a Home-based Freelancer

The following worksheet enumerates key benefits that have drawn many creative people into freelance careers. But every coin has two sides. Negative aspects of freelance life have kept other writers and graphic designers from starting their own home businesses—or have convinced them to abandon their efforts at self-employment. Ironically, what some people view as a benefit, others may percieve as a liability.

In order to evaluate your own motivations and potential problem areas as a freelance writer or designer, checkmark the benefits you find most attractive and the liabilities that most concern you.

## Working Toward a Business Plan

### BUSINESS SUCCESS WORKSHEET TWO

Concept: *Understand your motivations.*

*The benefits of freelance life must outweigh the liabilities for you if you are to succeed in a home writing and desktop publishing business.*

The benefits

Independence.

Opportunities to earn more than a predetermined amount.

Convienience—no commuting.

Control of your time.

Control of which clients you serve.

Control of what kinds of business you go after.

Control of your own ethics and business standards.

Integration of your business and personal life.

Freedom from office politics and gossip.

Opportunities for family involvement.

Opportunities to do personal creative projects.

The liabilities

Having to be a "self-starter" every day.

Uncertain income, cash-flow problems.

No paid benefits.

Having to market your own services.

Having to be aggressive in collecting money.

Work space that may be inadequate or lacking in privacy.

No time off without financial loss.

Difficulty getting credit.

Having to do everything yourself. No executive perks.

Loneliness.

May have to take whatever work comes in the door.

Family members may exert a negative or disruptive influence.

Unpredictable work schedules may disrupt family and personal plans.

May have less time for personal creative projects than when you were on salary.

# Getting Support on the Home Front

As we have seen, family members often make significant financial contributions to the start-up of a writer's or desktop publisher's business.

There is another kind of family support that is much harder to measure but even more critical for your home-based business success, and that is "buying into the idea," caring about your dream, hoping you will succeed, being willing to endure inconvenience on your behalf.

There's a hierarchy to this kind of support. Some of it is nice to have. Some of it is just about essential. Your parents, siblings, grown children, or close friends may not share your enthusiasm for risking your financial and professional future on a home-based writing/desktop publishing venture. That's too bad, but you can survive without their approval. Do not—I repeat—*do not* fight or argue with them. Instead, while you are in your fledgling stage as an entrepreneur, avoid discussing your business with them. Get professional advice instead from people who are truly informed about your industry and who know that a well-run home-based writing or desktop publishing business is a viable way to make a living.

In most cases, your success will bring these special folks around. Very likely they just had no mental model for what you planned to do and saw you stepping off into an abyss. When your business is running smoothly, risk showing them where and how you work and what you produce. Their praise will be among the sweetest you receive.

Now for the really hard part.

If your spouse or the significant other with whom you share your home is actively against your plans, you have a much more serious problem. To a great (and unavoidable) extent, a home business is a family business, and as you make your inevitable mistakes, that person's daily criticism and fault-finding can damage your self-confidence and even drive the two of you apart.

There are many excellent guidebooks on relationships and communication, as well as many supportive third parties—from friends to pastors to psychologists. Take this problem seriously and use all the help you can get. Remember that, for many entrepreneurs, running a home business is a deep source of joy. So can it be for you—and those you love!

## Working Toward a Business Plan

### BUSINESS SUCCESS WORKSHEET THREE

**Concept:** *Make sure your players want to be on the team.*

*Personal support from those closest to you can spell success or failure in a home-based business—especially one involving creative work.*

- Which people are part of your vital inner circle? Do they support your plans?

- If any members of your inner circle do not support your plans, what will it take for you to obtain their support?

- If you cannot obtain their support, can you succeed without it?

---

### Jack Fehr

*Jack Fehr Associates, Shelburne, Vermont*

#### Escaping to a New Life

In 1988, between jobs and fed up with city living, former sports writer and marketer Jack Fehr "escaped" from New York with his wife and three young daughters to a small town in Vermont. He soon found work in corporate communications with a Vermont insurance firm, but, two years later, downsizing threatened his position. After some careful planning, Fehr decided to open his own home-based writing business.

"During my first year," he says, "I had a variety of clients by using my New York contacts. I did a statistical newsletter for Avon Products, a white paper for Simon & Schuster, and a by-lined article for an insurance company. But I wasn't marketing myself very well, and I thought we were going to starve when my severance package ran out."

To find new clients, Fehr read "everything under the sun." He developed a mailing list of senior public relations executives, later realizing that most were government affairs specialists and not potential clients. He also targeted small local businesses. "I was calling on people who didn't have advertising budgets," he explains, "telling them I could give them agency-quality work for half the price. That just didn't ring true.

"Another mistake I made," Fehr recalls, "was trying to be everything to everybody. I claimed I could do speeches, AV scripts, anything—not realizing there are specialists who do each of these. I was going to be a generalist to Fortune 500 companies. But the more I decided that, the more I kept getting dragged into insurance expertise. After about a year, I decided I'd better accept it. Then everything just started clicking."

Now focusing on large firms, Fehr does ghost writing for executives, writes articles for trade journals and company magazines, and produces such non-advertising marketing materials as capability brochures, descriptive product pieces, and annual reports.

After briefly considering desktop publishing, Fehr decided writing was more profitable for him. He brings in a designer when he needs one and has the designer bill the client directly.

Fehr enjoys working at home and having control of his time. "I put in forty-plus hours a week, but twenty hours might be on a rainy weekend," he points out. "If I've got an article to write and the temperature is ninety degrees, I'd just as soon jump in the lake with my kids and write the article at night."

With his flexible schedule, Fehr has found time to write a book of anecdotes and essays on fatherhood. "It didn't dawn on me when I became a home-based writer that I'd have time to spend with my daughters," he says.

Fehr attributes his success to finding out what works by trial and error. "When you're marketing yourself, you can't take anything personally," he says. "If someone is not receptive, it just means they don't have time to be receptive today, but they might be receptive tomorrow. I've had people who refused to answer my calls contact me later with a job. I've had others tell me they'd love to hire me and I never got any work from them. I've given up trying to understand it. Now I just go with the flow."

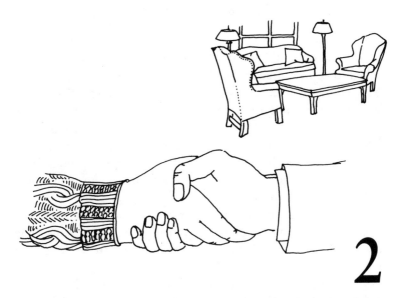

# 2

# What Will You Do and for Whom?

## Building on Your Strengths and Teaming with Other Professionals

## Why Define Yourself?

"I can write (or design) anything," is the brave cry some writers and desktop publishers issue to the world. Willing to tackle any work they can find, these fledgling entrepreneurs assume that a broad focus will bring them more business than a narrow one. Not so.

Dig deeper and you will probably discover that such home business operators have not done their homework. They don't know what they are best at or what they really want to do. Don't let this happen to you. An unfocused person is hard to remember and does not inspire confidence.

I think the real reason we creative types often fudge when asked to define ourselves is that we don't want to be locked into one definition. Many times we have a hidden agenda. The person writing a press release secretly wants to be a screenwriter. The person typesetting a menu would rather be illustrating children's books. And why not? Dreams are what keep us alive. Moreover, your home-based business is an ideal way to bring your daily work closer to your dream occupation—if you do it in small, carefully focused steps.

Developing a direction for your business will take time, and over the years, your emphasis may change. The important thing is to start *somewhere*—stake out a claim and start working it. If you don't find gold, try another claim.

*The Writer's Essential Desk Reference* (Writer's Digest Books 1991), a volume I highly recommend to both writers and desktop publishers, offers an exercise that can help you as you begin to ask, "What will I do, and for whom?"

> Take a conscious look around you today at written copy, wherever you are, beginning with what's right in front of your eyes—a calendar that has photo captions; an advertisement on the back of a cereal box; a button or T-shirt with a cute slogan on it—and continue throughout the day, wherever you are. Don't overlook the flyers posted on telephone poles by a local theater company, signs on the backs of benches or high up on billboards, and your own mail, especially your direct (also called "junk") mail.

Do you see the point? As *The Desk Reference* suggests, all of this material was painstakingly written, designed, and prepared for production by someone—possibly a freelancer. Maybe it could be you.

# My Search for a Business Identity

When I first started thinking about freelancing, I was making a professional transition from higher education public relations and publications into printing sales. As a sideline, I dreamed up a business called Logos Unlimited, designing logos and business letterheads. My service was focused—too focused, as it turned out.

Of course, I had a wonderful logo for my new business with gold-foiled business cards and letterhead that I could ill afford (I'm still using up that clay-colored letterhead for scrap paper). As a new part-time freelancer, I knew I lacked the experience and credibility to market high-ticket corporate identity programs. And, to be honest, I also lacked the confidence. So I went after more modest clients—new businesses and nonprofit agencies, as well as individuals—and I received quite a few logo assignments.

The problem was that a new business needs one logo and one set of stationery and maybe a flyer, and for a while, at least, that's it. What I had staked out for myself was endless marketing for a fairly inexpensive product with little repeat business—from clients who were very ego-involved in the product, had little to spend, and whose credit was often impossible to check. Many designers make this type of work pay handsomely—but they usually aim at high-paying clients.

Another early business idea of mine that fizzled on the launchpad (even though Logos Unlimited had designed a clever logo for it) was Growth Greetings. The greeting cards I envisioned were virtually unavailable in the late seventies—cards to celebrate nontraditional events like receiving a divorce, losing weight, getting sober, or having a spiritual experience. I still think it was a good idea, but working at it parttime, I lacked the funds to print cards in quantity and the know-how to develop distribution—to say nothing of the confidence to go out and get financial backing.

A friend who was an historian by training, Ashleigh Brilliant, did all of these things successfully when he established his offbeat greeting-card line, Pot Shots. Ashleigh passionately wanted to get what he then called his "unpoemed titles" out into the world—and he has done so! His firm in Santa Barbara, California, is now known as Brilliant Enterprises. I wasn't that passionate about either my logos or my greeting cards, but these ventures did teach me two things.

First, I learned to take the grim truism that *"most new businesses fail during the first year"* with a very large grain of salt. Those "failures" often represent a determined entrepreneur learning his or her craft, making a beginner's blunders, and bouncing back with new and better ideas. Colleges and universities are now offering theoretical courses in "being an entrepreneur," but I believe the best training is your own careful observations and inevitable mistakes when *your* capital is at risk.

The second thing I learned was the importance of identifying a market that I knew how to reach—one that spent serious money, paid on time, and had an ongoing need for my services. As a printing sales rep, I was selling to corporate and hospital communicators—people I already had a lot in common with. It was only natural that I turn to them for freelance work. At first I did whatever came to hand—articles for employee magazines, press releases, brochure and flyer designs, product literature, newsletters, workbooks, even logos.

With such assignments I managed to survive, and my list of corporate and hospital clients began to sound impressive, but I felt fragmented. It took me about two years to realize that newsletters were what I wanted to specialize in. In the first place, I like newsletters. I will always marvel at the persuasive power these homely, unobtrusive little publications have when they are done well. Newsletters call on both my writing and designing skills, giving me an advantage over freelancers who don't do both. Because they repeat regularly, I can spend less time marketing. They also match my previous experience in designing and selling two- and three-color printing. And they let me do what I do well—identify and fit in with my clients as a part of their teams.

Today newsletters account for about three-quarters of my work. I still do other kinds of projects, usually for established clients, and I am quite open to longer ones like this book, which may signal a new phase of my freelance career. Writing a book brings me closer to my lifetime interest in writing fiction and non-fiction, which drew me to a writing career in the first place.

# Finding Your Business Focus

As you begin your new home-based business, you will probably have a similar journey, defining and redefining what it is you want to do and for whom. Fortunately, some techniques are available to speed up the process.

You may have already done some freelance writing or graphic design that can provide a starting point—or you may want to get away from those assignments and turn to others. The key is to find the types of writing and design products that you feel comfortable with and are interested in. This will help you answer the question, *"What will I do?"*

At the same time, you need to identify the industries or subject areas that you would enjoy working in, such as banking, entertainment, real estate, medicine, local government, food service, or fashion. This will help you answer the question, *"...and for whom?"* Your client may be a business that provides goods or services in a certain area, an agency that provides services to such businesses, or a publishing firm that produces written material and graphics in the same field. You can serve all three.

If you choose an industry or field with care, you will be able to write or design well in these areas and enjoy your work over the long haul. Equally important, you will be on the same wavelength with your clients. They will feel easy with you and trust you with their material.

## Using your education

Review your educational background, including subjects you have studied but have not used in your work. For example, you may have studied biology in college, then switched to communications and wound up doing public relations for a government agency. If you still have a scientific bent, your background in biology can open doors to writing for laboratories, hospitals, and medical groups. If you're a desktop publisher, such training would allow you to approach scientific or medical clients. You don't have to master the subject, but it's important that you have a feel for it.

Make a list of the subjects you have studied, including short courses you have taken as an adult, and see what fields of writing or design they suggest. Did you do any writing or design projects as a student? If you enjoyed editing your yearbook, for example, you might also enjoy putting together community directories.

## Using your work experience

Even more important than your education is your work experience. Your most recent experience is the most viable, but go all the way back. I had done medical writing early in my higher education public relations career. Some twenty years later I trotted out those skills, very profitably, for freelance clients.

This time make a list of the industries in which you have worked and any tasks you have done that relate to writing or design. Have you had experience proofreading, designing or taking surveys, writing reports, preparing marketing materials, or designing labels? Write them down. They may help you focus on an appropriate specialty or an industry where you will find clients.

## Using your personal, family, and volunteer experience

Entrepreneurs often overlook areas where they have not had formal training or work experience when they are establishing their expertise. Do you speak a second language? If so, you have an edge with certain clients. Are you a member of an ethnic group? Special business or social organizations where you can meet clients may be open to you. Are you a member of a minority? Fifteen percent of federal contracts must go to minority firms. Seeking this business requires a minority business certification. (Unfortunately, the federal government doesn't consider women a minority, although some states do.) Do you have a disability or a past experience that gives you knowledge and a special ability to work with clients who serve these populations?

How about your interests? Did you ever study music or play in a local group? If so, you can talk to music stores, bands, nightclubs. Did you grow up helping out in your father's restaurant?

Then you are a food service insider. Your experience editing or designing your church newsletter, writing press releases about your club's social service program, or preparing handouts for your garden society also give you inside knowledge. In addition to the practical experience, you already have a special camaraderie with religious, social service, and horticultural clients.

## Exploring new areas

Now is a good time to start building expertise in areas that have long intrigued you but in which you have little expertise. Writing and designing are skills needed in every corner of our society. If you are fascinated by the worlds of sports or politics, if you would like to help the homeless, or if you would like to hang out with theater folk—whatever your interest—you can build up your knowledge through the learning techniques presented in Chapter One for improving your professional skills. These techniques include classes and workshops, special interest organizations, personal interviews and observation, and reading and sample-collecting.

Your initial contact may be on a volunteer or low paying basis—especially in nonprofit areas and highly competitive "glamour" areas—but you will find that with a careful study of the territory, your freelance skills can take you almost anywhere you want to go.

# Start with a Reality Check

If you know—or can arrange an introduction to people who are doing the kind of work you are interested in doing—ask for a little of their time or offer to take them to lunch for a brief reality check. Does it really work out, being a home-based freelancer? This query from new or potential entrepreneurs is very familiar to established home-based writers and desktop publishers. We did the same thing when we were starting out, and when we are not too busy, most of us are happy to advise beginners.

Find out how the established freelancers got started, what kind of work they do, where they get clients, and if possible, what they charge. Be tactful. Since these people may eventually be your competitors, they may be less than forthcoming with specific details. And be cautious about believing everything you're told. Your mentor may be having a bad day and feel negative about his work. Or he might decide to discourage competition by telling you the field is too crowded. Don't base important decisions on the input from one or two individuals.

## Working Toward a Business Plan

### BUSINESS SUCCESS WORKSHEET FOUR

Concept: *Build on your past skills and experience.*

*You already have knowledge and experience. Use them to help you focus your writing and desktop publishing business.*

- What education have you had relating to writing and desktop publishing? Consider both the fields you have trained for and the types of writing and designing you have studied.

- What interested you the most?

- What job experiences have you had relating to writing and desktop publishing? Consider both the industries you have worked in and the types of work you have done.

- What interested you the most?

- What personal, family, or volunteer experiences have you had that may translate into writing and desktop publishing? Again, consider both the fields you were in (for example, sports, religion, community government) and the types of work you have done.

- What interested you the most?

- What other types of writing and desktop publishing would you like to do? What other industries or fields would you like to be involved in?

- Based on your knowledge, experience, and interest, what could you specialize in as a writer or desktop publisher?
- What can you do to gain the knowledge and skills you lack?

# Setting Up Relationships with Other Suppliers and Associates

If you are not proficient in both writing and desktop publishing, you may decide to master the missing skill—or you may not. But in either case, you will soon be dealing with some clients who want to buy both services. You can leave them on their own to find a writer or a designer, running the risk that a new vendor will try to snatch away both parts of the job. Or you can set up relationships with competent vendors you can trust and offer their services in combination with your own. It's well worth the effort for the marketing advantage you will achieve by being a "full-service" supplier.

While you're thinking about other professionals, don't overlook the benefits of having a cooperative relationship with one or more colleagues who have capabilities similar to your own. Sure, they're competitors, but if you're sick or experiencing an overload, a trusted colleague could be a godsend.

## Finding reliable associates

Here are some resources to help you locate potential associates—and remember, you'll want more than one vendor to call on, in case your first choice is unavailable or isn't quite right for the job:

- Professional associations and directories.
- Referrals. Check with clients; other writers and desktop publishers; advertising, marketing, and public relations agencies; photographers; printers; and desktop service bureaus.
- Work you admire. Check with clients to find out who did the work.
- Your own advertisement for the needed service.

Here are some factors to consider in identifying associate vendors:

- Quality of work.

- Experience and interests. Do they fit your clients?

- Price range. Is it comparable to yours?

- Business style. Is it similar to yours? Are they comfortable with formal or informal agreements? Do they have similar policies in handling deadlines, revisions, extra expenses?

- Reliability. Check references, try a few small jobs, or trust your instincts.

- Ethical standards. An ethical associate will not steal your client, cheat you, or blame you if there is a problem.

## Setting up joint work agreements

When you team up with another vendor, your first consideration should be an agreement about each party's responsibility and liability. It's preferable to have these agreements in writing. At minimum, you must discuss and reach consensus on key issues. Points to be covered include:

- The relationship of the vendors to each other

- How fees are to be set

- The responsibilities of each vendor (in general or on the specific job in question)

- Any deadlines that must be met and who is responsible

- The legal and financial liabilities of each vendor

- How expenses are to be handled

- How invoicing and payment are to be handled

- The period of time covered by the agreement

- How the relationship can be terminated

## Handling a disaster

When a disaster occurs on a job—regardless of which vendor was at fault—never, never blame your associate when dealing with a client. The only professional thing to do is to present a unified front. After all, you agreed to team up, and one of you told the client that the other was reliable.

Privately, discuss the problem and your available options with your associate, and identify points of negotiation you can agree upon. Then meet with the client, define the problem clearly, negotiate any financial or other adjustments, and concentrate on getting the job done right as soon as possible.

## Bidding and billing

When bidding on jobs together, there are basically two ways to present your estimates—as two separate bids or one combined bid. The same applies to billing—two separate bills or one bill covering both services.

If you see yourself as a one-person operation and have no desire to expand, you will probably be more comfortable with the former. Some writers and designers would rather not worry about collecting from the client in time to pay a subcontractor or collecting any taxes due for the subcontractor's portion of the work.

But there is significant money to be made in buying a service or product at one price and selling it for more. That's what business is usually about! Many writers and designers take advantage of this opportunity to increase their incomes. Should you expand beyond your own capacities, you will often be hiring subcontractors, and it is certainly fair for you to profit by marking up their prices.

## Working with the client

You can handle all dealings with the client yourself, even though the bidding and billing may be handled separately, or you can introduce your associate to the client and have him deliver his portion of the job directly to the client.

As a rule of thumb, keeping your associate in the background is best for maintaining strong, personal client relationships—but it's not always best for every job. Some clients want to give you an assignment and receive back a finished product with as little in-between contact as possible. Don't bother bringing your associate to meet this customer. Other clients want to be involved in every step of the job, playing a major part in the creative process and often waiting to see the product before they decide whether it's really what they want. If such a client's instructions to the other vendor are complex, subtle, or vague, you will save time and needless aggravation by bringing your associate into this picture early.

## It's *your* client

However you handle the details, remember that the work is being done for *your* client and you want his or her entire experience to be pleasant and profitable. Stay in touch and in control. Make sure your associate's work is of the style and quality expected. Keep track of costs and see to it that the final bill is as agreed upon. If not, make sure your client has agreed to any added costs. When the job is being done for your associate's client, show both of them the same respect.

## Working Toward a Business Plan

### BUSINESS SUCCESS WORKSHEET FIVE

Concept: *Increase your business through joint ventures.*

*With the proper safeguards and a cooperative spirit, working with other independent professionals can help your business grow.*

- Does the idea of teaming with other professionals fit your business plans—assuming the other vendor will provide skills you lack?

- Would you be willing to use a colleague to handle an overload on your own work?

- Where will you find associates and how will you evaluate them?

- What kind of working relationship will you establish with such vendors? What are each party's legal and financial liabilities?

- How will you handle bidding, billing, and dealing with your client?

- How will you protect your relationship with your client?

---

## Claudia Miller
### *ADirections, Fullerton, California*

**Investing in Yourself**

While attending high school, Claudia Miller worked in her father's instant print shop, where she learned illustration and graphic design. After graduation, she became a printing estimator and took college graphics courses. When she decided to start her own graphic design business, she knew she had the necessary technical skills, but she lacked "knowing how to get out there and sell."

Miller had built up some savings and a part-time freelance clientele, but, divorced with a teenaged son, she wanted to minimize her risk. So she put $700 of her start-up funds into a Dale Carnegie course in sales and motivation and calls it "the best money I ever spent."

The hustle she learned at the course has kept her business growing since 1986. In 1992, at the height of the recession, Miller doubled her volume. Now remarried and working out of her Southern California home, Miller puts in seventy to eighty hours a week, providing graphic design, illustration, printing coordination, and desktop publishing services. Her clients include schools, medical firms, banks, and industrial companies.

Networking is Miller's "number one" marketing tool. "When you network," she advises, "you can't just go to meetings. You have to volunteer and get active." Another valued tool is persistence. "Don't be obnoxious, just persistent. It may take years, but it pays off."

Miller ran her graphic design business "the traditional way" for several years before moving into desktop publishing. She now works on a Macintosh Ilfx. Before buying a system, she took community college courses to "get a feel" for both Mac and IBM-PC systems and ended up heeding a teacher's advice: "Find the software that will do what you want and buy the hardware to support it."

Miller often subcontracts and coordinates joint venturing. "You need other people who can support your services," she says. "The more services you can offer, the more chance you have of getting the job." Since she "makes it easy for them to buy," clients often ask Miller to handle complete jobs, from inception to printed product. She uses freelancers and, to retain control, usually has them submit their bills to her. Relying on trusted relationships, she does not use formal contracts.

Miller's twenty-one-year-old son helps her three days a week. "A home business can't help but rub off on your kids," she says, adding, "when you own your own business, you do everything—paying bills, cleaning up, doing bookkeeping, researching new software and equipment, taking calls from vendors, making deliveries. Only a third of your time is spent on what you really want to do."

But that third can be sweet.

"My favorite days are in the winter," she says. "I'm in my studio with the heater on and soft music playing—and I'm working on a project where my client has said, 'Do whatever you want. Get really creative.' I'm playing and I'm getting paid for it. To top it off, I deliver the job and the client loves it. The client gives me praise, which I love, and then pays me. It doesn't get any better than that!"

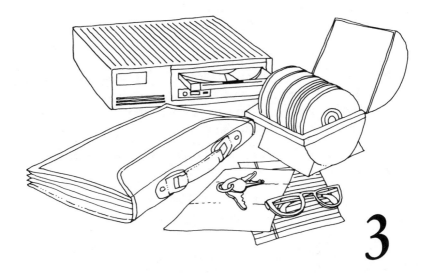

# 3

# Where the Work Is—
## *Key Writing and Desktop Publishing Products and Clients*

## What is the "Hidden Market"?

The more jobs you can do for the same clients, the more you will benefit from your marketing efforts. The key is identifying work you enjoy doing—and for which you can charge a profitable fee—and the clients who have a steady need for such work. Many writers and desktop publishers start out by taking any jobs they can get—and you may do so, too—but if you know which jobs and clients you really want, you will soon be guiding your business toward higher profits and greater satisfaction. This chapter will help you make your selection by analyzing "the hidden market" that exists in virtually every community.

The "hidden market" consists of a wide range of local assignments that allow you to be your own boss while doing what many writers and graphic designers do in salaried positions. I think of these as the meat-and-potatoes jobs. These are jobs that can start you off as a home-based writer or desktop publisher and sustain you for a lifetime, if you choose to stay with them. In general, these assignments meet three criteria:

1. They are assignments you can realistically expect to receive as a new freelance writer or desktop designer.

2. They are available in most communities.

3. They can add up to a full-time income.

To start you thinking across a wide range of options, this chapter lists sixty-three such jobs alphabetically. Writers will notice that articles and short stories for general-circulation magazines, nonfiction books, genre and mainstream novels, plays for stage and screen, poetry and song lyrics, essays, syndicated columns, and comedy writing are not included in this list. Why? Because these popular specialties are discussed in many excellent books on writing—to say nothing of writers' magazines, newsletters, and workshops, *ad infinitum*. Syndicated cartooning and other glamorous design jobs are omitted for the same reason.

Of course, the big bucks and ego rewards to be achieved in these specialties can be mind-boggling—so by all means, as your time and finances permit, purchase the books, take the workshops, and try your hand.

But remember that the money available for the plain-Jane tasks we are talking about here is often more substantial—and certainly more reliable—than the money earned writing moderately successful books or plays. It's not unusual for a good friend of mine, an experienced freelance writer, to make three thousand dollars writing one twenty-minute speech for the CEO of a locally based international corporation. Although doing high-profile writing and design can bring personal satisfaction, it is often at the expense of an entrepreneur's bottom line—at least in the short term.

In the list of writing and desktop publishing jobs that follows, look at each project description with these questions in mind, and check-mark as you go:

- Which assignments would I like to do?
- Which assignments can I do now?
- Which assignments could I do with additional knowledge and experience?

# Sixty-three Key Assignments for Home-based Writers and Desktop Publishers

1. *Advertising copy.* A big area with lots of opportunity. Both advertising agencies and the in-house advertising departments of large companies use help for their overloads. Occasionally they need special expertise not available on their staffs. In addition, small companies and professionals in solo and group practice often turn to outside professionals for advertising copy—and your rates can beat those of a full-service ad agency.

    ____ *like to do*   ____ *could do now*   ____ *could learn to do*

2. *Anniversary materials for corporations, organizations, institutions, municipalities.* Writing and producing company and organizational histories is a specialty that requires astute, long-range marketing, but one or several projects can provide a year's income. A California-based specialist in corporate histories told me that she looks for good-sized, privately held companies founded by strong, charismatic figures, with significant anniversaries coming up. Companies, universities, hospitals, trade associations, churches, cities, and other organizations also produce collateral materials such as calendars, flyers, and souvenir items in celebration of their anniversaries. Depending on the staff workload, the entire anniversary project may be bid out to a cooperative freelancer.

    ____ *like to do*   ____ *could do now*   ____ *could learn to do*

3. *Annual reports.* Producing annual reports for large, publicly traded corporations is not a place for a beginner to break in, although independent designers and writers are often employed for these prestigious, big-ticket jobs. Smaller companies and other organizations, however—community service agencies, colleges and universities, water districts, and government departments—often produce annual reports for their constituents that new freelancers can profitably produce.

_____ *like to do* _____ *could do now* _____ *could learn to do*

4. *Articles for employee magazines.* While the techniques for writing an article for an employee (or other internal) magazine are essentially the same as for any other magazine, the method of selling such articles is far less speculative. Basically it is work-for-hire, with the client owning all rights. Editors come up with the idea and assign the work for an agreed-upon price. One or more rewrites are included in the price; additional rewrites are extra. Often the fee is comparable to what a major magazine would pay. Since the editor generally has confidence in the writer, outright rejection of the completed work is rare.

_____ *like to do* _____ *could do now* _____ *could learn to do*

5. *Articles for trade journals and small magazines.* Payment is generally low for these articles, but your income can be multiplied if you rewrite the material and sell it to a noncompeting publication. The credibility you will attain from being published in a trade journal or small magazine will help you get jobs from other clients, and building a long-term relationship with an editor can result in repeated assignments or even a monthly column. If you want to sharpen your article-writing skills, you will find endless books and articles on how to write articles of all kinds. Whole books are devoted just to writing query letters to get article assignments. Another important market for business and trade journal articles is public relations and marketing specialists, who will pay you

very well to write articles about their clients. They, in turn, will try to place the articles with appropriate publications. If you are a writer who specializes in publicity, you can place your own work.

____ *like to do*    ____ *could do now*    ____ *could learn to do*

6. *Book design and production.* Desktop publishers have found this a profitable specialty. Business comes from local publishers, printers, and individuals wishing to self-publish. Established firms often serve a national clientele. Personalizing and binding pre-written, generic books for children and adults is a growing specialty.

____ *like to do*    ____ *could do now*    ____ *could learn to do*

7. *Brochures.* The workhorses of communication in every field, brochures provide work for both writers and desktop publishers. All organizations and businesses need brochures, as do seminar promoters, hospitals, medical groups, educational institutions, community and government agencies, churches, and fund raisers. The list is endless, as are the opportunities. Brochures are typically described by their format, such as a two-fold brochure or a three-fold brochure.

____ *like to do*    ____ *could do now*    ____ *could learn to do*

8. *Calendars.* Some desktop publishers have made a specialty of personalized calendars based on a standard format, but with the client's individual dates (birthdays, anniversaries, etc.) included. Personalized calendars are printed on a laser or color printer and individually bound. Of course, many businesses and organizations distribute promotional calendars each year to their constituents. National calendar companies have traditionally served such customers, selling standard calendars imprinted with the client's name, but local writer and desktop publisher teams can capture some of this business. In

addition nonprofit organizations and associations often produce calendars themselves for promotional and fund-raising purposes, but such calendars are far more successful when produced by professional writers and designers.

____ *like to do*  ____ *could do now*  ____ *could learn to do*

9. *Capability brochures.* Certain kinds of businesses, such as engineering firms, consultants, and management companies, need this specialized type of brochure as the core of their business solicitation. Capability brochures are usually more extensive than typical brochures in terms of text and illustrations, as well as more expensive in terms of graphics and printing.

____ *like to do*  ____ *could do now*  ____ *could learn to do*

10. *Catalogs and product sheets.* A lucrative workhorse of the business world offering plenty of business for both writers and designers. Businesses everywhere need catalogs and individual product sheets, with regular updates and reprints. If this work interests you, establishing a link with competent product photographers would be a plus. Business can come from individual firms, advertising agencies, photographers, or printers. The more you specialize in this area, the more business you are likely to receive.

____ *like to do*  ____ *could do now*  ____ *could learn to do*

11. *Charts, graphs, tables.* A good specialty for desktop publishers who have the skills and patience. New software makes accurate charts and graphs easier to produce. The graphic innovations of newspapers like *USA Today* have greatly increased the demand in virtually every field for imaginatively produced charts and graphs. Assignments may come from business owners; corporate communicators; public relations, advertising, and marketing firms; and publishers.

____ *like to do*  ____ *could do now*  ____ *could learn to do*

12. *City and newcomer guides.* Publishers of city guides need both writers and designers—or an enterprising writer and designer might develop a guide for a city that lacks a good one. Selling advertising covers the costs and provides the profit. City maps carrying ads are another option. If you are good at illustration or work with an illustrator, "cartoon-style" city maps are popular and profitable.

____ *like to do*   ____ *could do now*   ____ *could learn to do*

13. *Collateral materials.* "Collateral" is an advertising term that covers all the printed materials relating to a product or project—order forms, spec sheets, invitations, whatever may be needed. Such work may come from business firms or advertising and marketing agencies and requires the skills of both writers and designers. If you are assigned to one part of what appears to be a more complex project, ask about doing the "collateral."

____ *like to do*   ____ *could do now*   ____ *could learn to do*

14. *Conference and trade show materials.* Sales managers, associations, meeting planners, and other event specialists need a wide range of materials—including posters, programs, audio-visual and video scripts, workbooks, flyers, brochures, tickets, badges, and more—for the conferences and trade shows they produce. Writers and designers going after such business will find that local hotels and convention centers may help put them in touch with potential clients.

____ *like to do*   ____ *could do now*   ____ *could learn to do*

15. *Consultation.* Your expertise can be valuable to both individuals and organizations. I have been paid to help staffers plan a newsletter, to provide advice and training on desktop publishing, to critique and guide the redesign of an employee magazine. If, as this book assumes, your major emphasis is on selling your services as a writer or desktop publisher, con-

sulting assignments will usually come to you through networking and referrals. If you like doing this kind of
work—analyzing your clients' needs and advising them on
what to do and how to do it—you may want to move toward
communications or graphics consulting as your primary
focus, once you are well established in the field. If you can
speak publicly on the subject, so much the better.

____ *like to do*  ____ *could do now*  ____ *could learn to do*

16. *Contributing editor assignments.* Becoming a regular contributing editor for a local business publication or for a trade
journal in the field of your specialization can provide a regular monthly stipend—plus constant exposure to potential
clients.

____ *like to do*  ____ *could do now*  ____ *could learn to do*

17. *Direct-mail packages.* Another biggie. There's plenty of good
money to be made by both writers and designers who can
master the subtle and demanding skills of this results-oriented
specialty. Experts in direct marketing love knowing within a
few weeks exactly how successful their efforts have been and
delight in analyzing such measurements as cost-per-response.
If you can write or design packages that pull, you will have
plenty of clients. Direct marketers believe that only specialists
in their field know how to produce winning packages, so
study the many excellent books on the subject, take classes,
network in direct marketing organizations, attend conferences, snag any assignments you can to prove yourself, and
eventually choose a specialty: financial, consumer, business-
to-business, subscription sales, and fund raising are some of
the possibilities. Work is available on local, regional, and
national levels—and many of the best pros are freelancers.

____ *like to do*  ____ *could do now*  ____ *could learn to do*

18. *Directories*. Like city guides, directories require the efforts of both writer/researchers and desktop publishers. Business can come from directory publishers; chambers of commerce; associations; and institutions such as hospitals, colleges, and churches. If you do a good job, directories repeat on a regular basis.

    ____ *like to do* ____ *could do now* ____ *could learn to do*

19. *Editing*. Who does writing or deals with it? Book publishers, authors, and agents; undergraduate and graduate students; people preparing proposals, technical reports, newsletters, and employee benefits kits; consultants and engineers issuing studies for their clients; physicians, attorneys, and other professionals writing articles. The list goes on and on. Any of these nonwriters (and some writers as well) could be in the market for your editing skills. Editors specialize to some extent, so focus on the kind of editing you want to do. Editing can stay at the level of grammar, syntax, and clarity—or it can extend all the way to complete revision, with your price varying accordingly. Be sure you have agreement on what kind of editing is needed.

    ____ *like to do* ____ *could do now* ____ *could learn to do*

20. *Employee benefit materials*. As a writer, if you have expertise in this specialized area, or are willing to develop it, you can find work preparing employee benefit materials. Clients can include employers, as well as insurance companies and agents. This sort of work is ideal for a writer who prepared similar materials as an employee and is now seeking freelance work. If you are a designer, familiarity with the complex subject matter is not a major issue, though it would help. Your challenge will be getting the work away from staff designers or convincing buyers to invest in good design.

    ____ *like to do* ____ *could do now* ____ *could learn to do*

21. *Environmental materials.* If you are a writer, this is another area for experts. For designers, the main challenge will again be getting the assignment. As with medicine, investments, or any specialized area, if you're a writer with a professional background, job experience, or both, in the environmental sciences, you can capitalize on your background as a free-lancer. You can draft or help draft environmental reports, policies, guidelines, and informational brochures for companies, organizations, and government agencies. You can also write articles on environmental topics for a wide range of publications. If you lack specialized knowledge, but want to become involved, editing environmental materials for a consulting firm might be a place to start. A similar specialty for medical writers is the preparation of documents required for government approval of pharmaceutical and medical devices.

    ____ *like to do*    ____ *could do now*    ____ *could learn to do*

22. *Family histories and genealogies.* A growing specialty that uses both writing and desktop publishing skills. If you are a genealogy buff, so much the better. A fully researched, custom-written, professionally typeset and designed family history might be worth several thousand dollars to a wealthy client—even before the printing or duplicating charges. But simpler projects based on completion of a detailed questionnaire—either on paper or on a software program—can yield a more affordable product. Audiovisual specialists are also getting into the act, recording the memories of older family members and editing them into a videotape. Advertising in senior citizen and genealogy publications is a good source of business—as is local media publicity and networking in churches and other organizations.

    ____ *like to do*    ____ *could do now*    ____ *could learn to do*

23. *Flyers.* Most of what was said about brochures also applies to flyers. Though the terms "flyer" and "brochure" are often used interchangeably, a flyer is basically a single sheet, carry-

ing a simple message, while a brochure contains folded panels with more detailed information. Every organization and individual involved in communication with the public will need a flyer eventually. Residential and commercial real estate are especially voracious markets. Contact successful brokers to offer your writing and production services.

____ *like to do* ____ *could do now* ____ *could learn to do*

24. *Forms design and production.* This area basically belongs to the designer—though writers can contribute to good forms design by improving wording and organization. When you seek assignments, having both writing and design skills can give you an edge over nonwriting designers—if the client would like you to reword or reorganize the form. On a routine form order coming out of a purchasing department, however, the wording of the form will not be open to change. The forms industry is huge, with many printers specializing in forms production. While every organization, large and small, requires some forms, there are certain industries— insurance and direct marketing are examples—where forms are especially important.

____ *like to do* ____ *could do now* ____ *could learn to do*

25. *Fund-raising materials.* Prior experience can get you assignments here, both as a writer and as a designer, but if you lack experience, you can gain it over time through study, networking, volunteer work, and careful observation. Clients include large nonprofits such as colleges and universities, hospitals, zoos, museums, and performing arts centers, as well as fund-raising consultants. Materials needed include brochures, flyers, annual reports, posters, invitations, letters of solicitation, volunteer instruction and motivation, newsletters, forms, direct mail packages.

____ *like to do* ____ *could do now* ____ *could learn to do*

26. *Ghost writing and collaboration.* Many people want or need to write books and articles but lack the skill, the time, or both. Celebrities are an obvious example, but the list is much longer. Professionals publishing scientific papers often require much more than just editing to get their manuscripts in shape. Such clients can be reached through universities, professional associations, and professional journals—working with them usually requires some familiarity with the material as well as with the target publication's style.

_____ *like to do* _____ *could do now* _____ *could learn to do*

27. *Greeting-card writing and design.* According to the 1993 Writers Market, nearly 50 percent of all first-class mail consists of greeting cards, and while three large companies dominate 85 percent of the market, many smaller firms are serving special interests and breaking new ground. Read trade publications, locate lines of cards that appeal to you, and write to the companies for their catalogs and submission guidelines. Many card companies also buy ideas for gift products related to their cards.

_____ *like to do* _____ *could do now* _____ *could learn to do*

28. *Illustrations.* This is a vast field in itself, and really beyond the scope of this book—but as a desktop publisher, if you can provide your clients with quality illustrations, drawings, or cartoons, you can add significantly to your income—and you should certainly emphasize your capabilities in your promotional material. Be sure your work is professional—well-adapted clip art is far preferable to amateurish drawings. If you are good enough, you may eventually do nothing but illustration—and that is probably your long-range goal.

_____ *like to do* _____ *could do now* _____ *could learn to do*

29. *Indexing.* This specialty can be profitable for writers with a good eye for organization and detail. Clients include book authors, book publishers, or software publishers. Good computer skills help, since advanced word-processing programs provide indexing tools.

_____ *like to do* _____ *could do now* _____ *could learn to do*

30. *Instructional materials.* A good area for both writers and desktop publishers, but writers may need special expertise or on-the-job experience to qualify for assignments. Clients include textbook publishers, business and professional trainers, companies doing internal training, manufacturers providing instruction for customers, government agencies, religious organizations, and health-care providers. (Schools, colleges, and universities are less likely clients.) Locating clients will require well-focused marketing efforts for both writers and desktop publishers, but once a relationship is established with a vendor, repeat business is often forthcoming.

_____ *like to do* _____ *could do now* _____ *could learn to do*

31. *Investor-relations materials.* A profitable subspecialty in the corporate communications world. Previous on-the-job experience and financial expertise help qualify writers for such assignments, as does extensive knowledge of the industry involved. Desktop publishers would not require special knowledge, but both writers and desktop publishers would need to establish their credibility before a firm would give them investor relations materials to prepare.

_____ *like to do* _____ *could do now* _____ *could learn to do*

32. *Letter writing.* The sales letter is a vital part of most direct-mail packages, and successful direct-mail copywriters are highly compensated for letters that pull a strong response.

But there are other opportunities for writers to sell letter writing to clients. A firm might want standardized letters of all sorts written or updated. A marketing department might want letters that could be customized to accomplish various sales objectives. A writer with consulting and teaching skills might combine such projects with a contract to evaluate a firm's overall letter writing performance or train executives and middle managers in business writing. Individuals in business—such as architects and other professionals, independent sales representatives, financial consultants—might also need sales letters. Models for standard sales letters have long been provided in books and booklets on business methods, and the same kinds of letters are now available in software programs.

_____ *like to do* _____ *could do now* _____ *could learn to do*

33. *Logos, letterhead, and business card design.* A staple for desktop publishers and a truly fascinating one for any designer interested in symbols, history, and psychology. Human beings express their deepest beliefs and identities with graphic symbols and will, indeed, die for what those symbols represent (the cross, the flag). Seen in this light, logo design is part of a powerful human tradition. While designing high-end corporate identity programs can be a very profitable business, most desktop publishers will need to mix logo and letterhead projects with other jobs. Firms in some communities sell mailing lists of entrepreneurs who have recently obtained business permits—an obvious source of low-end logo business. Yellow Page listings will also yield business. For better-paying assignments, advertising in business publications can be a source of work.

_____ *like to do* _____ *could do now* _____ *could learn to do*

34. *Manuals.* A solid source of income for both writers and desktop publishers who specialize in these long jobs. Writers may need technical expertise to deal with certain topics, and both

writers and desktop publishers often concentrate on building expertise and contacts within specific industries. Repeat and referral work is often forthcoming from such frequent manual producers as manufacturers, software publishers, and government agencies.

____ *like to do* ____ *could do now* ____ *could learn to do*

35. *Menu writing and design.* An interesting specialty for writers and designers who have connections with the restaurant world and with printers who specialize in menus. When I talk with food and menu copywriters, I marvel at the number of enticing ways they find to say something tastes good.

____ *like to do* ____ *could do now* ____ *could learn to do*

36. *Newsletters.* An important source of income for both writers and desktop publishers—and an especially good niche for those with a good command of both skills. Newsletters come and go, so marketing must be constant in this specialty, as in any other. However, some newsletters provide steady business for years. Clients include trade associations, private clubs, residential communities, businesses of all kinds, human resources departments producing employee newsletters, professionals seeking to market their group or solo practices, hospitals, colleges and universities, large non-profit organizations, and government agencies. Some writers and desktop publishers become so successful at newsletters that they expand beyond one-person, home-based businesses and open offices where they employ staffs of writers, designers, and salespeople. Often they add a wider range of marketing services. Another approach is to produce a generic newsletter where only one page or one section is customized for individual clients. An informative generic newsletter can be an effective marketing tool for a real estate broker, a financial planner, a chiropractor, and others. The newsletter publisher signs up as many noncompeting clients as possible, usually

on a regional or national basis. The publisher may mail the newsletter, using client-supplied lists, or may ship a certain number of customized copies to each client for distribution. Yet another angle is to write or do desktop production for an entrepreneur who publishes a subscription newsletter on some specific topic, such as the oil industry, stock investments, wines, or travel. Be aware that many subscription newsletter publishers prefer to do all their own writing and often their own production in order to maximize profits.

____ *like to do* ____ *could do now* ____ *could learn to do*

37. *Newspaper feature writing, reporting, and stringing.* A source of extra income for writers skilled in journalistic techniques. While payment from all but the larger dailies may be low, published bylines give you credibility and may impress potential business or organizational clients. Being out and about covering stories, especially in a specific field of expertise, keeps you well-informed and gives you an edge over other writers. But beware of conflicts of interest. Should a newspaper ask you to write about one of your clients, better pass.

____ *like to do* ____ *could do now* ____ *could learn to do*

38. *Packaging design and copy.* A specialty that can be profitable. Every manufacturer who puts out a product requires words and design on the package. You will need contacts with manufacturers, advertising and marketing agencies, and packaging firms—and you should be familiar with relevant government regulations.

____ *like to do* ____ *could do now* ____ *could learn to do*

39. *Policies and procedures writing.* Previous on-the-job experience can qualify writers for these corporate and government assignments. Topics might include disaster planning as well as safety and environmental compliance and employee poli-

cies. Your assignment might come from a consultant hired to assist the client.

_____ *like to do* _____ *could do now* _____ *could learn to do*

40. *Posters and point-of-sale displays.* Often part of a larger promotional campaign, posters and point-of-sale displays are challenging design assignments. Outstanding posters can bring you professional recognition. Clients may include entertainment and sports promoters, advertising and public relations agencies, manufacturers, colleges and universities, nonprofit organizations, and government agencies.

_____ *like to do* _____ *could do now* _____ *could learn to do*

41. *Press releases and press kits.* A profitable public relations activity for writers. Elaborate press kits may also require desktop publishing skills. You may produce material according to your client's direction. If you are responsible for public relations strategy and media placement, you should also guide content and design. Clients may be individuals, corporate or organizational public relations firms, marketing departments, or advertising and marketing agencies.

_____ *like to do* _____ *could do now* _____ *could learn to do*

42. *Proofreading.* Writers and desktop publishers should not overlook this source of extra income when assignments are few. Earlier I mentioned a writer friend who receives $3,000 for a corporate speech. Early in her freelance career, I well remember seeing her in the offices of a typesetter we both used, making extra money as a proofreader. Anyone who produces large quantities of printed material may need a freelance proofreader—including typesetters, printers, publishers, consultants who issue long reports, and organizations preparing directories.

_____ *like to do* _____ *could do now* _____ *could learn to do*

43. *Proposals.* Another specialized area for writers with previous on-the-job experience or special training. Good teamwork and organizational skills, logical thinking, and clear writing are essential, as is security awareness since you will often deal with confidential information. Clients include fund-raising consultants, large nonprofit organizations, and a broad range of businesses. Payment varies widely.

    ____ *like to do*   ____ *could do now*   ____ *could learn to do*

44. *Public relations materials.* A writing specialty that often requires desktop publishing skills as well. Public relations is an excellent field of opportunity for the home-based entrepreneur—especially in the present economy, when many corporations have reduced or eliminated their in-house public relations staffs. With the right clients, you can be as effective as a large agency—and a lot cheaper. Solo public relations practitioners usually specialize in a particular area, such as entertainment, medicine, high tech, sports, social services, or fine arts. Narrowing your focus allows you to develop solid, long-term relations with media, government officials, and others whom you seek to influence. Payment is handled as a monthly fee for ongoing services or as an hourly or per-job fee for such specific assignments as a special event or the development of a public relations plan. There is a vast number of businesses, organizations, and individuals who need and can afford the services of a small public relations firm—either occasionally or on a regular basis. The challenge is reaching them and convincing them that they need and can afford you.

    ____ *like to do*   ____ *could do now*   ____ *could learn to do*

45. *Publication design and production.* This area represents a very significant source of desktop publishing business, coming from a wide range of clients. It includes designing formats and nameplates for newsletters and magazines, as well as providing such ongoing publication services as typesetting or data transfer, design, production, and even print brokering.

Publication design is a specialty within desktop publishing. The ability to enhance editorial content with good design that attracts and guides the reader's attention is a valuable skill that can command top rates.

_____ *like to do*  _____ *could do now*  _____ *could learn to do*

46. *Radio continuity and ads.* If you are a writer with previous experience in broadcasting or advertising, you can put that knowledge to work freelancing in this special area. Ads for radio require special wording, while "continuity" represents other scripted on-air material. Your clients will be radio stations, advertising agencies, or on-air personalities. If you want to get into this area, take a class in broadcasting or advertising copywriting, or contact radio station continuity writers or ad copywriters for advice.

_____ *like to do*  _____ *could do now*  _____ *could learn to do*

47. *Researching.* If you are a writer with good research skills, comfortable using primary sources, libraries, online databases, or any other appropriate informational source—you may be hired to help a book writer, a marketing team, a scholar, a publisher, a law firm, a government agency, or any client with special research needs. To build a career in this specialty, you will seek clients and referrals through networking and advertising in appropriate journals. Payment is by the hour or the project. Skilled use of on-line databases is emerging as an exciting new specialty.

_____ *like to do*  _____ *could do now*  _____ *could learn to do*

48. *Restaurant reviewing.* In virtually every community, there are restaurant reviewers who produce local restaurant guides and often conduct radio talk shows about the local restaurant scene. Even if you choose not to make such an all-out commitment to restaurant reviewing, doing a column for a local newspaper or magazine could be a gastronomically

enjoyable sideline that might also bring you to the attention of prospective clients in the restaurant field and beyond. Restaurants and restaurant chains require a wide range of promotional materials and media publicity. Some restaurants produce promotional newsletters for their clientele. If you are a restaurant critic who includes food service accounts among your freelance clients, guard against conflicts of interest.

_____ *like to do*   _____ *could do now*   _____ *could learn to do*

49. *Resumé writing.* Check your Yellow Pages to see how many fellow writers are already toiling in this vineyard—there's probably room for one more. Local and national firms hire writers to produce resumés, but individuals can compete effectively in this market. Directory, classified, and display ads are a vital source of business. Networking and referral programs are also effective. Speaking on resumé preparation before local groups and writing articles on resumé preparation for local business and organizational publications can also pay off.

_____ *like to do*   _____ *could do now*   _____ *could learn to do*

50. *Retail and mall promotions.* Brochures, flyers, posters, point-of-sale displays, and more are involved in retail and mall promotions produced every day in every community. As a home-based desktop publisher—possibly working with a writer colleague—you can produce this material for retail stores and malls in your region. When a good relationship has been established, there's lots of repeat business.

_____ *like to do*   _____ *could do now*   _____ *could learn to do*

51. *Reviews of books, records, concerts, theater, art.* You won't get rich, but you will get free review copies or free tickets plus lots of prestige from this kind of writing. Having your byline appear regularly in print can also help you attract freelance clients in other fields. If you want to be a reviewer for a local

publication but don't feel you have the necessary literary or fine arts background, start a self-study program or take some college classes—and try your hand at some free reviews for small publications or newsletters.

_____ *like to do*    _____ *could do now*    _____ *could learn to do*

52. *Sales presentations.* Writers who specialize in marketing materials and who have a strong relationship with a company or marketing firm may be assigned the job of preparing a sales presentation. Based on marketing research and product information, the presentation could include a verbal text plus a variety of audiovisual aids. Charge plenty.

_____ *like to do*    _____ *could do now*    _____ *could learn to do*

53. *Scripts and storyboards.* Rates for scripts to be used in audiovisual presentations and industrial or instructional videos and films are reckoned by the minute and vary widely, from really high to really low. Unless you are doing the work for little or no money, you will be expected to have solid experience in this specialty. If nothing in your previous employment and educational history has prepared you to write scripts, but you would like to enter this fascinating field, allow time to get yourself up to speed. Take classes. Ask professionals for information interviews. Volunteer to help crews on student and low-budget shoots. Check to see if your local cable station offers free technical training for public-access video. Your clients will be independent producers and in-house production teams.

_____ *like to do*    _____ *could do now*    _____ *could learn to do*

54. *Speeches.* An all-purpose public relations writer is expected to be able to write speeches, but specializing in speech writing for corporate executives, politicians, and other public figures can be a lucrative business. The best opportunity to make money is in the corporate world, but you will need to build credibil-

ity with the speaker and his or her public relations people first—perhaps by doing other kinds of writing for them.

_____ *like to do*    _____ *could do now*    _____ *could learn to do*

55. *Sports materials and services.* Local athletic teams need team books, programs, and other materials at the start of each season. The news media sometimes pay freelancers to report scores and do seasonal writing in areas their regular sportswriters can't cover. You won't make much for this kind of writing, but you'll enjoy doing it, and the contacts could lead to other business.

_____ *like to do*    _____ *could do now*    _____ *could learn to do*

56. *Teaching writing or desktop publishing.* Teaching can supplement your income while it builds your credibility and occasionally brings you an assignment. One approach is to teach adults through your local community college or any other adult education program. Or if you have a master's degree or the equivalent, you might become a part-time instructor for a local university or college, teaching a regular course for credit in communications or graphic arts. The huge amount of work required to develop materials for your first class may discourage you, but freelancers who persist as teachers find the experience both profitable and emotionally rewarding. And of course, you will have no financial risk and little or no responsibility for recruiting students. The downside is that halfway through the semester, when a big freelance assignment comes your way, you must continue to serve your students. A more entrepreneurial approach is to offer short-term workshops or seminars on writing or desktop publishing, financing and promoting them yourself. If you're good enough, eventually you can go on the road as an instructor for a business training firm. Since such programs usually attract working professionals, they may bring you a significant amount of business.

_____ *like to do*    _____ *could do now*    _____ *could learn to do*

57. *Technical illustration and design.* An important source of business for desktop publishers who have the patience and knowledge for this complex work. If your previous employment qualifies you for technical illustration and design, make the most of your background by approaching equipment manufacturers, technical publishers, laboratories and scientists, and others in your field of experience. If you are inexperienced, your science courses in school and your hobby interests may help you get started. If necessary, do work at a discount or for free to build a portfolio and gain experience.

_____ *like to do*  _____ *could do now*  _____ *could learn to do*

58. *Technical writing.* Many of the formats we have already looked at, such as books, brochures, and flyers, exist in the specialized area of technical writing. If you are familiar with (or are undaunted by) computer, scientific, and engineering jargon, technical writing can be a profitable specialty for you. Producing software and other operating manuals is an especially lucrative part of this work.

_____ *like to do*  _____ *could do now*  _____ *could learn to do*

59. *Telemarketing scripts.* Have you ever been a telemarketer—or are you willing to familiarize yourself with the large body of literature available in this growing field? Telemarketing firms and other advertisers who use this powerful sales technique need scripts for their telemarketers to follow. Some scripts are written by knowledgeable freelancers. Advertise your services through direct mail or network in professional organizations to meet those who buy telemarketing scripts. Or try telemarketing yourself.

_____ *like to do*  _____ *could do now*  _____ *could learn to do*

60. *Transcriptions and other word processing.* If you are reading this book, transcriptions and other word processing jobs are not your long-range goals. But while you're getting started as a writer or desktop publisher, you may take on such work to

make ends meet—especially if the work could lead to assignments that require your writing or desktop publishing skills. Make sure the work does not prevent you from doing your regular marketing. Then charge the going rate—which will be lower than your rate for writing or desktop publishing—and do the work to the best of your ability. Finally, let your client know about your real business goals and capabilities—and ask for a writing or desktop publishing assignment or referral. You may get it just because you did the word processing on time and with a good attitude.

_____ *like to do*  _____ *could do now*  _____ *could learn to do*

61. *Translations.* If you are a writer who is proficient in a foreign language, make the most of it. Translations can provide a source of income and give you an entree among foreign companies, publishers, trade representatives, and others that may eventually lead to bilingual writing assignments in the specialty of your choosing. If you can write professionally in English and in another language as well, your skills are worth more!

_____ *like to do*  _____ *could do now*  _____ *could learn to do*

62. *Travel writing.* This can be a glamorous full-time specialty, but not until you have solidly established yourself. At the very least, travel writing can be a way for astute writers to pay back some of the expense of their own vacations and weekend excursions. Markets are newspapers and magazines, including some membership publications (teachers' associations and auto clubs, for example), as well as general interest publications produced by airlines, insurance companies, and financial institutions for their clients. Producing and marketing a local travel guide (Anytown's Historic Sites, Where To Take Your Kids in Anytown) can be an enjoyable and profitable venture for a writer and desktop publisher.

_____ *like to do*  _____ *could do now*  _____ *could learn to do*

63. *Typesetting.* This is yeoman's work for any desktop publisher—although today's technology makes the term almost an anachronism. If the client's document is available on disk or modem or can be optically scanned, you will not technically be "typesetting," but flowing the text into pages and styling the type. You may be dealing with directories or price lists from databases, as well as books, booklets, manuals, and specification sheets. Although more and more typesetting is being handled in-house, your design skills can provide the client with a more attractive, more readable, and therefore more successful, publication. Announcements, invitations, resumés, and many other kinds of work will also come to you handwritten or typewritten, requiring keyboarding. Advertising typography is a very important subspecialty. If you're good at it, approach ad agencies and directory publishers, as well as individual advertisers.

\_\_\_\_ *like to do*    \_\_\_\_ *could do now*    \_\_\_\_ *could learn to do*

# Zero In on Your Areas of Specialization

Review the list of writing and design specialties and look for patterns in your responses—those you would like to do, those you can do now, and those you can learn to do. What common threads do you see among the kinds of jobs you want to do? If you *can* do something but don't *want* to do it, should you eliminate it? Probably you should, if your feeling against it is strong. If you want to do something but are not currently qualified to do it, what will it take to become qualified?

## Working Toward a Business Plan

### BUSINESS SUCCESS WORKSHEET SIX

### Concept: *Define your niche*

*Having a business focus (one or more areas of specialization) will give you credibility and better access to clients.*

Here are some ways to establish your business focus. Based on your responses *(like to do, could do now, could learn to do)* to the key assignments for home-based writers and desktop publishers listed in this chapter—and to other types of work that may occur to you—answer the following questions.

- What types of writing and desktop publishing work would you like to do?

- Based on your knowledge, experience, and interest, what could you specialize in as a writer and desktop publisher?

- Is this type of work going to be profitable? Can it predictably provide a satisfactory return for the time you must invest?

- How much competition is there for this type of work in your community? You'll learn more about how to evaluate the competition when you study marketing in Chapter Seven, but for now, what is your best educated guess?

- Will this type of work lead to repeat or related business?

- Is the work seasonal? Is it related to popular trends that may shift?

- What is the long-range outlook for this type of work? Is it related to growing or at least stable industries or technologies?

- Will you need additional knowledge or training in order to succeed at this type of work?

- How will you get the knowledge or training you need?

# Who Buys the Meat-and-potatoes Jobs?

Once you have focused on the kinds of work you will do, you can define your marketplace and begin to identify and make contact with potential clients. The following list gives you a cross section of many businesses, organizations, and individuals in your community who may buy services from professional home-based writers and desktop publishers.

Recall that in Chapter Two you analyzed your education; your work experience; your personal, family, and volunteer experience; and the areas you would like to know about—both in terms of the work you would like to do and the clients you would like to serve.

As you go through the following list, rate your interest in serving each client. Then look for a pattern in the clients you have rated "high."

If you would like to serve a client category, but do not feel qualified to do so, highlight that field for future study. For example, attorneys often attract clients by sending out informational newsletters, and a writer would need some background in legal terminology and procedures in order to serve an attorney. A desktop publisher seeking to produce a newsletter already written by an attorney would not have that limitation. On the other hand, a desktop publisher undertaking a highly technical scientific document would need some familiarity with such material. This is just one more reason for specializing. When you have special knowledge in a field, you can work more quickly and accurately—and you can charge more.

## Sixty-three Key Writing and Desktop Publishing Clients
MY INTEREST IN SERVING SUCH CLIENTS

|  | High | Average | Low |
|---|---|---|---|
| 1. Accountants | ___ | ___ | ___ |
| 2. Advertising agencies | ___ | ___ | ___ |
| 3. Architects | ___ | ___ | ___ |

|  | High | Average | Low |
|---|---|---|---|
| 4. Art galleries, public and private | \_\_\_\_ | \_\_\_\_ | \_\_\_\_ |
| 5. Associations | \_\_\_\_ | \_\_\_\_ | \_\_\_\_ |
| 6. Athletic teams, sports promoters | \_\_\_\_ | \_\_\_\_ | \_\_\_\_ |
| 7. Attorneys | \_\_\_\_ | \_\_\_\_ | \_\_\_\_ |
| 8. Churches (large), denominations, religious organizations | \_\_\_\_ | \_\_\_\_ | \_\_\_\_ |
| 9. City guide publishers | \_\_\_\_ | \_\_\_\_ | \_\_\_\_ |
| 10. Colleges, universities, and private schools | \_\_\_\_ | \_\_\_\_ | \_\_\_\_ |
| 11. Concert promoters | \_\_\_\_ | \_\_\_\_ | \_\_\_\_ |
| 12. Conference planners | \_\_\_\_ | \_\_\_\_ | \_\_\_\_ |
| 13. Consultants | \_\_\_\_ | \_\_\_\_ | \_\_\_\_ |
| 14. Convention centers | \_\_\_\_ | \_\_\_\_ | \_\_\_\_ |
| 15. Corporate human services departments | \_\_\_\_ | \_\_\_\_ | \_\_\_\_ |
| 16. Corporate marketing departments | \_\_\_\_ | \_\_\_\_ | \_\_\_\_ |
| 17. Corporate public relations/communications departments | \_\_\_\_ | \_\_\_\_ | \_\_\_\_ |
| 18. Corporate purchasing departments | \_\_\_\_ | \_\_\_\_ | \_\_\_\_ |
| 19. Dentists, dental practice groups | \_\_\_\_ | \_\_\_\_ | \_\_\_\_ |
| 20. Design firms | \_\_\_\_ | \_\_\_\_ | \_\_\_\_ |
| 21. Direct marketing firms, especially direct mail | \_\_\_\_ | \_\_\_\_ | \_\_\_\_ |
| 22. Directory publishers | \_\_\_\_ | \_\_\_\_ | \_\_\_\_ |
| 23. Engineering firms | \_\_\_\_ | \_\_\_\_ | \_\_\_\_ |
| 24. Fitness centers | \_\_\_\_ | \_\_\_\_ | \_\_\_\_ |
| 25. Fund raising departments and consulting firms | \_\_\_\_ | \_\_\_\_ | \_\_\_\_ |
| 26. Government departments—federal, state, county, township, city | \_\_\_\_ | \_\_\_\_ | \_\_\_\_ |

|  | High | Average | Low |
|---|---|---|---|
| 27. Goverment-funded special agencies, including water districts, school districts, education departments, libraries, and other specialized programs | _____ | _____ | _____ |
| 28. Greeting card and gift companies | _____ | _____ | _____ |
| 29. Health insurance firms | _____ | _____ | _____ |
| 30. Hospitals, medical centers | _____ | _____ | _____ |
| 31. Hotels, resorts, casinos | _____ | _____ | _____ |
| 32. Importers, exporters | _____ | _____ | _____ |
| 33. Individuals, families | _____ | _____ | _____ |
| 34. Labor organizations | _____ | _____ | _____ |
| 35. Laboratories | _____ | _____ | _____ |
| 36. Lettershops, quick-printers | _____ | _____ | _____ |
| 37. Magazines/newsletters—business and trade | _____ | _____ | _____ |
| 38. Magazines/newsletters—consumer, including regional, local, hobbies, how-to | _____ | _____ | _____ |
| 39. Magazines/newsletters—employees, alumni, organizations | _____ | _____ | _____ |
| 40. Marketing agencies | _____ | _____ | _____ |
| 41. Medical professionals, including those in solo or group practice, or health maintenance organizations; and other medical specialists, both traditional and non-traditional | _____ | _____ | _____ |
| 42. Museums, public and private | _____ | _____ | _____ |
| 43. Newspapers—community and regional | _____ | _____ | _____ |
| 44. Newspapers—business and trade | _____ | _____ | _____ |

| | High | Average | Low |
|---|---|---|---|
| 45. Performing arts centers, theaters, performing groups | ___ | ___ | ___ |
| 46. Printers, quick-print and commercial | ___ | ___ | ___ |
| 47. Private clubs—yachting, golf, etc. | ___ | ___ | ___ |
| 48. Producers—industrial/educational/ promotional films, video, broadcast | ___ | ___ | ___ |
| 49. Psychologists/counseling groups | ___ | ___ | ___ |
| 50. Public relations agencies | ___ | ___ | ___ |
| 51. Research organizations | ___ | ___ | ___ |
| 52. Restaurants | ___ | ___ | ___ |
| 53. Resellers | ___ | ___ | ___ |
| 54. Retail stores | ___ | ___ | ___ |
| 55. Shopping centers, malls | ___ | ___ | ___ |
| 56. Small manufacturing businesses | ___ | ___ | ___ |
| 57. Small service businesses | ___ | ___ | ___ |
| 58. Social service agencies | ___ | ___ | ___ |
| 59. Software publishers | ___ | ___ | ___ |
| 60. Theme parks, recreation centers | ___ | ___ | ___ |
| 61. Transportation/shipping firms and agencies | ___ | ___ | ___ |
| 62. Travel agencies | ___ | ___ | ___ |
| 63. Wholesalers | ___ | ___ | ___ |

# Writing and Design-related Agencies

While some employment agencies specialize in communications skills and may be able to place you in a temporary job, in my experience, they are a last resort for a freelancer—use them only to keep the wolf from the door. Unless you learn valuable new skills or make new contacts, such a job is a setback because working in an employer's environment will keep you from seeking new business. Only in technical writing is it common practice—and the stuff of which a freelance career can be made—to take temporary full-time assignments.

There is, however, another type of agency that brokers freelance writing and design services. Often these writing-related agencies specialize in technical communications, as does The Write People in Dayton, Ohio, and Joy Mieko White's firm, Infoteam/ Ecrivons, Inc., in El Toro, California. Some writing-related agencies or groups emphasize medical, public relations, or other specialties. Some have a broader focus. Cincinnati-based Creative Consortium, Inc., is a full-service marketing communications agency dealing with associated writers and graphic artists across the nation.

Writing and design-related agencies may provide you with work for a percentage of your fee or, like an advertising agency, they may pay you for your work and bill the client directly. Either way, they will require that your work meet their professional standards and that you follow their business practices. Check your regional Yellow Pages and other directories under such headings as "writing," "graphic design," and "marketing communications" to see if you have such a resource in your area.

Rank your interest in working with a writing-related agency. Is it high, average, or low?

# Matching Jobs and Clients

At this point, go back over your responses on the list of jobs and the list of clients and compare the kinds of work you would like to do with the kinds of clients you would like to serve. Do the clients you like buy the jobs you prefer? If not, what jobs do they buy? Let your mind float over the material and look for connections you may not have seen before. Look for patterns that will help you decide *what you will do—and for whom.*

## Working Toward a Business Plan

### BUSINESS SUCCESS WORKSHEET SEVEN

### Concept: *Identify your market*

*Identifying who your potential clients are is vital to your home business success.*

- Have you already done some independent writing or desktop publishing (either free or for payment)? Who were your clients?

- Would it be profitable for you to continue serving these clients and others like them? (If not, samples of your work for them and testimonials from them may help you approach more profitable clients.)

- Within which industries  do you plan to seek business?

- Will you need any special preparation in order to work in these industries?

- Within these industries, what types of clients do you plan to serve? Consider all the individuals who customarily buy printed materials—owners, marketing directors, communications specialists, art directors, human services directors, and purchasing agents. Which ones can you work most effectively with?

- How can you prepare yourself to call on buyers whose specialties may be unfamiliar to you?

- How credit-worthy are the clients you are interested in serving?

- How promptly will they pay?

- Do they offer repeat or related business?

- How much competition are you likely to encounter in serving these clients?

- Is the business seasonal or dependent on trends that may shift?
- What is the long-range economic outlook in your region for the industries you are considering?

---

## Alan S. Horowitz

### *Business Writer, Salt Lake City, Utah*

### Creating Business Opportunities

"You never know where business will come from," says Salt Lake City business writer Alan S. Horowitz. Horowitz traces the growth of his own writing career through a web of introductions and seemingly opportune connections, yet he insists that "thinking and initiative are all that are required. You don't need inside information."

Horowitz didn't start out as a writer. A native of New York City, he earned advanced degrees in economics and theater management, but, while writing theater public relations material, he realized that writing was his true love.

Horowitz worked as a writer for a Los Angeles public relations firm and an in-house ad agency, wrote academic term papers, and then got a job at *Entrepreneur Magazine* where he met an editor who had started an investment newsletter. The editor hired Horowitz to write for him full-time, and when the newsletter business moved to Salt Lake City, Horowitz went along. When it moved again following the 1987 stock market crash, he decided to stay put as a freelance writer, pursuing a longtime dream.

Horowitz' initial strategy was to "go all over the place," writing on health, travel, business, theater. "But after a while," he says, "I saw the benefits of focusing on a couple of markets." Today, Horowitz specializes in business with an emphasis on small business, personal finance, and the business side of the computer industry. He writes articles and newsletters and recently ghost-wrote a book on personal financial planning.

A web of connections has helped his business grow. For example, a friend introduced Horowitz to the editor of *Selling Red,* a magazine for computer resellers. It was his entré to computers. Later, he used his articles from *Selling Red* to approach *Reseller Management,* a national computer trade journal for which he still writes.

"In any industry you write about," Horowitz explains, "you build up a knowledge base along with a database of contacts, information, and quotes."

Often it is simple research that gets Horowitz the job. Reading *The Wall Street Journal,* he learned of a new entrepreneurial magazine being started by American Express. He got in touch with them and sold them several articles. In the local office of the Small Business Administration, he noticed *Small Business Success,* a magazine published by Pacific Bell. He called the editor, put together a query letter with three story ideas and clips of his work, and received a positive response.

In another venture, Horowitz and a desktop publisher colleague created a marketing newsletter for an East Coast computer reseller. It was a turnkey operation and the two divided the income based on the hours each had put in.

Horowitz, who is single, has his office in one bedroom of his apartment and uses a 486 PC, a transcription machine, and a modem.

"I'm not what you would call disciplined," he says, "but I try to spend up to half my time doing something that could lead to new business, whether it's sending out pitch letters or queries, researching new markets, thinking up story ideas, or calling prospective customers."

# Making Your Business Legal

## The Basics of Setting Up a Business

Many writers and desktop publishers start selling services out of their homes part-time—and even full-time—without ever taking a serious look at the fundamentals of choosing a suitable form of business organization, selecting an appropriate business name, and obtaining the necessary business licenses. *Not a good idea!* Be serious about your business from the beginning. Your customers will sense the difference—and, down the road, you will avoid such potential disasters as property use violations, fines, back taxes, business name lawsuits, and issues of business ownership.

Selecting the organizational structure on which you will build your business is a vital first step, and there is no shortage of information on the subject. Most books on starting your own business explain the three basic types of business organization—sole ownership, partnership, and corporation—as well as procedures for establishing a name for your business and obtaining the necessary licenses. Since regulations in these matters vary from state to state, county to county, and city to city, what follows will be a general guide to the points with which you must be familiar. Eventually, you will have to obtain forms and file papers with specific government agencies—but the more information you have in advance, the better.

For recent information about starting a business in your state and community, go to your library and ask for relevant books or pamphlets. Another good move at this point is to attend free or low-cost seminars about starting a business. Many organizations offer such training. Watch the business section of your newspaper, and check with your library, chamber of commerce, and local office of the Federal Small Business Administration (SBA). In addition, adult education classes on starting a business are offered by many school districts and colleges. The information you obtain in these programs will be current and specific to your locality. Often local accountants, bankers, attorneys, SBA spokespersons, and representatives of the Internal Revenue Service (IRS) are asked to address seminars and classes on starting a business. They will give you materials and be available to answer your questions, and they would not be on the platform if they were not interested in making contact with new business owners. You may find your own future accountant, attorney, or business banker this way. Talking with other new entrepreneurs in the audience may also provide you with information and resources.

As a writer, I love and live by the printed word, and I rely on books, magazines, and newspapers for much of my mental sustenance. But I am also a strong believer in networking. When you are exploring a new area, face-to-face contact is a better way to gain a foothold.

# Sole Proprietorships

Most of the small businesses in this country are sole proprietorships. Basically, if you do not form a partnership or file articles of incorporation, a sole proprietor is what you are. This is where you will probably start and where you may very well stay, although you can always change your form of business organization later on.

## Characteristics

As a sole proprietor, you are solely responsible for your business. You are the boss. You make the decisions, pay the bills and taxes, and may keep the income that is left. Any debts or obligations your business incurs are your personal responsibility. Hiring employees to work for you does not change the status of your business. If you decide to move your residence, your business can move with you. When you die, your business will end. You may operate any number of sole proprietorships at the same time—or in addition to any role you may play as a partner in a partnership or an officer in a corporation.

## You pay taxes on net earnings

As the owner of a sole proprietorship, you will pay taxes via your personal tax return, calculating the net earnings of your business on Schedule C of Form 1040, and reporting that amount as personal, taxable income. You will also be required to pay your own Social Security taxes.

## You can't hire yourself

One of the most common misunderstandings on the part of individuals new to business is how an entrepreneur actually "pays" himself. A sole proprietor cannot hire himself as an employee, but may withdraw any amount of money from the business as a "draw." This is not a wage and is not subject to payroll taxes or to any unemployment or disability requirements. At tax time, the profit of your business, as calculated on Schedule C, is your actual wage and is reported as income, regardless of how much or how little "draw" you took during the year.

## Federal Identification Number

If you have set up your sole proprietorship under a name other than your own—such as The Write Stop, Peterson Desktop Publishing, or Hometown Editorial Services—you will need to obtain a Federal Identification Number (FIN) from the IRS. Contact your local IRS office for the necessary form. Clients will need this number to report the payments that they make to you. At the end of the year, you will receive statements from your clients (those who keep good books), showing the totals that they have reported. If you work under your own name, you can obtain a FIN or you can use your Social Security number.

## Advantages and disadvantages

A sole proprietorship has many advantages. It is easy to start and to discontinue. Because fewer documents and no legal fees are required, it is the least expensive form of business to start. It is freer of government regulation than a corporation. And your tax rates may be lower than corporate rates.

A sole proprietorship also has disadvantages. Unlike a corporation, it provides no shield for your personal assets—one reason why the letterhead used by your physician in solo practice down the street may say, "Ann Smith, M.D., Inc." Damages from any lawsuits brought against your business as well as debts incurred by your business can be taken from your personal assets. You will also encounter more difficulty than a corporation or partnership raising capital or obtaining business loans. Barring a major improvement in the U.S. health care system, you will probably pay more for health insurance than a large business would pay, and you cannot deduct the premiums as a business expense. Instead, they are itemized as a personal tax deduction. Finally, a sole proprietorship "dies" when you die. You can, of course, leave your business to your survivors, but the assets of your business could be subject to inheritance taxes.

## Husband-and-wife arrangements

If you are a husband and wife running a business together, you may form a partnership, but you may also designate one spouse as the sole proprietor and consider the other an employee, deducting his or her wage as a business expense. The wage of the employee spouse is taxable income, and all required federal and state deductions and payments must be made. A simpler but perfectly legal option exists, however. In this scenario, the employee spouse works in the business but is not on the payroll, saving federal and state payroll taxes and avoiding all the paperwork. The "draw" taken by the employer spouse covers the needs of both. The main drawback to this simple, inexpensive solution may be a serious one at retirement time: The employee spouse earns no Social Security credits for working in the business.

# Partnerships

When two or more people go into business together but do not form a corporation, they are in partnership. From a tax standpoint, there is little difference between a partnership and a sole proprietorship except that an annual notice of the revenue distributed to the partners must be filed with the IRS, and a partnership must have its own Federal Identification Number (FIN). Partners pay their taxes in the same way sole proprietors do, and the personal assets of partners are at the same risk as those of sole proprietors to meet business debts or judgments. Since partners, like sole proprietors, cannot be employees of the business, arrangements for paying them must be agreed upon in advance. Each partner may draw a regular guaranteed payment or may share in profits—or some combination of the two.

When one partner dies or withdraws or a new partner is added, the partnership is legally terminated. The business need not be liquidated, however. All that is needed is a new partnership agreement.

## Advantages

Obviously, the talents, energy, contacts, and ideas of two or more professionals can be a great asset to any business. A writing–desktop publishing team is an especially winning combination. Having a partner can even out workload peaks and valleys and make it easier for owners to schedule vacations and deal with personal emergencies. Each partner may bring different pieces of equipment into the business, reducing start-up costs. When funds are needed, a partnership will usually find it easier than a sole proprietorship to raise money, since lenders and investors see less risk when several entrepreneurs are committed to the venture. Government regulations for a partnership are less stringent than for a corporation. And partnerships are easy to start—though less easy to dissolve.

## Disadvantages

Since the breakup rate for partnerships is even higher than that of marriages, a partnership poses some very real risks. Partners may not have compatible working habits and may not agree on long-term goals. Lines of authority may be in frequent dispute. Issues relating to unequal initial investments may be hard to resolve. And all partners can be held personally liable for the acts of any one partner relating to the partnership business—whether it be borrowing money in the name of the business or mishandling a job so that a lawsuit results.

## Partnership agreements

From a legal standpoint, a partnership is a real entity, even if a written partnership agreement does not exist. Unfortunately, many small partnerships get under way with no written agreement—and such casualness can be costly. In their book, *Working From Home* (1990), Paul and Sarah Edwards state, "Anyone entering into a partnership should have an attorney draw up a partnership agreement first and obtain partnership insurance as soon as the agreement goes into effect." Other authorities take a less extreme position, providing guidelines partners may use in drawing up their own agreements for possible review by an attorney.

Whether or not you seek an attorney's help, your agreement should cover the following:

- the nature of your business and its goals
- what each partner will contribute in labor and property

- how earnings are to be distributed, procedures for withdrawing funds and paying profits
- a clause specifying the financial and legal powers of each partner
- provisions for continuing the business if a partner leaves or dies
- provisions for adding a new partner
- procedures for mediation
- provisions for revising the partnership agreement and keeping it current

A good reference on this topic is *The Partnership Book,* published and periodically updated by Nolo Press of Berkeley, California, (800) 992–6656. Nolo has also introduced a software program, Partnership Maker, which can be used in any state to prepare a legal partnership agreement.

## Partnerships in the home

When partners share a home—whether or not they are a married couple—there should be no special problems housing their business in their residence. However, when a business is housed in the home of only one partner, this significant contribution to the business—and its financial and management implications—should be carefully discussed and clarified in the partnership agreement.

## Limited partnerships

A limited partnership allows investors to become partners in a business without assuming unlimited liability, while at least one general partner bears full legal and financial responsibility. Limited partners don't take part in the daily operation of the business but do share in profits. Since government regulations at the federal, state, and even the county level are much more stringent regarding limited partnerships, you should consult a tax accountant or an attorney familiar with the rules in your area before entering into an agreement.

As a writer or desktop publisher getting started at home, bringing in a limited partner might work if you have a friend, relative, or other investor willing to help fund your new business. However, in line with the wise old business adage, "KISS: Keep It Simple, Stupid!", I would strongly advise you to handle such an investment as a loan, perhaps paying only the interest for the first few years.

### Limited liability partnerships

A new partnership structure, available in some eighteen states, is the limited liability company (LLC). An LLC is a partnership that works like a corporation with respect to liability, limiting liability to the assets of the enterprise, but when it comes to income taxes, it works like a traditional partnership. If you are considering a partnership, find out if your state offers this option.

# Corporations

A corporation is a legal entity in itself. It suggests stability and strength to potential investors and can extend beyond your lifetime. The corporate form of business limits your liability and may enable you to obtain insurance benefits not available to a sole proprietorship or partnership. The days of incorporating small businesses as a tax loophole, however, ended with the Tax Reform Act of 1986. Establishing a corporation today is expensive and time-consuming and will almost certainly require the help of an attorney, unless you want to gamble your future and that of your business on a do-it-yourself kit. Since corporations are regulated by several levels of government, running even a small one requires extensive paperwork. Corporations are also subject to higher taxes and could increase your insurance costs.

For these reasons, very few writers or desktop publishers will start their businesses as corporations. The only exception might be an entrepreneur who sees his or her home business as the first step in a much larger enterprise. In that case, incorporating at the onset could be simpler and less expensive than incorporating later. *Small Time Operator* by Bernard Kamoroff, C.P.A. (1993) is one of many books for new entrepreneurs that go into the specifics of starting a corporation.

# Naming Your Business

Even though naming your business is a marketing function, I'm going to take it up now because filing a fictitious name statement is one of the basic steps of setting up your business, and it's required in most states if you're using a name other than your own. Bearing in mind that you can modify, or completely change your business name later as your business evolves, consider these general suggestions while you engage in one of the fun parts of starting a business.

## Just your name

You can work under your own name—a simple "Mary Sanchez" at the top of your letterhead. This is typical of writers and designers serving such traditional markets as magazines, publishers, and advertising agencies. If you are entering the local business marketplace, however, your business will be better accepted if its name clearly suggests what you do. You are not dealing exclusively with editors and art directors, but with a wide range of buyers, some of whom may never have encountered a writing or desktop publishing service before.

## Adding to your name

For a single, home-based entrepreneur, adding a term such as "enterprises" or "group" to your name suggests a larger, more permanent organization. Calling yourself "president" instead of simply "owner" has the same effect. A young friend who operates a marketing firm out of his home calls himself "vice president" to suggest an even bigger organization. I must admit that I have mixed feelings about trying to appear larger than you actually are. I have been given assignments from some very large corporations who know full well that I am just one person working out of my home, and they are happy to get good work for less money by hiring me. On the other hand, a person working alone is less credible in soliciting a large assignment than someone who has a team backing him up—which is why some form of networking among trusted colleagues is so vital.

## Multiple identities

For a different perspecive, however, let me share something I learned years ago in an E. Joseph Cossman seminar for small entrepreneurs. Since most of these business people were planning to sell products by mail, Cossman recommended they use multiple company names on multiple letterheads—even listing one "firm" as a "division" of another. After all, the impression made at the other end is all that really counts (along with, of course, the price, the service, and the final product). If this advice fits your operation, give it a try.

## Elements of your name

One popular approach to selecting a name is to use an element of your own name followed by a business description, such as: "Wong Communications" or "Bruce Wong Public Relations" or "BW Graphics" (your initials) or "W & J Resumé Service" (you and your partner, Nancy Janowitz). Since I do not plan to add assistants or associates, and since I feel that *I* am what I sell, I use my full name followed by a business description—"Lucy Parker Writing/Design." But this, too, has caused problems. When a large hospital issued a check to "Writing/Design," I had to ask them to cut another check made out to me so that I could cash it.

## A play on words

If your name lends itself to a play on words, you're lucky. Such tricks help clients remember your business name—as long as the moniker is not too cute! Good (fictitious) examples would be Wright Writing (owned by Jean Wright) or High Voltage Designs (owned by Sam Volt). Be careful to avoid trendy words that may soon sound dated.

## General or specific?

Some writers and desktop publishers elect to sound like an organization, while not suggesting what they do—for example, Betty

Jones & Associates. I understand the dilemma of a new entrepreneur who is not sure what his or her area of specialization will be, but I also believe strongly in clear communication. Vagueness may turn out to be a mistake when a potential client tries to recall what that nice woman he met at the networking breakfast really does.

### A separate name

Another valid approach is to give your business a completely separate name, perhaps suggesting your locale or the quality or tone of your work, such as "Tri-Counties Copywriting" or "Speedy Desktop Publishing" or "Word-Tech Company." This, too, suggests a larger, more permanent organization.

### Being cute

Before we leave the ego-titillating topic of naming your business, let me stress again that writers seem especially prone to inventing cute names—no doubt because we like to play with words. Unfortunately, a cute name may convey an unprofessional image. If you are aiming at a market segment that will appreciate an off-the-wall name, go for it! But if corporations are part of your marketing mix, it's usually better to be businesslike than amusing.

### Check for duplication

Whatever name you select, even your own, run a check of local competition in Yellow Pages and business directories to see if another firm is using something very similar. You can carry this search further by checking the sources listed below under Trademarks.

# Fictitious Name Statements

As I mentioned earlier, in most states, if you are doing business under anything other than your own name (that is, just "Robert Schwartz," not "Robert Schwartz Editorial Services"), you will need to file a fictitious name statement, also known as a DBA ("doing business as"). Without filing a DBA, you will probably not be able to obtain a city business license or open a bank account in the name of your business. Check, first, however, in case your state is one that permits the addition of descriptive words to the entrepreneur's own name. Often the filing of DBAs is handled at the county level.

Filing a fictitious name statement helps to protect the community from shady operators who might not want their identities known. It also helps protect your business name from use by others because it establishes the date and place you first used the name. For full protection, however, you will need to register a trademark or service mark.

Filing a DBA is a two-step process. You must obtain and register a form with the appropriate government agency, paying a nominal filing fee. And you must publish your fictitious name in a general-circulation newspaper. The easy way to do this is to observe which local papers carry fictitious name statements and then contact one. In many locations, small newspapers keep DBA forms on hand and will handle all the paperwork for you.

# Trademarks

Both the wording of your name and its typographic representation as well as any graphic symbol that is part of your business identity can be legally protected through a trademark or service mark (a trademark for a service). If there is an infringement, however, you must still front the legal costs to fight it. You can also trademark the name of a specific product. Some states register trademarks, giving you statewide protection. The U.S. Patent and Trademark Office (see Source Directory), currently registers trademarks nationally for $200. The process is fairly lengthy. About 48,000 trademarks were registered with the U.S. government in 1991, and 6,400 were renewed. A trademark includes "any distinctive word, name, symbol, device, or any combination thereof adopted and used, or intended to be used, by a manufacturer or merchant to

identify his goods or services and distinguish them (from others)."
The term of registration or renewal is 10 years. Since a trademark
is an intangible asset, it can be sold with your business, but it cannot be depreciated, as can patents and copyrights.

Registering a trademark involves a search of existing trademarks, and one valuable resource is *The Trademark Register*,
published each year and containing all federally registered U.S.
trademarks. A trademark research firm, such as Thomason and
Thomason in North Quincy, Massachusetts, or Trademark
Research Center in New York City (see Source Directory) will
search all state and federal trademarks plus additional sources.
Fees range from $120 to over $1,000. An online database, Trade-
markscan, produced by Thomason and Thomason, is updated
weekly and accessible through CompuServe—you will be charged
by either the minute or per record.

Do you need a trademark? Most home-based writers and desktop publishers do not—or at least not right away. However, if you
offer a unique product or service, and especially if you serve a
widespread clientele, registering your trademark may be advisable.

# Business Licenses and Zoning

Almost certainly, you will be required to get a local business
license, which is a permit to do business in a specific city or county.
Usually this involves going to the appropriate office, filling out a
form, paying an annual fee based on the volume of business you
expect to do, and then renewing your license each year by mail.
Often you will be required to post your license in your place of
business—a small but special moment for the new entrepreneur!

## Rules against home-based businesses

Unfortunately, this otherwise routine procedure holds some pitfalls
when you plan to work at home: Many communities have zoning
regulations against home businesses—or against certain types of
home-based businesses. Also, your municipality may require you

to obtain a "home occupation permit" before you can apply for a business license.

With the recent boom in home-based business, these restrictions are easing, rather than tightening. But bite the bullet and learn the rules in your area. You don't have to explain why you want to know. How is your neighborhood zoned? Single-family residential? Multiple-family residential? Light industrial? Commercial? What does that mean in terms of a home business? Can you put up a small sign? Can you have a business telephone listing? Can you advertise your home address in the Yellow Pages? What are the penalties for zoning violations? If the business licensing department does not have this information, the zoning department will. Check also with your chamber of commerce or local Small Business Development office. Or you may want to consult an attorney.

Fortunately, neither writing nor desktop publishing is characterized by the objectionable features that zoning restrictions are designed to prevent—large numbers of people coming and going, parking problems, noise, smoke, odors, hazardous materials, commercial signs, and unsightly exterior equipment or storage. Some communities also distinguish between a business and a profession in granting home business licenses, in which case you may qualify as a professional writer, artist, or consultant. If you live in an area zoned for agriculture, you're in luck! Such zones rarely ban home business.

## What if home business is prohibited?

If establishing a home business is prohibited in your area, you may decide to ignore the restriction, as many home entrepreneurs do— bearing in mind that if a neighbor files a complaint, you may be vulnerable to being fined, or worse. And if your state requires you to charge sales tax on any of your products, applying for a state reseller's permit may result in your city's being notified of your business address.

If you want to play by the rules, you can apply for a variance. This may also be necessary if you live in an apartment complex, condominium, or private community that has its own regulations against home businesses.

Another alternative is to obtain an address through a private mailing service, or if you work in close association with a colleague, you might use your associate's address. You could also move. Your new career as a home-based writer or desktop publisher is very, very important, so if the obstacles in one community are too great, go to a community that is more hospitable. Two adjoining towns may have completely different regulations. Be sure to let your old community know why you had to move! As home-based entrepreneurs, we must all work to improve zoning, tax, and other regulations that affect our success or failure.

# Seller's Permits

Sales taxes are imposed today by most states and some local governments. If you sell products or services on which your state charges sales tax, you are required to collect this tax and turn it over to the state annually, quarterly, or monthly depending on your volume of business. To comply with these regulations, you must apply for a seller's permit (also known as a resale permit). What is taxed varies from state to state. Writers providing copy for their clients' use are generally in the clear since such writing would probably not be considered a taxable product. Not so, however, with desktop publishers. Camera-ready art may be considered taxable in your state. And when you supply printing to a client, you will certainly be expected to collect tax unless your client plans to resell the material.

Again, bite the bullet. It's part of doing business. Find out from your state and local governments what regulations apply to your products and, if necessary, obtain a resale permit. When you do so, you may be required to deposit cash against the taxes you will collect. Your clients will accept the sales tax as a necessary burden, and if your volume of taxable business is small, you may have to file and pay only once a year. On the plus side, when you purchase raw or finished material for resale, you can avoid paying sales tax if you put your resale permit on file with your vendors. Likewise, you must keep your clients' resale numbers on file when they purchase products tax free from you, planning to resell them.

## Working Toward a Business Plan

### BUSINESS SUCCESS WORKSHEET EIGHT

Concept: *Set yourself up right.*

*Choosing the most suitable form of business organization, selecting an appropriate business name, and obtaining necessary licenses are the right way to begin.*

- Do you plan to organize your business as a sole ownership, partnership, or corporation?

- How will you handle ownership if you are a husband-and-wife team?

- What names are you considering for your business? List your best ideas.

_____

_____

_____

_____

_____

- How can each of these names benefit you from a marketing standpoint? (See the discussion about business names in Chapter Seven.) Do you see disadvantages to any of the names you are considering?

- Try the names out on some potential clients. Which name will you select?

_____

- Will you need to file a fictitious name statement? Do you know how to file one? When do you plan to do it?

- Will you need a trademark? Now or later? State or federal?

- What local zoning regulations will apply to your home-based writing and desktop publishing business?

- Do you live in an apartment, condominium, or private community that regulates home-based businesses? How will these regulations affect you?

- If any potential zoning or regulation problems exist, how do you plan to handle them?

- Do you know how to obtain a local business license? When do you plan to apply?

- Does your state and/or local government collect sales tax? Are any of the products you plan to produce taxable?

- If you will need a seller's permit, do you know how to obtain one? When do you plan to apply?

## Joy Mieko White
### *InfoTeam, Inc., Irvine, California*

### Establishing the Right Foundation

"Engineering firms pooled their resources to build Hoover Dam because one firm couldn't do it alone, so why couldn't we do the same thing as communications professionals?"

This was the idea buzzing in Joy Mieko White's brain during the mid-1980s, as she struggled to put together teams of writers, illustrators, and word processors for CalComp, a large computer hardware manufacturer. Because of a hiring freeze at the southern California firm, White, as technical documentation manager, was forced to call on independent contractors. "I had to spend days trying to find people who could work together," she says. "It was ridiculous. I felt that I should have been able to place just one call."

White began thinking about starting her own business, and she and her husband "worked lean and mean" putting a year's worth of net pay into their credit union. In 1986, she "took the big leap out of the corporate world."

Since White's background includes a communications degree, teaching credentials, and two years of high school teaching, she initially hung out her shingle as a seminar broker. At night, she taught technical writing at the University of California, Irvine, and local colleges. She also purchased an IBM PC system and began developing desktop publishing skills.

"To keep the business alive, I moved into technical writing," White recalls, "but as I started meeting other freelancers and understanding their skills, I finally acted on my real goal."

In 1989, the year her daughter was born, White refined her procedures, researched laws and regulations, studied the market, hand-picked ten writing and desktop publishing professionals, and invited them to become part of her organization. All but one signed up.

On Valentine's Day, 1990, she incorporated InfoTeam, a consortium of writers, editors, and workgroup publishers specializing in technical publications for business and government. "What a valentine!" she says.

Per a written agreement, all members must be in business and must satisfy a twenty-point set of criteria. Any member may withdraw or be asked to leave at any time. White handles most marketing and sales, calling on the technical skills of other members as needed, and earns a 10 percent commission. If another member brings in a sale, that person earns the commission. InfoTeam charges 15 percent for overhead.

The ten consortium members are encouraged to continue serving their own clients. "If InfoTeam provides more than eighty percent of any consortium member's livelihood, that person would be viewed legally as an employee," White explains.

The consortium holds monthly teaming meetings to share technical expertise, make plans, and talk things over. Each project has its own teaming agreement, which details the work expected, fees, and a timetable. Each project also has a manager—a job that rotates between White and several consortium members.

Since White's mother is Japanese and part of her heritage is American Indian, she applied for and received federal certification as a minority business owner along with certification as a woman business owner in California. "Being a minority or woman-owned firm doesn't get you the job. You have to prove your technical skills," she stresses. The certifications, however, may have helped her firm earn several large contracts.

With a growing business and a burgeoning technical library, White feels she may be outgrowing her home office. She predicts that "this may be the year that tells us whether we need to move outside."

# 5

# Office Space and Equipment

## What Will You Need to Get Started?

This chapter deals with office space and office equipment for the home-based writer or desktop publisher (with the exception of computer hardware and software, which will be discussed in Chapter Six). It's designed to help you determine what you will need to do a professional job from Day One without squandering precious start-up funds on nonessentials.

In areas where you are not sure ("Should I tear out the closet?" "Will I need a scanner?"), you may wish to do some additional research, such as reading and visiting stores. You can also collect opinions from your mentors and other knowledgeable people.

Heading into the exciting (but stressful) phase of creating and equipping your home office is like setting sail on a choppy sea in an untested boat. You're leaving dry land as you start to commit money, space, and time. And you're not 100 percent sure your plans will work. For a safe voyage, navigate by this lodestar: The goal is to be IN business, not to have your business perfectly set-up. Once you start earning money, you can refine the rough edges. Until you start earning money, you have nothing to refine.

There are expenses involved in starting any business—but there are also ways to keep costs down. Remember, "conserve cash" is a vital rule of thumb for new businesses.

At the end of the next chapter, after you have given detailed consideration to space, office equipment, and computer hardware and software, take a look at Business Success Worksheet Twelve. This worksheet will help you balance your needs and start-up costs against the funds you have available.

# Space for Your Home Office

Back in my university public relations days, long before I dreamed of working for myself at home, my English-teacher husband and I became friends with a novelist and his wife. As a couple, they also wrote TV scripts, working in a tidy, attractive, air-conditioned building in their backyard. How we envied that creative space! It seemed the epitome of a writing life.

Today, a close friend of mine in Orange, California, has successfully ghosted ten books and nine book proposals—plus four books under her own name—from a home office in an open corner of her living room, about 12 feet from her front door and 5 feet from where her young daughter often sits with neighborhood children watching TV.

As I work now at my Macintosh in my cool, quiet, albeit cluttered basement office—with my own children grown and gone—I honestly do not know how my friend does it. But she does—with style and high-volume production!

At another extreme, *Home Office Computing* recently reported on a successful graphic designer in Philadelphia who "shares his two-story, 2,000-square-foot home with his wife, his brother, and his brother's wife—as well as five graphic designers, two or three regular freelancers, and a steady stream of models, photographers, print reps, clients, and other visitors." Whew!

With its high-tech design, this spacious home office is mobile and convertible, reflecting the owner's wanderlust. He's moved three times in three years as his company has grown.

In other words, there are as many kinds of home office arrangements as there are home entrepreneurs. And each arrangement is a compromise stitched out of five basic elements that must be taken into account:

- the space you have available
- your existing equipment and start-up funds
- the requirements of your business specialty
- your own work habits
- your family's lifestyle

Keep them in mind as you go over the following topics related to office space.

# Basic Space Needs

Although a desktop publisher needs more equipment than a writer, there are several functions that your home office must support regardless of your specialty. Don't shortchange yourself on these requirements or you'll regret it as you struggle over the years with inconvenience and mislaid materials.

- Desk, chair, computer, and telephone for you
- The same for any other frequent workers
- Storage areas suitable for files, books and periodicals, computer materials, art materials, and office supplies
- Space for large pieces of equipment, including access to the equipment and handy storage for supplies

Be aware, also, that the Internal Revenue Service requires you to have a separate space in your home dedicated solely for office use in order for you to deduct home office costs. If necessary, this could be part of a room, even though the rest of the room is used for nonbusiness activities. But keeping the IRS happy is just one of many reasons why a separate room is preferable.

## Working area and storage

Get as much square footage for your office as you can. Be aware that, according to tax authorities, your office should not exceed 50 percent of the total area of your home, however. Consider creating an L- or U-shaped work area where you can easily reach your computer and other materials—you'll save time. For storage, a walk-in area adjoining your work area is just about ideal. It's handy and keeps clutter out of sight. A wall of cabinets (similar to those in your kitchen) will also serve—or you can even hang drapes or shutters in front of open shelves.

If your work area is too small to provide good storage, commandeer part of a guest room, garage, basement, or outside building for your needs. You must have storage—and even the inconvenience of storage in a detached building is preferable to the frustration of having no place to put things. Good storage promotes productivity. It allows you to keep and find what you need—when you need it!

## Locating and relocating to suit your work style

Many new entrepreneurs don't choose the best place for their home office on the first try. The problems may be subjective. For example, a desktop publisher sets up work in her living room, but she and her husband soon hate having business clutter "in their faces." A writer locates his office on the street side of his apartment and finds that traffic noises break his concentration. Another writer feels claustrophobic after three months in his basement. He misses having windows with fresh air and a view.

The problems may be objective. An office may be in a family traffic path. It may lack a door, inviting children or animals to enter and do damage—or visitors to look at confidential papers. A basement may flood in winter. An attic may become a summer steam room.

Don't be surprised if you end up relocating to another part of your house, remodeling your garage—or even erecting an outside building. I moved to the basement after deciding that my bedroom was incompatible with an office. Sleeping in the same room with my freelance materials and client records did not give me the sense of "going to work" that I seem to need.

To avoid the cost and bother of a move, try to anticipate such problems in advance, taking your work style into account. Do you like having people around? Then you may want to be in the traffic flow. Do you like taking your work to the living room or patio? Then you may need phones and small work areas in other parts of the house. Would you enjoy having a window—or would that be a distraction? The only "right" way to set up your office is the way that makes you feel most comfortable and most productive.

# Space Factors to Consider

If you can't afford to do all the necessary construction and buy all of the equipment you need for your office all at once, develop a written plan outlining each stage of the project, with materials lists and cost estimates. This is especially appropriate when converting a patio, porch, or basement; adding a dormer to an attic; or creating a loft above a high-ceilinged room. Consider seeking an architect, contractor, or handyman's advice. When you know what you're going to need, it's amazing how often you will spot low-cost supplies and equipment in ads and at garage sales.

What follows is a list of factors you can use as a planning guide in setting up your home office, based on my research and my own experience.

## Bulletin boards and pegboards

A bulletin board is a practical and businesslike addition to your office. Beyond the usual wall calendar, monthly or yearly planner, cartoons, and inspirational sayings, your bulletin board can hold a job status chart or reference materials pertinent to your work, such as maps (including one showing time zones and phone prefixes), current postal rates and regulations, type samples, and printing paper charts.

For years, I have made inexpensive bulletin boards by stapling colored fabric tightly over half-inch fiberboard. Sold by building supply stores in 4-x-8-foot or 4-x-4-foot sheets, the fiberboard is easily cut to fit the space available. Rich, dark cork is also nice—but beware of self-adhesive squares of cork that start crumbling as soon as you get them up and are almost impossible to remove. A better solution is sheet cork glued to a same-size piece of pegboard, which can be hung over nails or with wires. Or you can always buy a traditional bulletin board, framed in aluminum or wood.

For small tools and supplies—especially art supplies—a panel of the same pegboard that you use in the garage is perfect. Pegboard hooks and shelves come in a wide range of designs to fit your needs.

## Your communications system

Telephones, fax and modem connections, computer networks, and intercommunication systems (if needed) must be part of your office plan. Good advance planning will help you avoid changes later on, saving you downtime and frustration. How many phone lines will you need? Tax experts often advise home entrepreneurs to install a separate business telephone line to avoid any IRS questioning of business costs. I have not found this necessary. I take half my phone costs for business and answer my phone with a business message during business hours and a personal message during nonbusiness hours. I do, however, have a separate fax–modem line so that clients and others will never have a problem faxing me and, if necessary, I can communicate with a client or vendor on my regular line while sending a document via modem. An added benefit is that I have an extra call-out line.

Where will you place phone outlets? If you have several lines, will all phone instruments be able to access them? If you have a separate line for your business, will you need phones for it in other parts of the house? Will your fax–modem require its own line? How will your computer and peripherals be networked? Do you need an intercom to other parts of the house? Do you need a listening device (such as to a children's nursery)? What about your front door? Can you hear the doorbell from your office? If not, will you need a special buzzer or communication line?

If you are going to do even minor remodeling, consider running phone and computer networking cables through walls or ceilings to meet a variety of future needs.

## Toilets

You'll need convenient access to toilet facilities for yourself and any workers.

## Exterior access and parking

If you expect to receive many clients or vendors and can arrange a separate entrance for your business, it might be worth paying for some remodeling. However, most home offices get by without such access. Since exterior signs are likely to be prohibited, make sure your address is clearly marked. If you are hard to find, make up a small businesslike map that you can supply to those who will be visiting you.

To create a businesslike impression, keep up the appearance of your entry as well as the interior areas your visitors pass through. You'll also need a place for visitors and delivery persons to park—especially if unauthorized parking could cause conflicts with your neighbors. If street parking has restrictions, be sure your visitors know what to do.

The comings and goings of visitors are a potential mine field, and complaints from nearby residents can cause serious, long-lasting problems—even in a city where home businesses are allowed! In general, it's best to be friendly with neighbors and to keep them informed, probing for and correcting any potential sore points.

## Safety and emergency procedures

In 1991 I did an article on telecommuting (employees working from their homes) for a computer marketing newsletter. One of my questions was, "How do employers handle on-the-job injuries at home?" Several employers replied that they specifically define the employee's home work area and inspect it for safety, requiring that the employee correct any hazards. Then they insure the employee for the time he or she is doing company work in that workspace.

Take the same approach to providing safety in your home office and you will be ahead of the game. You'll be protecting yourself as well as any employees, freelancers, vendors, customers, or other visitors from injury.

Your local library can provide you with guidebooks to home and office safety. Look them over and take an inventory of potential problems, such as stairs without handrails, poorly lighted areas, scatter rugs or slippery floors that might cause falls, low beams that might cause head injuries, bookshelves that might fall over (we think about that a lot in earthquake-prone California), and hazardous materials. Correct problems when you can and put safety notices up when you can't—just as you would in a commercial setting.

Your office should have an emergency exit if possible. For example, a roll-down ladder can serve as an exit for an upstairs window. Your office should also be equipped with a smoke detector, a flashlight, and a fire extinguisher. (There are several types of extinguishers, so read up or talk to your vendor. Personally, I wouldn't advise calling the fire department.) Some health-and-safety authorities suggest putting a low-radiation screen in front of your computer monitor to reduce electrical emissions. Finally, you, your family, and your employees should agree on what to do in case of a fire, earthquake, flood, hurricane, or any other likely disaster and periodically review these procedures.

## Power

I had two dedicated electrical circuits added to my basement office for the security of knowing that my power-hungry computer, printer, scanner, copier, waxer, space heater, and anything else I might plug in will have enough juice to avoid catastrophes. That may not be possible for you—especially if you are in an apartment. But at least study your circuits and try to equalize the power loads. You don't want to lose computer documents when your microwave and washing machine kick in at the same time. If you cannot fully protect yourself from such a disaster, my best advice is, "When using your computer, save, save, save!"

## Light

Industrial research has shown that productivity drops when lighting is poor, and we usually think of an office as a place with plenty of light. But too much light can make it hard to adjust back and forth between your desk and your computer screen. Since the goal is to prevent eye strain, a balance between ambient (room) lighting and task (area) lighting is the answer. Set up different arrangements to see how they work at different times of day before you install permanent fixtures. Like other home-based writers and designers, you may soon be meeting deadlines at 2:00 A.M., so your office must provide good lighting at all times.

Another factor to consider is the positioning of your computer screen. Place a small mirror where your screen will be. If lights are reflected in the mirror, distracting reflections will also show up on your screen. Try another angle or location. If you're a desktop publisher who plans to work with color printing, you'll have a special interest in maintaining even light where you view your color work.

## Temperature control

An office in a spare room will probably share the existing heating and cooling system. But if you are converting a garage, attic, basement, or external building, you will have to equip it for temperature control. A small electric heater in winter and an oscillating fan in summer may do the job—but don't stint on comfort in the space where you will be living eight to ten hours a day. Remember, this is where you must perform at your best! Installing a wall heater, a room air conditioner, or some other permanent system could be a very good investment.

## Ergonomics

With recent attention focused on such on-the-job difficulties as carpal tunnel syndrome (a wrist disorder afflicting some computer users), ergonomics has become a hot topic. I think of ergonomics as the science of fitting form and function to the human frame. Industrial designers use it in establishing specifications for chairs, desks, counters, and other equipment. They design for average human dimensions, however, and one of the nicest things about planning your own office is that you can base your design on your own height and arm length or back problems. Your home office can be the most comfortable office you have ever worked in.

## Decor

Shelter magazines, furniture manufacturers, and interior decorators have staked out home offices as a new frontier. The theory is that if an office is in your home, it should meet a higher standard of decor than in an office building. I don't buy this one bit! All my office furniture, except the drawing board and a very good desk chair, is secondhand, much of it from the Goodwill and Salvation Army. My L-shaped work area consists of two large hollow-core doors from Home Depot mounted on filing cabinets. Commercial metal shelving (also pre-owned) sits on the doors to hold my books, periodicals, and many supplies. I do try to coordinate colors, but the fact is, I get a bigger kick out of saving money than decorating. On the other hand, I paid an electrician plenty to install recessed lighting for my eyes.

But don't let me talk you out of decorating your office. If it's in a high-traffic area, or if you have frequent visitors, or if the esthetics of your surroundings are very important to you, go to it—assuming you have sufficient start-up funds!

## Using design software or to-scale drawings

Interior design software is available to help you plan your home office. If you're a desktop publisher, you can save money by creating desk-sized and file-cabinet-sized boxes in a page layout or drawing program and moving them around a floor plan of your office drawn to scale to try out various options. Or, of course, you could also do that the old-fashioned way—on paper. Such planning will keep you from damaging the floor—or your back—as you experiment with furniture arrangements.

## What if you have "no space?"

Don't give up. If you must stay where you are, convert a closet or the area under a stairway. Divide a room with a screen or a combined desk and shelf unit. You may be surprised what good lighting and a carefully planned desk surface and shelves can do to transform a cubbyhole into a businesslike space. Later, as your business prospers, you can move to larger quarters or build a room addition.

## Working Toward a Business Plan

### BUSINESS SUCCESS WORKSHEET NINE

Concept: *Plan an office that suits you.*

*Your home office will be a compromise between your available space, existing equipment, start-up funds, and specific business requirements; your own work habits; and your family's lifestyle.*

- What space do you have available to meet the following needs?

    Your personal workspace and that of other frequent workers

    Well-organized storage

    Equipment and room to use it

    Comfortable meeting space to accommodate clients and vendors

    Assembling materials

- What percent of the square footage of your home will you use for your office and business storage?

- Will your work and storage areas be together or separate?

- What features of your office location might cause problems for you or other family members?

- In converting space for your office, what can you adapt or build yourself?

- Will you have to do significant remodeling? Can you do it in stages? Do you have a written plan or design? What outside assistance will you need?

- Have you considered the following factors?

  Bulletin boards and pegboards

  Your communications system: telephone lines, computer networks, and intercoms

  Toilet facilities

  Exterior access and parking

  Safety and emergency procedures

  Electrical power

  Lighting

  Temperature control

  Ergonomics

  Decor

- If you have "no space," is there anything you can do to create some?

- Make a list of the expenses you think you will incur in preparing your office space.

# Determining Your Equipment Needs

Whether you're a writer or a desktop publisher, the equipment you have on hand, plus the money you can invest, will determine the equipment you have when you start your business. If you're a desktop publisher, the equipment you have will determine the work that you can do. Setting ego aside, the real goal at this point is for you *to become functional and credible* as a home-based writer and desktop publisher. Much as you might like to have them now, a new oak desk and foil-stamped letterhead can usually wait.

## Furniture, files, shelving

Let's take a look at furniture, filing cabinets, tables, bookshelves, and storage shelves first. You will probably pay too much for these items if you shop at traditional office equipment stores, geared to furnishing large offices. Go there to get ideas. Home furnishing stores, such as the international chain, Ikea, also offer attractive but, to me, rather "lightweight" furnishings for the home office. Their showrooms are another good source of ideas, however. If you want to pay a little less for a wider selection, check the catalogs of large office supply mail-order houses. In my experience, you will pay even less at the big office-supply discounters, such as Staples and Office Depot. Discounters have thousands of products in stock and can order many thousands more through catalogs on file in their stores.

By the way, these stores are a great source of large, inexpensive plastic wastebaskets. Get several.

To make your money go as far as possible, consider buying used furniture, files, and shelving whenever possible. Check used office equipment stores and thrift stores such as the Salvation Army and Goodwill Industries. Look into government and corporate surplus sales. Check newspaper classified ads and "recycler" publications.

One caveat: If you can't find a used desk chair that suits you, pay whatever you must to get one that will be comfortable for you eight to ten hours a day. One friend with back trouble happily paid $400 for a lumbar support chair at an office discount store. Other back-pain sufferers also experiment with special cushions, available from orthopedic suppliers. Still others swear by "knee chairs," where body weight is said to be better balanced. A knee chair with casters will scoot you around in style.

As you lay out your office floor plan, remember that using lateral files (similar in shape to bookshelves) are sometimes preferable to traditional file cabinets, which require an open area for their pull-out drawers. Plastic crates designed to hold hanging files and sturdy cardboard "transfer" files and storage drawers can also help handle file storage. Rolling carts can hold frequently used files or supplies—or materials related to a current project.

Adjustable metal bookshelves, available at hardware and home supply stores, are a good investment. These shelves typically are black or gray, 3 feet wide by 1 foot deep, with uprights in 3-foot segments. Thus their height can be 3 feet or 6 feet, and their width can be 3 feet, 6 feet, 9 feet, and so on. You can set 3-foot shelves on a deep desk or table, securing them to a wall. To create an inexpensive counter height work and storage area, you can wire several shelving units back to back, topping them with a 24- or 30-inch-wide door or plywood sheet. The result? An inexpensive counter-height work and storage area. Since you are likely to relocate your office at least once, the "Tinker-Toy" flexibility of this kind of shelving is a big plus. And when disassembled, it's easy to transfer and store.

## Poor man's "fire-proof" storage

In *Tools of the Writer's Trade*, compiled by the American Society of Journalists and Authors (1990), one writer advises fellow writers not to discard an old refrigerator or small freezer. Instead, he suggests you put it in your basement or storage area. "It may not be as efficient as a costly fireproof safe, but it will protect computer disks and one-of-a-kind manuscripts from flames, smoke, and a considerable amount of heat should you have a fire in your home." Your guests may be disappointed, however, when they open it to find software instead of sodas.

## Typewriters and word processors

Still handy for addressing envelopes and labels and for filling out forms, typewriters retain a place in today's offices. I have to say that the electronic versions do not enchant me—with their slow carriage returns and inscrutable modes and codes that I am always forgetting. I still think the IBM Correcting Selectric II was the best typewriter ever made—and there are other old electric workhorses out there, too, including solid portables that take up little space. Used ones are easy to find.

If you are a writer, you could make do with a word processor as your main working tool. These hybrid-looking electronic devices provide a keyboard, a small screen eighty characters wide, and a built-in printing mechanism. They offer letter quality output, using strike-on or bubble-jet technology, but have very little typographic flexibility. Spell- and grammar-check features may be included, along with a small internal memory. The better word processors have a floppy-disk drive for storing documents, and (very important!) some are DOS compatible. That is, their disks can be converted for use on IBM-style personal computers. If you have a word processor, use it until you can afford a computer. If you don't have one, think carefully before buying. For about the same money, you could get an early-model used Mac or IBM PC and a dot matrix printer. They would be a much better buy.

## Telephones

Since you already have a phone in your home, you may tend to overlook typical business options when planning your telephone system. Such options do cost extra, but they can pay for themselves in convenience and the businesslike impression you make when people call you. They range from hold buttons and multiple-line phones to intercommunication systems and the ability to play music or a commercial message while your caller waits.

If you use the same line for business and personal use, as I do, consider this tip: I equipped all the phone outlets in my home with instruments that have a hold button, so that I can gracefully get to my office to handle a business call no matter where I pick up the phone. Also, when I put in a second phone line for my fax and modem, I bought two two-line phones for my office and ran the fax line to them. I use the second line only for outgoing calls. Having two lines conveniently at hand has proved well worth the investment. If a fax comes in while I'm on the line, the sender receives a busy signal and tries again.

Local phone companies are ecstatic about the home office boom and many provide special services, literature, and advice for home-based entrepreneurs, including 800 (toll free) and 900 (caller pays) numbers. Check it out—but be sure to learn whether you will be required to pay a higher rate if your number is identified as a business phone.

## Car phones

The gadget appeal and prestige of car phones are undeniable, and they are easy to purchase now—but they are still expensive to use, since you must pay by the minute for every call you make or receive. If you are often on the road and your work involves quick turnaround and fast answers, your clients will definitely appreciate being able to reach you in your car. However, a pager (see below) would do the same job for much less money. Some mobile entrepreneurs even equip their cars with faxes—a most impressive feature—but one that is probably quite dispensable for a writer or a graphic designer.

## Pagers

More and more small-business people are using pagers to stay in touch with their clients. The small devices clip on your belt or purse and beep or vibrate when you have a message. Most display the number, and sometimes a message, of the caller. At $50 to $100 and up for the unit and under $10 a month for the service, an "electronic leash" might be a good idea for a writer or desktop publisher—depending on the kind of work you do. Or it might be a bad idea. You may dislike interruptions from people who really don't need immediate attention.

But a pager is something to consider. For a small additional charge, paging firms can provide you with a custom message, voice mail, and other services. When you travel, they may be able to set you up with a temporary paging service out of town.

## Answering machines and answering services

As a home-based entrepreneur, you *must* have a convenient and dependable way to receive phone messages. A good answering machine is the usual choice. You can screen calls when you're busy (that is, you can listen to the caller start to leave her message and pick up the receiver if you want to accept her call). When you're away, you can pick up your messages and even change your own outgoing message. Some machines have two or more "voice mail boxes"—handy if you share a home business with a spouse or roommate: *"If you're calling Ted Garcia Copywriting, press 1. If you're calling Annie Garcia Design Service, press 2."*

A friend with a marketing firm clings to her old-fashioned live answering service. She hates machines on principle and thinks it's more prestigious to have a real person answering the phone when she's away. But I fume every time I want to leave a message too detailed for the operator to take down. If you prefer a live answering service, consider one with a voice mail option: *"Bob Okamura is at a trade show today. I can take your number and have him call you—or would you like to leave a message on his voice mail?"* Very professional!

My son, who does computer consulting out of his home in northern California, has come up with a slick combination of phone services. Using Delayed Call Forwarding (a relatively new phone option), he has his calls automatically forwarded to his paging number after the third ring. There, a message in his voice invites callers to leave him a recorded message or to page him by entering their phone number. This seamless system requires callers to keep track of only one number.

## Fax machines

A few years ago, I thought I could get by without a fax machine. The machines then were $600 or $700, and my nearby fax service (in a stationery store) charged only a dollar a page to send or receive. Then one Friday before a holiday weekend, a good client, the employee communications director for a major bank, called to say she had a rush project—a newsletter that was written but needed to be laid out. Could I do it by Tuesday? "Sure," I said. I was already familiar with the newsletter's format and asked her to fax it to me. Since I was busy all day Friday, I planned to pick up the work on Saturday morning. But when I got there, the stationery store was locked up tight with a sign in the window saying, "Closed for the weekend." On Tuesday, after apologizing to my client for blowing the job, I went out and bought my own fax machine.

Faxes are a basic part of communications today. Who could fail to be inspired—and even amused—by brave Chinese demonstrators faxing reports out of Tiananmen Square during the 1989 uprising, circumventing China's rigid information controls? With fax modems available for your computer for under $100, why not join the movement? Personally, I still prefer my stand-alone machine—but when I come home and find fax paper spilling all over my office floor, I wish it had a paper cutter. I also wish it didn't have to be hand-fed—since its ten-page document feeder likes to spit several pages through at a time.

If you buy a stand-alone fax, make sure all the features work. In addition to a paper cutter and a document feeder, other common features include preprogramming for frequently called numbers, automatic redialing, and the ability to automatically send a transmission (such as a press release) to a list of numbers at a predetermined time (such as at night when rates are lower and faxes are less busy). A machine that uses a paper roll larger than the standard 98-foot roll saves money and the bother of changing rolls, as well as lost faxes when you run out of paper.

Don't be impressed by manufacturers' claims that your fax can serve as a copier. It can, but only in a pinch.

## Phone–fax–modem managers

Several of my home-based writer friends manage all their phone-related activities on one line with the help of a phone–fax–modem manager. These devices can detect what kind of call is coming in (voice, fax, or modem) and they direct incoming calls to the proper instrument. At least, they're supposed to. In my experience, some of them give you a fax tone when you want to talk with someone, or put someone on the line when you want to send a fax. If you buy a phone–fax–modem manager, make sure it works!

## Copiers

I am surprised how many writers do not own a copier—fewer desktop publishers seem to get by without one. When I was short on cash, I managed without one for almost three years, running to the copy shop almost every day. Out of frustration, I began studying the classifieds and finally bought a used copier that turned out to be a nightmare of paper jams, toner smears, and repairs (thank God the seller took it back). Chastened, I bought a new 11x17-inch enlarging and reducing Sharp for almost $2,000. It was one of the best purchases I ever made! The quality on this machine, properly maintained, is so good that I often pasteup its output directly into low-budget layouts. Today I can't imagine life without a copier.

Next time you take off for the copy shop, consider what your time is worth. Personal copiers start at about $500.

## Calculators

No doubt you have a pocket calculator—that's all I use to this day. But a larger printing calculator might be useful. If you work with financial material, it might be essential. If you handle technical material, you may need a scientific calculator.

## Postal meters and scales

If you do a lot of mailing, a postal meter is a labor- and money-saving tool, since you can dial in the correct postage instead of hunting for the right stamps. Pitney Bowes leases an inexpensive unit to home entrepreneurs and small businesses. (But consider whether doing a mailing is really a good use of your time—small mailing houses are set up to do it much more efficiently.)

Even if you don't have much outgoing mail, a mechanical postal scale ($20 and up) is a necessity. You certainly don't want your material returned for insufficient postage, nor do you want to waste money on excess postage. An electronic calculating postal scale (over $100) calculates the necessary postage with the help of a pop-in rate cartridge that can be updated. It would be nice to add later as an efficiency upgrade.

## Binding machines

Office-supply discount stores and mail-order catalogs provide several bindery options, including plastic comb binding machines (about $500), which produce bound documents that will lie open, and various other units that bind documents on the side. I picked up a plastic comb binding machine in OK condition at the Salvation Army for $5.00. (They didn't know what it was.) A new or used unit might be a good investment if you often prepare material for presentation—writing proposals, for example. Presenting your own samples in a neatly-bound package also makes a dynamite impression.

## Color copiers

Color copiers print from reflective originals or slides and are too costly for most home offices as prices start at around $14,000. They offer enlargement, reduction, and even some color correction for about $1.00 a page. The quality is surprisingly good—good enough for comps to show your clients—and may even be good enough for your own promotional materials.

## Tape recorders and transcribers

If you're a writer who does taped interviews, you already have a tape recorder. If not, an inexpensive unit (either standard or microcassette) of any reliable brand will cost $30 to about $100 and will do just fine. When I'm taping phone interviews from home, my recorder is hooked up to a reliable $20 device from Radio Shack that can turn my remote-controlled tape recorder on automatically as soon as the receiver is lifted and produces good quality recordings.

Transcribing these interviews is, unfortunately, a time-consuming pain in the neck! You can't bill for it at your normal creative rates, and it's hard to find vendors to do it without losing both time and money—to say nothing of the difficulty getting an accurate transcription. A professional transcribing machine, with a foot pedal and speed control, sells for $200 to $300 new—and anything that makes transcription easier is a bonus in my book.

## Graphic arts equipment

Though few realized it at the time, the 1984 Super Bowl ad that introduced the Macintosh irrevocably changed our lives as graphic artists. Desktop publishers who, like me, got into graphics in pre-Macintosh days will recall antiquated tools like T-squares, triangles, drawing boards, waxers, and X-acto knives. No, just kidding—I still use those tools. But the truth is, I use my drawing board less and less. Rarely do I sit there now, doing thumbnail sketches or noodling with ideas, as I did so often in the past.

Today we can scan anything into a document, enlarge it, reduce it, redraw it, combine it—until it is a finished page ready to be made into film—completely bypassing, if we choose, the once-essential off-screen steps of "camera-ready art." What an amazing capability!

As a desktop publisher, will you equip your office with a drawing board and other graphic arts equipment for manual page assembly?

## Working Toward a Business Plan

### BUSINESS SUCCESS WORKSHEET TEN

Concept: *Buy only the equipment you need.*

*The funds you have available will determine how extensive your initial setup can be—but remember that as you become established and find your focus, your needs may change.*

- What usable office furniture and equipment do you already have?

- What additional office furniture and equipment will you need during your first year?

    Furniture, files, shelving

    Typewriters, word processors

    Telephones, including car phone

    Pager

    Answering machine vs. answering service

    Fax machine (or fax-modem)

    Copier

    Calculator

    Postal meter

    Binding machine

    Tape recorder, transcriber

    Graphic arts equipment

    Other?

- What will this equipment cost if you buy it new? Can any of it be bought used or obtained through trading or surplus sources? How much can you save?

- Can you use a copy center to avoid buying a copier during your first year?

- What equipment can you wait until your second year to purchase?

# Donna Donovan

*Real Good Copy Company, Glastonbury, Connecticut*

## Finding Yourself through Your Business

"Self-employed people have often held a lot of different jobs in their careers," observes Donna Donovan. "It's the 'finding oneself' process." Donovan, who founded her home-based writing and desktop publishing business 11 years ago, is a case in point. "I've been in business for myself longer than any job I ever had," she says.

Donovan's first position after college was as a newspaper reporter. She became a copy editor, did some page layout, switched to corporate communications, and attended law school but didn't finish—most of this as a single mother. Her last job was writing industrial advertising copy. But when Donovan describes how her business has evolved, a pattern of incremental change appears.

She first planned to specialize in industrial accounts, building on leads from her last employer. "I was going to give industrial advertising a consumer spin," she recalls. But during her first two years, she found selling engineers on her approach "a real uphill battle."

She joined organizations, networked, and did a lot of thinking. "I was trying to fit in," she says, "but I didn't feel comfortable in a navy blue suit, so I decided to be myself." With this in mind, Donovan chose her company's name, Real Good Copy Company, because she found it "memorable and unusual" even though it didn't sound corporate.

Building a new client base, she began writing copy for real estate developers. "I enjoyed the challenge of creating 'a sense of place' about a place that didn't exist yet," she says, "but the economy changed that."

In a shrinking economy, Donovan was convinced that "clients were looking for new options." Drawing on her newspaper design experience plus knowledge gained from her father, a graphic designer, she began desktop publishing newsletters.

Today, desktop publishing has given her a profitable niche in the thriving direct response catalog business. Clients send Donovan a designed document on a cartridge, and she writes and fits the copy. "I know what else is on the spread, so I can avoid repetition," she explains, adding that "some firms produce four, eight, even ten catalogs a year. Unless I screw up, they'll be back, leaving me time to do fun projects."

These have included composing board game cards and writing stories to be made into jigsaw puzzles. Donovan's legal background has helped her work with law firms and small businesses. "I enjoy it because a Yellow Pages ad or a direct mail piece is so important to them," she says.

Donovan often joint-ventures with designers—usually on a verbal agreement.

A "morning person," the writer-designer averages sixty-hour weeks in her glass-walled office overlooking the wooded acreage she and her semi-retired husband own. She uses a Mac SE 30 with "as much memory as possible" and a laser printer upgraded to 600 dots per inch.

Recently, Donovan was recruited for a job that appeared to offer security. "I turned it down," she says. "The only security is what you create yourself. I could pack up and go anywhere in the country and within two months, I would be up and running with a good flow of business."

# 6

# Computer Hardware and Software

## An Overview of a Controversial Subject

Computer hardware and software is a massive topic, full of trade-offs and compromises—

> *"No, this wasn't the printer I wanted, but I got a great deal on it."*

personal preferences—

> *"Mac! Are you kidding? I wouldn't use one on a bet!"*

> *"DOS? You mean as in DOSappointing, DOSagreeable, and DOSgusting?"*

disasters—

> *"Hello? Day and Night Computer Service? Can you help me? All my data disappeared."*

and endless change—

> *"You should have said you were using System 6.7 when you placed your order. The $649 version of OmniPage we shipped only works on System 7. Well, I can't help it if you promised to scan a ninety-page manual."*

My purpose in this section is not to review the mass of products flooding today's market, but to give you, as a writer or graphic designer, some idea of the kinds of hardware and software you will need to do various kinds of work—and further, to suggest techniques for shopping smart and obtaining reliable information.

From here on, incidentally, I'll be calling categories or types of computers "platforms," since that's how the industry refers to them—as in, "What platform are you on?" This is not a question directed at diving champions or politicians, but at computer users.

# Mac vs. PC—Is the Platform Controversy Fading?

The operating system that runs the Apple Macintosh (Mac) computer is based on a graphical user interface (GUI) that uses pull-down menus, accessed by a point-and-click mouse, making it more user-friendly than the character-based DOS (disk operating system) that has traditionally run the IBM-PC (personal computer) and its clones. DOS requires keystroke commands, which must be memorized or looked up. And even though it's much, much faster to issue commands via keystrokes than with a mouse, no combination of keystrokes can do what a mouse can do in graphics applications.

An application, or program, is an electronic environment designed to perform certain kinds of work. In graphics programs the mouse is ideal for such activities as positioning elements, drawing lines, and applying shading. For writers, however, the PC has often been the platform of choice because of its lower costs and greater speed.

Today, Microsoft's improved versions of Windows have made the Mac versus PC controversy less intense, providing the PC world with its first popular graphic interface. Windows operates on top of DOS and is similar in many ways to the Mac environment. At the same time, prices continue to drop on all personal computers. This includes IBM-PCs and clones, with their 80 percent share of the U.S. personal computer market, and Apple Macintoshes with their seemingly endless array of short-lived models, accounting for 12 percent.

Further reducing the conflict between the two platforms is a variety of Mac-PC conversion techniques that permit users to move documents from one platform to the other.

So which platform is better? Nearly ten years after the Mac's 1984 debut, no less an authority than *PC Magazine* rated Apple's system software superior to DOS/Windows in terms of elegance of design, functionality, and ease of use. This evaluation came as part of an exhaustive comparison of high-end personal computers and small workstations (June 1993). However, the magazine found the elegant Macs significantly slower than rival PCs.

In 1994, the old controversy is taking an entirely new turn with the introduction of the PowerPC, a RISC (reduced instruction set computer)-based microprocessor family created jointly by Apple, IBM, and Motorola. PowerPC developers claim significant improvements in price, performance, power, and functionality. In the Mac camp, Apple states that affordable PowerPC upgrades will run most existing Mac software as well as DOS and Windows programs plus new programs written specifically for PowerPCs. If users embrace the PowerPC, the whole microcomputer scene will be interesting to watch during the next few years—and, for once, the users may be the winners.

## The writer's Mac–PC dilemma

If you're a writer, a wide range of computers—fast and slow, costly and inexpensive—can meet your needs. Even if you have important documents already formatted on one platform, you need not be locked into buying that computer, since a service bureau can probably convert your documents, preserving the data even if the formatting is lost. (Service bureaus are a business category that has sprung up to serve desktop publishers. In addition to high-resolution electronic imaging, they often provide scanning and disk conversion, as well as traditional typesetting and graphic film work.)

Basically, you need only ask yourself three questions:

- Which computer do I already know how to use—and which do I prefer?

- Do I already own or have access to a certain platform—and is that an important factor in my start-up costs?

- Will compatibility with my clients' computers be important? What computers do they use? (Many writers send their material to clients electronically over the telephone by modem, making the platforms largely irrelevant.)

## The desktop publisher's Mac–PC dilemma

Today's desktop publishers are free to select the platform they prefer or can best afford. In their most recent survey of desktop publishers for the *Pricing Guide for Desktop Publishing Services* (1993), Brenner Information Group of San Diego noted a move away from the Mac dominance, evident in their first survey, toward a more equal distribution between Macs and PCs.

Because of Apple's early efforts to market the concept of desktop publishing, Macs are widely used in print communications. Much of the software and peripherals for high-end color printing, as well as for presentation graphics, have been designed for the Macintosh, which is also central to the exploding field of multimedia. But if you are already skilled on the PC, if you expect to interface with PC-based clients, if you are involved with spreadsheets or other applications in which the PC excels, or if you just want to spend a little less money—a PC could be your best choice.

Although they are beyond the scope of this book, there are several other PC operating systems that may be of interest to desktop publishers. These systems include IBM's OS/2, Windows NT, and NeXTSTEP. Unix workstations are used to produce large, complex publications in some business research and government settings.

*In the sections on hardware and software that follow, prices quoted are approximate street prices for 1993.*

# Computer Hardware

The next section is addressed to writers, but it also applies to desktop publishers. Both need a basic computer setup. Desktop publishers require additional bells and whistles, which will be dealt with separately.

At minimum you will need a computer to process your words, a hard drive for storing them (a hard drive is a device for storing large amounts of electronic data), and a printer to print them.

Computers are alien and scary to many people, and you may be among them. A recent study by Dell Computer Corporation showed that 32 percent of U.S. adults are intimidated by computers and worry about damaging one if they use it without assistance—while more than 25 percent "would not use a computer unless forced to." As an independent writer, you are your own boss, so no one will force you to use a computer. But do the forcing yourself. It's vital!

*A word to the wise:* The best way for an adult to learn to use a computer is with a real project that is not critical in terms of time or quality.

## Computer

If you are looking in the classified ads for a computer, you'll undoubtedly come across a listing like this: "IBM 486, 33 MHz, 4MB RAM, 80 HD."

Ugh! Translated into English, that means:

IBM  Probably IBM-compatible, but it might mean that IBM is the manufacturer.

486  The Intel processing microprocessing chip, or "heart" of the PC computer.

33 MHz  The speed of the microprocessor in megahertz.

4 MB RAM  4 megabytes of random access memory (RAM). More RAM can be added to most computers and some printers. In general, the more RAM, the more speed and efficiency.

80 HD 80 megabyte hard drive. That is, the hard drive will hold up to 80 megabytes of data.

An older used computer (such as a 286 PC or a Mac Plus or SE—selling for $350 and up) could get you started if funds are short. To buy an inexpensive new PC or Mac, expect to pay $1,300 and up.

In general, the higher the number of the microprocessor, the newer and faster the computer. Today's fast PCs use 486 or Pentium Intel microprocessors. (Chips competitive to Intel products are also in use, with different numbers.) Macs use Motorola chips. Starting with 68000 in 1984, top-of-the-line Macs were using 68040 microprocessors in 1993, with a new Mac PowerPC chip on the horizon.

If you crunch numbers or deal with large documents or graphics, you will need more power and memory than you need for basic word processing. Or you may just crave more speed. Color is also nice—and it's standard in PCs and most new Macs. A color computer can operate some monochrome monitors, but not vice versa, so you might save money by buying a monochrome monitor initially and adding a color monitor later. Check compatibility before you buy.

## Notebooks and smaller

If your work involves travel, you may need a notebook computer ($1000 and up, up, up). If you own a good one, you really don't need a separate desktop computer—unless someone in your office must use it while you are gone. Many notebook computers can be turned into desktop computers by plugging in a full-sized keyboard and monitor. (Some Macintosh PowerBooks require monitor adaptors; PowerBook Duos require a docking station at extra cost.) Notebook computers that can run a large monitor are great for off-site presentations.

New palm-sized computers ($400 and up) take even less room than notebooks, virtually fitting into your coat pocket. They function as personal organizers and note takers and are usually PC-compatible. Apple's much ballyhooed Newton MessagePad ($700 and up), which operates with a pen, debuted in 1993, and is launching a new category of "digital personal assistants."

*Caution:* If possible, wait to buy supplementary computers. While helpful and fun, they are usually not essential. Conserve cash now.

## Hard drive

A hard drive is a data storage device that looks something like a miniature record player. Your hard drive may be mounted inside your computer or in an external box with its own power supply. It holds your operating system, your applications, and any other data you load on it.

The operating system is needed to start and run your computer each time you switch it on. You don't have to have a hard drive to do this job. You can "boot" (start-up) many computers from a floppy disk containing your operating system. Without a hard drive, however, your computer will run inefficiently—and many programs will not work at all.

Since word-processing documents are much smaller than graphics documents, as a writer you could probably get by with a small (40-megabyte) hard drive. But buy a bigger one if you can. For more storage, you can link several hard drives together.

## Printers

Your printer is controlled by your computer. Dot matrix printers are the least expensive ($200 and up). They use pin-fed, continuous-sheet computer paper, but usually can also accept hand-fed single sheets and envelopes. Type is formed from dots made by pins striking the paper through a ribbon. Quality is poor to medium, even with the better-quality 24-pin printer. (Don't even think of getting a 9-pin printer.)

If you start with a dot matrix, you will probably want to produce better-looking output before long. Some clients demand high quality output—and all appreciate it.

An ink-jet printer ($300 and up) is a step up in quality, but laser printers are now so inexpensive ($800 and up) that if you can buy one now, you should. That way, you'll have professional-quality output from the beginning.

If you work with lists, you may want a pin-fed dot matrix printer to print roll labels (affixable by machine). Ink-jet and laser printers can print only sheet labels, which must be hand-affixed.

## Label printers

Some full-size printers do not handle envelopes well. As a result, small auxiliary label printers ($200 and up) have become popular as a quick way to address envelopes and packages. You must use the manufacturer's proprietary (and expensive) labels in these machines, which makes them uneconomical for long runs. (Their formats are not compatible with commercial label-affixing equipment anyway.)

Another approach to the ever-frustrating envelope problem is a small ink-jet printer dedicated only to envelopes and cards (about $700)—a costly solution unless you print a great many envelopes. Some software programs also address the problem. After hand-feeding an envelope two or three times through my Apple LaserWriter NTX and either having the envelope rejected or incorrectly printed, I usually turn to my tried and true IBM Selectric II typewriter.

## Modems

What else do you need? Probably a modem. Connected to your computer and to a telephone line, a modem translates digital computer data into telephone signals. At the other end of the line, another modem is needed to receive the transmission and convert it back into computer-speak.

You'll pay $70 and up for a standard 2,400 bps modem. ("bps," or its baud-per-second, refers to the modem's transmission rate. A few years ago the standard was 300 bps.) You'll pay $200 and up for a fast new 14,000 bps model—which might be a good investment, since your 2,400 bps modem will one day be obsolete. A fast modem can slow down to connect with a slower modem, so you don't need to worry about the equipment on the other end of the line.

Your modem will probably come with communications software to run it, but for a powerful, high-quality communications program, you may have to make a separate purchase.

Why does a writer need a modem?

Computer-savvy writers are frequently on-line. Their modems connect their home offices to the world via telephone lines, which can link them with CompuServe, America Online, and many other networks. All day (and all night) they are receiving electronic mail (E-mail) and data from clients, information sources, and colleagues. They are sending out finished work. They are schmoozing and sharing advice and opinions through bulletin boards and forums, using such computer programmer expressions as : ) and : ( (sideways smiling and frowning faces indicating the sender's mood). And—very important—they are doing research through on-line information sources. While most of these services cost money (usually billed in fractions of a minute to your credit card), they save enormous amounts of time compared with traditional library research. They also represent extra profit when on-line writers do customized data searches for clients.

Often these on-line writers are otherwise nontechnical people who would never try to install a spark plug or assemble a bicycle. *But they want and need this new avenue of communication!* There is a whole new universe of information exchange going on—and most of the population is barely aware that it exists! But make no mistake—to those who live in an environment where E-mail is commonplace, not having E-mail is like not having a telephone. To those used to gathering instant statistical data, bibliographies, article printouts, and other information from on-line services such as

CompuServe or LEXIS/NEXIS, not having electronic information is like not having a public library.

This being the case, certain clients—especially publishers, the research community, and some corporations—may expect or even require you to have a modem capability. Receiving your copy electronically saves them time, money, and errors, since it allows them to edit and use what you have written without their having to rekeyboard it.

## Fax–modem feature

Fax–modems are now widely available for Macs and PCs. A fax–modem allows you to send and receive faxes through your computer, eliminating the need for a separate fax machine. You simply print to "FAX."

Some business people prefer not having a stand-alone fax, which accepts whatever it is sent, sometimes using up your fax paper on unsolicited material. One writer–desktop publisher told me he got rid of his stand-alone fax and refuses to treat faxes as an emergency demanding his immediate attention. His computer collects faxes as they arrive, and he reviews them on-screen, at his convenience, when he reads his E-mail. Some optical character recognition (OCR) software can convert on-line faxes, which your computer receives as graphic documents, into text documents that you can edit.

## Large monitors

If I were not a desktop publisher as well as a writer, I would probably never have bought a 19-inch monitor—but now I can't imagine writing without it. Try a large monitor (17 inches and up) in a store or at a training center sometime and see how it feels. This could be something to save for!

Working with a large monitor in Windows or on a Mac, you can see one or two full pages at a time. Some applications (such as Microsoft Word) allow you to open several documents at the same time. You can move them around on the big screen, layering them behind one another and pulling them forward as you need them.

You can make corrections in related passages, and copy material from one document to another. Working on this book, with each chapter set up as a separate document, my 19-inch screen has been invaluable! If your operating system allows multi-tasking, you can also work on documents from more than one application at a time.

"Portrait" monitors allow you to view one full page. They look like a regular 14- or 15-inch monitor turned on its side, and, in fact, the popular Radius Pivot one-page monitor can be used either way. Two-page monitors are usually 19, 20, or 21 inches. You will pay $900 and up for a 19-inch black-and-white monitor, plus $200 and up for a board that goes into an expansion slot inside your computer, equipping it to drive the large monitor. For a 17-inch color monitor, you'll pay $1100 and up, plus $400 and up for the card. For a 19-inch color monitor, you'll pay $1,800 and up, up, up, plus $800 and up for a board. Used monitors are a less expensive option. Some computers come equipped to drive a large monitor and do not require an extra board.

Monitors are difficult to compare and shop for because their specifications are complex. Read up in your computer magazines. Publications like *MacWorld* and *PC World* report periodically on monitors for various platforms. Check the back files in your library.

One caveat about monitors: *Beware of flicker and distortion.* A poor monitor can cause eyestrain after only a few minutes—to say nothing of staring at it for eight or ten hours. Make sure you can return any monitor you buy—even a used one—if it does not perform satisfactorily with your system! The prices I have quoted are low end, and you may have to pay more for the monitor you want. But for the sake of your eyes and your productivity, it's worth it.

## Keyboards, input devices, wrist supports

You don't have to stick with the keyboard that came with your computer. A variety of custom keyboards is available ($50 and up). One of the most unusual is Mac's two-part adjustable keyboard ($200). Mice, too, come in a variety of custom models, as do track-balls, which many people find more convenient than mice. Since you will spend a lot of time at your keyboard, invest in one that suits you.

The accessory section of your computer store will also offer several wrist supports ($10 and up)—or you could make yourself one. I recommended them for avoiding wrist fatigue—and they are vital if you already have wrist problems.

To give myself more desk space, I installed a keyboard drawer, which pulls out from under my worktable and comes with a convenient wrist support. Working on this book has made me aware of another benefit of a keyboard drawer. My cat has begun to resent being ignored and has taken to walking back and forth in front of my monitor. When I leave my worktable now, I push the drawer in so he can't walk on the keys.

## Scanner for optical character recognition

As a writer, you will almost certainly find the optical character recognition (OCR) capabilities of today's scanners useful—although this is a purchase you can defer. (Scanning services are available at service bureaus and large copy centers to meet an occasional need.) With OCR software, a scanner can "read" clean printed or typewritten text—such as your client's manual that needs editing, a long quote from a printed source, or a list of parts for a catalog. Good OCR software can read in several languages. You can create a separate document of the scanned pages, or you may be able to insert the scanned material directly into the document you are working on.

Using special graphics software, scanners can also translate photos, illustrations, and drawings into digital images that can be edited (with still more software) and used in publications and presentations.

Hand-held scanners ($200 and up) read a 4- or 5-inch pass. If one pass does not take in the entire subject, the software allows passes to be combined. These scanners are sold with basic OCR and graphics software. Full-page scanners ($700 and up) are available in several styles—flat bed (the most popular), sheet-fed, and overhead. Scanner options—important for scanning graphics—include gray-scale or full-color. The color scanners vary in their color precision and in their quality of resolution, measured in dots per inch (dpi). Three hundred dpi is the current standard, but that's already beginning to change. Better scanners offer higher resolution.

If the scanner you buy does not provide it, you will need OCR software ($180 and up). Shop carefully. OCR can be a great convenience, but the results are sometimes unusable.

## CD–ROM drive

CD-ROM technology is taking off for the stratosphere. Looking like familiar audio CDs, CD-ROM disks have a 600-megabyte capacity, allowing them to carry a vast amount of digital information. And incidentally, they represent an emerging market for computer-savvy writers and graphic designers, since material must be tailored to this medium's unique capabilities.

Works on CD-ROM (what to call them?—they're not books, they're not records) come complete with color visuals and sound, quickly and randomly accessible. With an internal or external CD-ROM drive ($200 and up, up, up), you can view a growing number of surprisingly inexpensive disks (like a full encyclopedia promo-priced at $50). Access time, currently ranging from 200 to 400 milliseconds, measures how quickly the drive can find a file. The lower the number, the faster the search. Another measure of a CD–ROM drive's speed is its "sustained transfer rate"—the number of kilobytes (KB) of data the drive can read off the disk each second. (This measurement is probably of more interest to desktop publishers who must access photos and graphics on CD–ROM disks.) Older drives had a transfer rate of about 150 KB per second, requiring at least seven seconds to read a 1 megabyte file. Newer double-speed drives boost that rate to 300 KB. Faster CD–ROM drives cost more, but if you use your drive often, extra speed could be worth the cost.

## Photo CD

If you provide your clients with photos, you should be aware that Kodak has developed technology for digitizing photographs and putting them on photo CDs. This topic is discussed in more detail under hardware for desktop publishing.

## Networking

If your office has more than one computer or printer, a network can link these devices so that all computers can access all printers. But that's just the beginning. Computers can be linked to share files and send E-mail—even across platforms, from a PC to a Mac or vice versa. Such linking is called a local area network (LAN). Networking takes technical savvy, so check with a consultant.

## Power controls

Surge suppressor power strips ($12 and up) are widely sold for use with computer equipment. If your computer is connected to your household power through a surge suppressor, occasional power spikes cannot harm your hardware or your data. For even more protection, units are available to provide a few minutes of reserve power, during which you can save your data in case of a power failure ($180 and up). If your area experiences frequent power outages, such a fail-safe device might be a wise investment.

## Accessories

You can add many other accessories to your computer arsenal—including mouse pads, copy holders, dust covers for keyboards and computers, monitor stands, printer stands, CPU stands, computer traveling cases, floppy disk cases and wallets, floppy disk mailers, security devices to prevent computer theft, antiglare monitor filters, reference guides listing commands for specific applications, computer tool and cleaning kits, power converters to plug your notebook computer into your car cigarette lighter, and more and more. A favorite accessory can be a delight and well worth its price. But shop carefully.

# Desktop Publishers—Hardware for One-, Two-, or Three-color Work

If you are doing one-, two-, and three-color desktop publishing, you can succeed with relatively simple equipment. Compared to a writer's computer setup discussed above, you will need a more powerful computer with plenty of RAM (random access memory), a much bigger hard drive, and a good laser printer. You don't have to have a modem, a large monitor, a scanner, a CD–ROM drive, or mass data storage devices to get started, but a general plan for upgrading and acquiring equipment is a vital part of your strategy. That way you can be on the alert for equipment bargains that suit your plans and your budget.

A portrait or two-page monitor, either mono or full-color, is almost essential today. If you are using memory-gobbling electronic art and scanned photos, you will soon need expandable data storage—the removable cartridge system is the most popular. Rewritable optical disks are a newer option. Tape cartridge systems give you the most storage for the money, but access is much less convenient, so they are used mainly for backup.

For nearly three years, I conducted my writing and desktop publishing business working on the nine-inch screen of a Mac 128 upgraded to a Plus, proofing on an ImageWriter (Apple's original dot matrix printer), and driving 10 miles to a Kinko's Copy Center, usually after midnight, for all of my laser output. And my clients included several national corporations, a large hospital, a major health-maintenance organization, an international educational program, a retail store, and a national computer security group.

I can't believe I even tried to do it. But I was a single mom, pinching every penny, determined to make my business succeed.

Desktop publishing has advanced a lot since those days—the biggest change being the advent of good-quality color work—a development that has linked Macs, and more recently PCs, to high-end prepress technology. Today both vendors and buyers are more sophisticated, so you will certainly need ready access to a laser printer. Printer access is vital in order to make subtle design changes based on printer output. WYSIWYG (what you see is what you get, pronounced "wizzy-wig") on the screen is usually accurate only up to a point.

## Laser printers

Laser printers are essential components in the desktop publishing revolution, and they are truly amazing devices! At 300 dots per inch (dpi), an 8½ x 11 page is made up of nearly 9 million dots, each of which is individually controlled by the printer. The widely used PostScript laser printers ($900 and up) use the PostScript page description language developed and licensed by Adobe. They are more expensive than ordinary laser printers because they are more complex internally, with increased graphics capabilities. Add-on cartridges (about $400) are available to convert some printers, such as the popular HP LaserJets, to PostScript.

Determining which printer will meet your needs will require some research. If you handle complex documents, you'll need a printer with at least 1.5 to 2 megabytes of RAM to make it operate at a reasonable speed.

If your printer is equipped with a SCSI (small computer system interface, pronounced "scuzzy") port, you can connect a separate hard drive to the printer. Using the hard drive to store fonts for downloading will save processing time and space in your main hard drive; otherwise, your computer must download any fonts that are not resident in the printer.

Consider buying or upgrading to a printer that prints at least 600 dpi (instead of the current standard 300 dpi). Higher resolution is definitely where things are headed. You will give all of your clients better quality proofs and, in some cases, you will be able to use the 600 dpi output as camera-ready copy, saving the cost and trouble of going to a service bureau for 1,200 dpi Linotronic output. For maximum sharpness in your final camera-ready pages, use special laser printer paper.

## Ink-jet color printers

Ink-jet color printers are inexpensive ($450 and up) and can be used for making low-end comps (a comprehensive layout shown to the client during the design phase) and proofs.

## Scanners

Scanners have been valuable desktop publishing tools for reproducing line art from the beginning. Until recently, however, scanned black-and-white photos could not approach the quality of traditional halftones.

Today's inexpensive scanners—assisted by such software as PhotoShop and Digital Darkroom—can turn out not only high quality black-and-white photos but usable low-end color separations as well.

When a good-quality color separation is needed today, the scan is made commercially by one of several processes. The complete scan is kept on file at the service bureau, and a low-resolution version (a much smaller document) is given to the designer to use "for position only."

If you are doing scans, you will eventually need a scanner, since running to the service bureau takes both money and time—and the results may be less than satisfactory on something as subjective as a scan. (Designers often scan a graphic several times, using different settings, before getting the exact output that they want.)

Since scanning is a complex subject, you will need to do research to determine which equipment best suits the work you do. Some successful desktop publishers who use only an occasional bit of line art get by with a low-cost hand scanner ($200 and up). However, a flatbed scanner ($700 and up) would be the more likely choice. Since color scanners cost little more than gray-scale scanners, you may want to buy a color scanner even if you don't currently need it.

## Data storage

Eventually, as a desktop publisher, you will need a mass storage device—especially if you are doing scanning or color illustrations. Formats available include removable cartridge, rewritable optical disk (also called a "floptical"—cheaper than a cartridge and with ten times the shelf life of magnetic media), and tape (cheaper still). Tape is not suitable for active storage, however, because retrieving files is slower than by other methods.

## Special input devices

Mouse pens and graphics tablets, including pressure sensitive tablets, can help provide the special control needed in some graphics programs. Illustrators are more likely to need these tools than graphic designers.

# Desktop Publishers— Hardware for Four-color Work

If you plan to do high-quality, four-color work for such clients as ad agencies, manufacturers, publishers, and catalog firms, you will need even more computer speed, memory, and data storage than desktop publishers who do one-, two-, and three-color work.

As a high-end desktop publisher, you will also need a scanner (probably with a slide attachment) and a good color printer—or convenient access to such equipment—in order to produce comps and proofs. You'll also need access to a color photocopier, available in most large copy centers.

## Photo CD

If you work with color photos, you should familiarize yourself with Kodak's well-publicized new technology for putting digital photos on CDs. The image scans are inexpensive and of high quality. The storage medium is also inexpensive. To process a 24-exposure roll of color film and transfer it to a Photo CD costs about $20.

Here's how a Photo CD works: The processor takes your film and scans all photos on the roll at various resolutions (a set of resolutions is called an "image pack"). You receive your slides or negatives (and prints if you wish), along with a Photo CD that may be used to put photos directly into page layout programs, presentations, or multimedia—gobbling masses of memory in the process. Additional photos may be aded to the CD later, and one Photo CD can store 100 to 150 images. Since you can't erase the images, you may want to have your photos developed first and digitize only selected photos.

Kodak's entry into the world of CD–ROM provides a needed link between photography and electronic publishing—and the technology is still evolving. When you buy a CD–ROM drive, make sure it's multisession photo compatible. "Multisession" refers to the practice of adding photos to a CD at a later "session." Photo CD technology is expected to play an important role in the stock photo industry. Kodak has also recently launched Picture Exchange, an on-line resource for accessing stock photos from agencies.

## Electronic prepress

In addition to design, you will be doing electronic prepress—and a working relationship with service bureaus and printers who will output your final film or digital printing plates will be important to your success.

Electronic prepress involves doing all the work to prepare the film used for burning metal printing plates. Today, the film process itself is sometimes skipped and printing plates are created digitally, making fast, low-cost, short-run color printing possible for the first time. In either case, color photos must be color corrected. All elements of the page must be assembled. Colors must be "trapped" so that adjoining colors overlap slightly to avoid any white gap. Reverses and silhouettes may need to be created. Until recently, skilled printing industry craftspeople did this work. Now you can do much of it yourself at your computer. Electronic prepress has become widely accepted because of its many advantages: more color for less money, more artistic control, more convenience in making corrections, faster turnaround. But it also has disadvantages, among them computer failure, proofing difficulties, and the long time sometimes required to process the final film.

To continue refining your electronic prepress skills, work closely with your service bureau and your printer, ask questions, and learn everything you can. Designers who either don't know or choose not to consider the complexities of printing technology can saddle their clients with huge and unnecessary costs—and may still end up delivering a disappointing job. Every printer has seen this happen.

# Software for Writers and Desktop Publishers

## Word processing—the writer's home environment

Most word processors have more features and more power than we users take advantage of—which is our loss. The trend is for word processors to add more page layout features and for page layout programs to add more word processing features, bringing the two closer together. But they still have their distinct roles to play. Of course, desktop publishers use word processing programs, too.

If you do general business writing, you might save time on certain assignments with special software programs like an employee manual maker, a job description maker, or a company policy maker. If you write about specialized subjects, watch for software designed to serve them. One Southern California book author, who includes cats and genealogy among her writing specialties, uses a program that handles pet pedigrees (she noticed that it was used by a national cat registry service), as well as a "family tree" program she learned about in a genealogy magazine. You won't find such specialized software in the big software mail order catalogs, but tracking them down could be worth your while.

Leading word processing programs include

- Microsoft **Word** (PC DOS $210 or Windows $320, Mac $300)

  I use Word by default, not having tried many others, but it's a good, solid program.

- WordPerfect Corporation **WordPerfect** (PC DOS or Windows $290, Mac $290)

  Another widely used program, especially in the business world.

- WordStar International, Inc., **WordStar** (PC DOS $299 or Windows $119)

  An old workhorse featuring good file interchangeability with other programs and platforms.

- Lotus **Ami Pro** (PC Windows $260)

  Handles graphics better than most competitors and has more typographical functions.

- Claris **MacWrite Pro** (Mac $170)

  Easy to use, many desktop publishing features.

  All of these programs incorporate at least some of the following:

  Extensions to specific word processing programs, adding graphics, page layouts, and other features

  Grammar and spell-checking

  Dictionary

  Thesaurus

  Quotations

  Foreign language support

  Bibliography and footnote making

  Resumé making

  Forms making

  Envelope addressing

  Legal and sales letters

  Merging (with database files)

  Optical character recognition scanning and editing

## Page layout—the desktop publisher's home environment

Here's a quick rundown of the programs most used by desktop publishers to combine text and grahics. *The Pricing Guide for Desktop Publishing Services* (see Bibliography) lists software used by survey respondents by platform and program, indicating what percent reported using each program. If you buy this useful resource, be sure to check this section.

Page layout programs include

- Aldus **PageMaker** (PC $490, Mac $500)

  The leading seller and a very solid program, a good choice if you design for both Macs and PCs or must interface with clients' files, but not the best choice for long documents.

- Quark **XPress** (PC and Mac $550)

  My personal favorite. Very powerful typography control, very stable, efficient use of memory.

- Corel Corporation **Corel Ventura** (PC Windows $249 list or $99 upgrade from previous versions of Ventura Publisher or Corel-DRAW!). Package includes Ventura Publisher, Ventura Database Publishers, Ventura Separator, CorelDRAW! 600 fonts, and 10,000 clip art images. A lot for the money! Ventura works best when dealing with large amounts of information.

- Frame Technology **FrameMaker** (PC $580, Mac $540)

  Well suited for long documents.

- Manhattan Graphics **Ready,Set,Go!** (Mac $250)

  This venerable program is making a new bid for attention. Offering most of the features of PageMaker and Quark XPress at half the price, **Ready,Set,Go!** could be a bargain for some users. One desktop publisher I interviewed uses **Ready,Set,Go!** exclusively and says the firm provides excellent customer support.

## Fonts and Graphics

All desktop publishers need some graphics software, but the type and amount vary greatly. Listing the major vendors and programs is beyond the scope of this book, and since offerings and their features change constantly, the only way to keep up is to stay informed. Skim the many books and articles available, attend demonstrations, study catalogs, and discuss programs and their features with fellow graphic designers.

*Fonts.* Certainly you will need an assortment of fonts to fit the work you do. PostScript fonts, the established standard, can be scaled up or down to virtually any size without "jaggies" (the stairstep edges caused by pixel definition in bit-mapped fonts). True-Type fonts, PostScript's leading competitor, offer the same features.

A wide range of font accessories is also available including font management programs that help you organize, preview, and access your fonts; programs that help you style fonts with special effects, including 3-dimensional images, shading, and curving; and programs that allow you to create your own fonts.

*Illustration.* A variety of illustration, drawing, and painting programs is available. The early distinctions between these general categories is now blurred, with the leading programs offering many of the same features. Designers seem to gravitate to one or two favorites that best fit their work such as Illustrator, published by Adobe; Freehand, published by Aldus; or CorelDRAW, published by Corel. These powerful programs can take months or years to master. Accessory programs allow you to remove jaggies and add 3-dimensional effects, brush strokes, pencil lines, and many other special features.

*Image processing.* Image processing is another major category. This includes software for scanning photos and other images; image manipulation programs such as the industry leader, Photoshop by Adobe; color editing and color scaling programs; and filters for special effects. Programs that change images from one storage format to another are available. Programs such as Morph by Gryphon Software transform one image into another—a dazzling effect. Kodak is developing a line of image processing programs related to its Photo CDs including Kodak Shoebox, which helps you manage thousands of Photo CD and other digital images.

*Clip art.* Clip art (so called because the illustrations were originally printed on paper to be cut out and pasted into layouts) is an important tool for most desktop publishers. A vast array of electronic clip art is available from simple line drawings to maps to complex color illustrations and color photos. With illustration, drawing, painting, and various image processing programs, you can combine and manipulate clip art in virtually endless ways. Purchase only what fits your line of work, but check your sources regularly to keep up with current offerings. You may need database software to organize your image library. Don't forget that printed clip art is still available. It is far less expensive than electronic art and can be scanned as necessary.

*Chart and graph making.* Special programs are available for chart and graph making. The subject introduces two completely different software categories—spreadsheets and databases. You will need to familiarize yourself with programs that manage statistical data if you work extensively with graphs and charts. Specialized programs also exist to create flow charts, organizational charts, genealogical charts, and more.

*CAD, presentation, and multimedia software.* Branching out in related directions are major graphics programs for CAD (computer-assisted design), used primarily by architects, engineers, and industrial designers; presentation, helping you to create slides and overhead transparencies for platform speeches and point-of-sale displays; animation; and multimedia, combining video, animation, graphics, text, and sound into multimedia shows.

Even forming a mental picture of this ever-expanding array of graphics software is mind-bending. Studying the categories used by vendors to organize their product offerings in large software catalogs can help.

## General business software

You should be aware that software is available in the following categories to help you run your business. Read reviews. Attend formal demonstrations or ask for demonstrations in the store. Talk to colleagues. Which categories fit your needs? Within those categories, which software packages appeal to you?

**Communications**
   Telecommunications (modem operation)
   Computer fax
   Phone dialer
   Remote control for computer
   Online information services

### Financial

Personal and small business accounting, check writing, payroll

Tax preparation (may be integrated with accounting program)

Estimating (general, no *specific* programs are offered for either writing or desktop publishing—to my knowledge)

Time/job recording, client billing

Financial planning, investment management

### Organizational

Daily planning, scheduling, calendar making, on-screen reminders

Project managing

Message managing

### Utilities

Desktop builder, computer work space organizer, menu builder

Screen saver (the only fun item on this list!)

Antivirus protection

Security, passwords, file access

File backup

File retrieval and browsing

File managing, cataloging

Reconciling different versions of files

Universal file viewing

High speed file transfer

Data compression

Data recovery

Diagnostics, file repair

System status check

Memory allocation

Hard disk optimization and reformatting
Utility package (combining several utilities)

## Connectivity
Mac–PC file transfer
Networking
E-mail

## Database managers
Large, multi-purpose database programs
Contact managers
Other simplified and custom databases
Address, label, and directory making
Bulk mailing
Simplified and custom databases
Report creation

## Spreadsheets
Financial reporting, analysis, projections
Charting
Business modeling
Works (integrated application packages that contain
limited versions of programs for word processing, spread-
sheets, database, drawing, telecommunications, etc.)

## Miscellaneous
Brainstorming, outlining, idea generation
Business plan making
Sales and marketing forecasting
Publicity generating
Interior designing (for office planning)
Address list sorting and postal coding
Print sideways (good for spreadsheets)
Banner making

HyperCard (unique Mac environment with many creative uses such as custom databases, educational programs, to-do lists, record keeping, and more)

Training programs
Specific to applications

Information resources on floppy disks or CD–ROM disks (including marketing databases, atlases, medical references, U.S. history, fact books, Bible, encyclopedias.

# Computer Shopping

The most important thing I can tell you about computer shopping is to view all hardware and software as disposable. You will never be completely set up, and you will never be finished buying.

Whenever possible, leapfrog over versions of both hardware and software. Take pride in doing so. If you can jump from PickyPage 3.0 to PickyPage 5.0 without laying out your hard-earned cash for versions 3.01, 4.0, and 4.2—*and* do it without your business suffering—you're ahead of the game. And by the time you buy the upgrade, you will be buying a proven new version.

Don't buy new hardware or software unless there is a vital task you can't perform without it or unless you find it significantly faster or more convenient. When I am tempted to buy something that I really don't need, I think of the $100 I laid out for ThinkTank, an outlining program that I have not used once and the Kensington Turbo Mouse for $109, which I disliked from the start, that now sits in the closet while my old mouse rolls along.

Stay on a single platform as much as possible. Converting files between platforms will cause unnecessary problems.

Look for hardware and software that offers maximum compatibility with what most clients are using and most service bureaus can support.

For desktop publishing buy as much speed, memory, and disk

capacity as you can afford and then increase them later. It's like the old saying, "you can never be too rich or too thin."

Don't be afraid to buy used. If the word "used" scares you, remember that dealers who specialize in used computers provide guarantees. Better bargains are available from individuals (check classified ads, recycler publications, user groups, and swap meets). I am no techno-whiz able to spot a faulty circuit at ten paces, but I have bought many pieces of used hardware from individuals, saving many, many dollars, and never once have I been burned. Companies getting rid of surplus equipment are another source of used bargains, one that is often overlooked.

When you must buy new, compare prices and service. There's a "street" price for almost everything in the computer world. But don't underestimate the value of a live person who will help you solve problems after you get the equipment (or software) home. The big mail-order firms offer discounts, as do the computer superstores emerging in many cities. Smaller, older computer retailers compete by advertising sale prices (often in the Saturday sports section of your newspaper). These are the vendors who may lease you what you need, if you qualify.

After a recent trip to the bright, cold, crowded confusion of a major computer discount store, where the clerk I finally lassoed knew nothing and seemed offended at the interruption, I have decided that comparing computer products in the store is hopeless. Mail-order catalogs are the only way. Do you agree? I'm not sure. One competent, friendly clerk could change my mind.

## Getting help when you need it—consider a consultant

Wherever you buy, ask if the vendor, manufacturer, or publisher offers follow-up customer assistance (beyond the usual repair or replacement if the product does not work). Some mail-order firms, like Zeos International of Minneapolis, offer 24-hour phone technical support for their systems.

If not, consider having a consultant, preferably one who doesn't have an interest in selling certain products. To find a consultant, check the Yellow Pages, look for consultants' cards posted in computer stores (or ask a store for a referral), check classified newspaper and business journal listings, ask friends and colleagues. You'll probably find that your consultant is another home-based entrepreneur—a good person to do business with! Paying for several hours of a consultant's time is a prudent way to get your system set up properly. And you'll know whom to call when your inevitable computer crisis occurs.

## Finding reliable information

The secret here is—there is no secret. You just have to do it! Learn to be alert for information about the hardware and software you use or plan to use. Attune yourself to news of bugs, new versions, and discontinuations. The biggest source of this information is computer magazines. Subscribe to one or more, and keep back issues for at least two years. If you take formal computer training, ask the advice of your instructor. Attend free product demonstrations held in computer showrooms and training centers. Join a user group and ask associates what hardware and software they use and why.

One day people will begin calling you—just as some friends and business associates now call me—to ask your advice about a hardware or software purchase. Maybe you won't know everything—I certainly don't. But you may be surprised at how much you do know!

## Working Toward a Business Plan

### BUSINESS SUCCESS WORKSHEET ELEVEN

Concept: *When buying computer hardware and software, buy smart.*

*View all computer hardware and software as disposable. Leapfrog over versions whenever possible. Buy only what you really need. Stay on a single platform if you can. In general, stay with widely used products. Desktop publishers: get as much speed and memory as you can afford. Don't be afraid to buy used. When you must buy new, compare prices and service.*

- Make a list of the usable computer hardware and software you already have.

- Make a list of the additional hardware and software you will need during your first year.

 Computer
 Hard drive
 Printer
 Fax–modem
 Large monitor
 Special keyboards, input devices, wrist supports
 Scanner
 CD–ROM drive, including Photo CD
 Networking hardware and software
 Data storage devices
 Power controls
 Accessories
 Software in the following categories
  Word processing
  Page layout
  Graphics, including scanning and image editing
  Computer-assisted-design (CAD) presentation
  Communications
  Financial
  Organizational
  Utilities
  Connectivity
  Database managers
  Spreadsheets
  Training programs
  Miscellaneous, including applications for special subjects
  Specialized information on disk or CD–ROM

- What will this hardware and software cost if you buy it new? Can any of it be bought used? How much can you save?

- Can you borrow or rent any hardware or software during your first year?

- Do you have a general plan covering key hardware and software products you will need later—what to get, when, how much to spend?

# Revisiting Start-up Costs

Now that you have considered all of the expenditures you will need to make to get your business started, you can put your start-up costs into perspective. Read Business Success Worksheet Twelve, below, and follow the directions for matching expenditures with funds available.

## Working Toward a Business Plan

### BUSINESS SUCCESS WORKSHEET TWELVE

Concept: *Conserve cash*

*The goal is to be IN business, not to have a perfect business setting. Your business focus will probably change. Invest only what you actually need to get started.*

- Based on the kinds of work you plan to do and the kinds of clients you plan to serve, what kinds of space, office equipment, and computer hardware and software will you need during your first year in business?

- Which of these needs can you meet—even temporarily—without spending money? For example, what can you borrow—perhaps a relative's typewriter or the occasional use of an associate's scanner?

- Can you use business services to avoid large capital outlays?

- Would leasing equipment help you get started quickly, or would it cost too much in the long run? (You probably will not qualify for a business lease for two or three years, but you may be able to arrange a lease based on your consumer credit.) If you lease, will your lease payments apply to a purchase?
- What must you actually spend to get started?
- What cash do you have available—or what cash can you raise—to cover these costs without borrowing?
- If you must borrow, which sources will you draw on now and which will you leave in reserve? What is the maximum risk you are willing to take to get started?

# Start-up Costs vs. Funds Available

To balance your needs against your resources, set up two tables headed:

| *Essential Start-up Costs* | *Start-up Funds Available* |
| --- | --- |

On the first go-around, include under start-up funds your savings (reserving a portion for emergencies), anticipated income from items or property you can sell, securities you can liquidate (other than your retirement funds), and any anticipated surplus from your own full- or part-time income and that of your spouse or significant other during the start-up phase.

Will these funds cover your start-up expenses?

If not, take another look at your costs and pare them where you can. Since small business loans are difficult to obtain for creative start-ups like ours, a business loan is not a likely option—but to make sure, talk to your mentors, your accountant, your banker, or a Small Business Administration counselor.

To meet your start-up expenses, you may have to turn to higher-risk sources of funds, such as personal loans from relatives or friends; borrowing on your home, insurance, or retirement investments; and funds from credit cards and signature loans. A gift of up to $10,000 can be given annually without tax consequences to donor or recipient (nice if you can get it!). If you decide to borrow from relatives or friends, financial experts offer these guidelines:

- Determine an interest rate and a repayment schedule, and put the agreement in writing.

- Have a witness sign your loan document.

- If possible, secure the loan with some form of collateral. This can benefit your lender if you default. If your lender attempts to collect the money or the collateral, whether successful or not, the IRS may consider the loan a capital loss for income tax purposes. Discuss this with your accountant.

Finally, be careful. You may feel that if you're not willing to gamble a second mortgage on your home against the success of your business, perhaps you don't have faith in your own dreams. But successful entrepreneurs know the maximum risks they are willing to take, just as they know when to cut their losses.

Think about it this way: If you can get your business started, grow it, and clarify its goals without maxing out your credit cards or taking on a second mortgage, you'll have those sources of funds in reserve if you ever need them. And by the time you do need a more powerful computer system—perhaps to fulfill a profitable new contract—you may be able to qualify for a regular business loan.

## Wayne Kaplan

*CompTutor Desktop Publishing Services,*
*Huntington Beach, California*

### Combining Technical and Creative Talents

Wayne Kaplan entered desktop publishing through the technical door, and his firm, CompTutor, is a business in transition. Currently he does 40 to 50 percent computer training/consulting and 50 to 60 percent graphics, but he's moving in the graphics direction.

In 1987, Kaplan found himself burned out as a senior project engineer. A skilled tennis player, he decided to teach tennis for a time to think things over. Then he became a computer hardware and software instructor at a Los Angeles adult learning center.

At the same time, the former mechanical engineer became fascinated with computer graphics. His original introduction to graphics had been "cranking the mimeograph machine as a student activist." Later, he produced a newsletter on a "primitive IBM PC page layout program." When he was given a demo copy of Ventura Publisher to evaluate, he "got hooked."

After 18 months of teaching at the adult school (classes too large, pay too low), Kaplan decided to become an independent trainer/consultant.

"My concept was to go out to hapless souls—the laymen—and help them understand a machine designed for techies," says Kaplan. "I was aiming at home business and home users. I didn't want anything to do with the corporate world. But I didn't consider that these clients had very little money to spend."

Fortunately, he was able to pick up an accounting firm and other small businesses as consulting clients. He also bought a copy of Ventura Publisher and began doing occasional ad layouts and brochures. His sister, a writer, suggested a joint venture with her, designing a logo and brochure for a medical clinic start-up. The client's positive reaction encouraged him. In fact, the firm now has ten locations and remains a solid customer.

To help himself find focus, Kaplan joined a Ventura Publisher user's group. Today, he says the group played a significant role in his business growth. He later added expertise in CorelDRAW! and now uses the program for up to 60 percent of his design work. Giving back some of the help he received, he has become a local and national leader in the Association of CorelDRAW! Artists and Designers.

A move from Los Angeles to Orange County in 1992 gave Kaplan a chance to develop a new desktop publishing clientele, and he now focuses his training and consulting on Corel-DRAW! and Ventura Publisher.

Living alone in a three-bedroom townhouse, Kaplan uses one bedroom as an office and another for business storage. He prefers to work at night "when the phone doesn't ring" and balances the loneliness of design time with mornings on the tennis court. "One element of engineering that has stuck with me is being very structured," he observes.

When he first starting taking work to service bureaus, Kaplan was asked, "if you're serious about desktop publishing, why don't you get a Mac?" His answer: "There's a ten-to-one ratio between IBMs and Macs in the business world." Now he's glad he didn't switch.

"Windows has opened up graphics and desktop publishing to small and mid-sized companies that are solely using IBMs, and that creates a great opportunity for people like me," he says.

# 7

# Marketing Your Services

## Marketing Makes the Difference

The thing to remember about marketing is that what you do today pays your bills in three to six months. Even if you *have* business now, if you *seek* no new business now, you will have no business three to six months from now. Marketing is your most important investment in the future.

Years ago I took a marketing workshop from a freelance photographer who began his presentation by scribbling these words on a chalkboard: *If you're there, you'll get your share.* At first I resisted his homely slogan. I found it hard to believe that just by showing up in the marketplace, I would get business. But I have learned that he was right. Nevertheless, most freelancer writers and designers I have talked with worry more about marketing—and fail more often at marketing—than any other aspect of their business.

It's tough to put yourself out there where you can be rejected. It's tough to meet with a prospect, build rapport, analyze a job, contribute ideas, develop a good price, outdo yourself presenting your proposal, start counting on that $2,000 to meet upcoming bills—and then, when you phone a week later, to receive a casual, "Oh! Didn't anyone call you? We went with someone else."

But you know what? You can survive that kind of rejection. Within a year, you can learn not to take it personally and to understand that, no matter how solid your foothold seems to be, you may not get the job.

You learn by experience that a competitor may underbid you, or conversely, that your price may have appeared too low. Or that the owner stepped in and decided to give the work to his brother-in-law. You learn that the project may be cancelled or deferred—or that there may never have been a project, just a planning exercise at your expense. And—painful but true—you learn that some prospects will not like your samples—or your personality. (In which case, you probably wouldn't have liked them either.) Above all, you learn never to *plan* on income without a firm job commitment—and never to *count* on income until the work is done.

If most freelancers can learn these difficult lessons, why does marketing often plague them throughout their careers?

I think there are two problems, and neither of them is insoluble.

First of all, as writers and designers, I think we often expect too much of ourselves. "Just being there" isn't good enough for us as creative types, trying to break out of the competitive clutter. We need something smashing, something unforgettable, the kind of thing that will get written up in designers' or writers' magazines.

If you can come up with such a promotion, go to it! Too often, however, the perfect project hangs out of reach in our imaginations, and in the meantime, it's best to do some of the meat-and-potatoes marketing this chapter describes.

The second reason freelancers fail at marketing is simpler, but more frustrating. When we have more work than we can handle, we do the most urgent things first, and put our marketing aside.

Again, a meat-and-potatoes approach is the answer. Whatever marketing strategies you adopt, make them as routine as possible. Just as you clean your office, do your filing, pay your bills, so you do your marketing. Every day, every week, and every month. If a killer deadline kept you from paying bills when you had planned to, would you stop paying them for three months? No, but many of us do that with our marketing.

## Marketing versus selling

When you're a home-based entrepreneur, you wear every business hat from janitor to CEO—and two of the most important are marketing manager and sales representative. Both of these jobs are concerned with selling your services, but they are different in focus.

Marketing is everything you do to make the sale possible—before your first contact with the prospect. Selling is what you do to make that contact and close the sale. When you identify a professional organization whose members could use your services, you go to their monthly meeting and put your brochures on the literature table, and then stand up and give your name and your ten-word business description, you are marketing. But when you make a point of meeting the communications director of the Ajax Corporation, find some common interests, pocket her card, call her, and make an appointment to discuss her needs, you are selling.

The marketing process for the home-based writer or desktop publisher involves
- Research
- Strategy
- Determining and presenting your image
- Publicizing yourself and your services
- Advertising your services
- Evaluating and updating your marketing plan

The selling process involves
- Prospecting
- Follow-up
- Presentation
- Close *or...*
- Additional follow-up and close *or* appropriate disposition of the prospect from your active files
- Solicitation of additional business

The following case study is fictional but based on experience. Whether you are a writer or desktop publisher, whether you are selling to large clients or small in a city or a rural area—this example shows how each step in the marketing and selling process can lead to the business *you* want.

# Marketing and Selling— An Entrepreneurial Example

Rob is a desktop publisher who has decided to make his lifetime interest in athletics a part of "what he does and for whom." A former high school athlete who worked as a sports publicist in college, he would like to be around competitive athletics as more than just a fan. With this goal in mind, he undertakes a marketing effort.

## Marketing research

Rob's research turns up seventeen high schools, two colleges, and a state university in his region. Many of these schools have a recurring need for game programs and printed media guides for major sports, along with such recurring collateral material as posters, flyers, and schedules. He collects samples of typical programs and learns by phoning school athletic departments that some are produced by outside vendors. As far as he can tell by questioning prospects and checking the ads of his competitors, no local desktop publisher is specializing in sports programs and team media guides.

The booklet format used in sports programs is similar to work Rob has already found profitable. He also believes he can fit seasonal projects into his work flow.

Rob knows that season programs are usually financed by advertising, so when calling the schools, he inquires about their advertising procedures and finds that a few schools engage outside professionals to sell ads, while others rely on students or parent volunteers to do the selling.

Rob researches ways to reach decision makers and and learns that it will be difficult to reach coaches, athletic directors, and sports information directors through local organizations. Local luncheons held occasionally for college sports officials and media representatives are not open to him. He discovers, however, that the annual College Sports Information Directors of America will be meeting in his region next year, and he investigates attending as a vendor. He also identifies several professional journals in the field.

## Marketing strategy

Rob recognizes that becoming a specialist in sports programs and media guides requires long-range effort, but he believes it will pay off in seasonally recurring work. In addition, working regularly with local coaches could lead to contacts with such potential clients as athletic equipment manufacturers, specialists in sports medicine, professional sports promoters, and summer sports camps.

Studying the samples he has collected, Rob determines what he would have to charge to design and produce sports programs and media guides, and he decides that he can lower his prices if he is assured of several jobs a year from the same school—a sales benefit to the prospect. He also notices that most of the samples could be improved by professional design, which he can offer—another sales benefit.

So far, Rob's research has determined an ongoing need, his strategy has determined what appears to be a fit with his capabilities, and he has thought of several benefits he can sell. Encouraged, he goes on to develop more detailed strategies. What else can he sell? How can he make it easier for clients to deal with him? What could set his service apart from others?

Rob considers buying printing at a discount from trade printers (those dealing only with resellers) and reselling it for more money, but he quickly tables the idea because of the large cash outlay required and the risks involved if a printing job should be unacceptable or if a client should fail to pay. Instead, he decides to offer production supervision as a compensated part of his service.

Since Rob is interested in having more control of the job as well as in making more money, he considers joint venturing with Amy, a friend who formerly sold newspaper ads and is now anxious to make money part-time at home. After discussion, Rob and Amy agree that if she sells program ads for one of Rob's customers, she will give him a percentage of her profits.

Because schools may require writing or photographic services, Rob lines up a writer and a photographer. Both have experience in athletics, and Rob knows them to be reliable. In this case, he does not propose a percentage fee, but looks at these referrals as aids in making the sale. Rob figures that any assignments he directs to the writer or the photographer will come back to him in referrals.

## Determining and presenting a business image

Rob decides to build an athletics capability into his business image by including athletics programs and media guides in his basic list of business services and adding a sentence about his background in athletics to his business resumé. He also creates a new, sports-oriented slogan for his business: *"Win with peak performance."*

## Publicizing himself and his services

Since he is doing volunteer work as a Little League coach, Rob seeks ways to capitalize on this activity for business publicity. He writes an article for his local chamber of commerce newsletter about volunteer opportunities in youth sports. Although the school coaches, athletics directors, and sports publicists he needs to reach are unlikely to see this article, Rob plans to use reprints of it in his presentation.

Business networking groups also give Rob an opportunity to put his athletic experience and desktop publishing capabilities in front of potential buyers. His knowledge of athletics begins to impress prospects who share his interests—but he has yet to sign up a school to design a season program or media guide.

## Advertising

Rob considers placing his own ad for desktop publishing in local game programs, but he rejects the idea. Consumer ads will not bring him business. Instead, he decides to take one-line listings in his local business Yellow Pages and in the services directory of a regional business magazine. Even though these listings are too brief to mention his specialty in athletics, Rob believes they enhance his general credibility in the marketplace. Shortly after placing these ads, he receives calls from several new prospects in other fields.

## Sales prospecting

Moving into the selling phase, Rob begins prospecting, using his research to set up prospect files on his computer. His lists include local high school and college coaches in major sports, as well as directors of athletics and sports information.

All of this effort has taken Rob about six months, involving a few hours of work a week. Now he begins calling his prospects for appointments and finds this to be the most difficult task he has tackled so far. It is hard to find time to make the calls, hard to reach the busy prospects—and really hard to convince them to see him, since most do not perceive an immediate need for his services.

## Sales follow up

Rob knows that business people often fail to get the order—even when they have the names of prospects who need and can afford their products—because they fail to follow up. They fail to get an appointment for a presentation. They fail to get a bid request after making a presentation. They fail to get a purchase commitment after bidding. And finally, they fail to solicit repeat orders after completing the initial order.

Determined to work in athletics, Rob brainstorms about ways to break through the resistance he has encountered. He could prepare and mail a flyer about his services. He could try to meet some prospects through professional or social activities. He could call and offer to design a small job free as an introduction. He could mark up his sample of the team's current program, showing how he would improve it, and send it to the prospect. Rob is intrigued with the latter idea until he realizes that he might antagonize a prospect by criticizing designs the prospect likes.

Finally, Rob prepares a mailing, offering to show the prospect—in a fifteen-minute interview—five ways that professional design can improve the image of the team, while being cost-effective. Phoning for appointments a week after his mailing, Rob finally lines up some interviews!

## Sales presentation

Even though none of his previous work is athletics-related, Rob selects the best samples he can find and pulls together an outline of the features and benefits of his services, aiming at what he believes are the needs of the market. Then he adapts his material to a fifteen-minute benefits blast and heads for his interviews. In the back of his mind is an idea for a brochure and maybe a journal article based on his presentation—"five cost-effective ways professional design can improve your team's image."

Sitting down with his prospects, Rob finds that most of them voluntarily extend the brief interview when they begin talking about their own needs. Since athletic needs are seasonal, he takes care to find out when he can check back for upcoming projects— and he gets each prospect's permission to do so. (Months later, when the reminder pops up on his computer tickler file, he can say, "Coach Smith asked me to call him this month regarding the season's program.") Rob also probes to find out who else may be involved in purchasing decisions and later contacts many of these prospects.

Rob makes notes about each interview and modifies his presentation, dropping some points and adding others. He also notes which samples created the best impression or provided the best openings to discuss his strengths.

## Close

Rob makes his biggest inroads at a small liberal arts college where he and Amy are asked to bid on media guides and programs in three sports. Knowing that the college is accepting competitive bids, Rob calls the decision makers to ferret out any price problems after he presents his bid. Following some price negotiation, he is able to close the deal. Now he is actually doing the work he has been seeking!

## Additional follow-up or appropriate disposition of prospects

Using news of his assignment at the liberal-arts college as an opening wedge, Rob telephones his other prospects. He realizes that most of the high schools cannot afford him and removes them from his active prospect file. Since he has gotten to know several of the high school coaches through phone conversations, he keeps their names in an inactive file. Who knows? Someday he may need to contact one of them.

## Solicitation of additional business

Within a few months, Rob is asked to do a seasonal booster club newsletter for the liberal arts college. He is also selected to design a basketball program for the state university—and, as he anticipated, side benefits of his marketing campaign start coming in.

Rob is hired to prepare promotional materials for several sports camps. Through a client introduction, he picks up work from a professional soccer team—and designs a poster that wins an award. He sends press releases about the award to local news and business media and receives coverage. Then he mails reprints to his prospect list with a friendly note. As a result, two previously resistant prospects agree to meet with him. With his growing credibility as a designer for this specialized field, Rob calls on a local athletic equipment manufacturer and receives a lucrative assignment when the marketing director, in frustration, pulls a catalog away from the company's high-priced ad agency.

## Evaluating and updating your marketing plan

Where Rob goes with this new business will be up to him. As he compares the profitability of various jobs, he may put less effort into college athletics and more into assignments from professional teams or athletic equipment firms. With his increased cash flow, he may start bidding on printing—adding a profitable sideline. He could become a regular exhibitor at conferences for athletics professionals, perhaps scaling back his other work to concentrate entirely on athletics. Or he could use these projects to impress clients in other fields. He could begin to seek work from a wider geographic area, could hire assistants, or subcontract work to other home-based desktop publishers.

Any and all of this is possible—if Rob continues to make marketing a regular part of his business routine!

# What Can Marketing Research Do for You?

"Marketing research" sounds intimidating. It has overtones of focus groups, surveys, and statistical analysis. But business decisions cannot be made without answering such simple questions as: "Is there a market for it?" "What features do clients like or dislike?" "What should I charge?" And in point of fact, an informal focus group is easy to arrange. Just buy a pizza for a few clients or prospective clients, throw out some provocative marketing questions, and listen to the enlightening replies!

When I was selling printing for a local, family-owned firm and thinking about starting my own business, I noticed that most of our business came from a relatively small group of repeat clients in our own geographic area.

While you never want all of your work to come from one or two clients (a good rule of thumb is to make sure no single client accounts for more than 20–25 percent of your work), you, too, are likely to be doing most of your work for a small number of clients in your own geographic region. Even if you serve many nonrepeating clients—running a resumé service, for example—the bulk of your business will come from a few key sources. Even if you serve clients nationwide—perhaps doing specialized technical writing—a few networks will provide your business contacts. Thus, your marketing research need not be massive. One or two weeks of serious, full-time study—or its equivalent—can provide the planning data you need as you begin your writing and desktop publishing business.

# Where and How to Get Marketing Information

## What you're looking for

Basically, you are looking for client categories and names of potential clients, along with any information you can find out about them—their products or services, sales volume, number of employees, branch locations, affiliated companies, and their prospects for stability or growth. You also want to know who is serving these clients now for their outside writing and desktop publishing needs, what these competitors charge, and how crowded the field is.

## Standard reference sources

Some easy sources of such information include your own previous employers and business associates, professional organizations, and "leads" clubs, where business people gather to share leads. Another possible source are the sophisticated and usually expensive databases available from computerized list companies. But most home-based entrepreneurs begin their serious marketing research with directories—telephone books, industry directories, and other compilations available in most libraries.

Your reference librarian will be helpful. So will your chamber of commerce. Chambers often sell local business directories—printed or on disk. College and university libraries may have good business resources. On-line data bases can connect you with huge amounts of information, but may have limited ability to provide you with details specific to your region.

Looking for potential clients by name? Perhaps they belong to a trade association. Most chambers of commerce maintain lists of local organizations. Your library will have a national directory of associations, whose national offices can provide information about local chapters.

Association membership lists are often available only to members, but joining may be worth it if the organization includes many potential clients. Or a guerrilla marketer might borrow the directory from a member friend.

Your daily newspaper's business pages are a gold mine, as are local business periodicals and trade journals. These inexpensive resources are often insufficiently appreciated by home-based entrepreneurs. Read them carefully and save clippings. The information adds up.

## Set up an information retrieval system

To retrieve the information you are collecting, set up a filing system, using a computer database program, file folders, loose leaf notebooks, 3 x 5 cards—whatever works for you. You may be using this information for a long time.

## Test the waters with a phone survey

As you gather information about potential clients, make a dozen or so calls—to buyers by name or to job titles. Explain that you are doing marketing research for a start-up business and draft two or three brief questions to find out whether and how they use the services you plan to provide. If the answers are discouraging, take another look. You may be offering the wrong service or going after the wrong clientele. If they do use the services you provide, ask who they use and whether they have trouble finding good writers or desktop publishers. If you establish really positive rapport, you might ask about prices for typical jobs, but many buyers will refuse to share such information.

## Will you need to create a market?

You may find that you want to provide a service for which a market must be created. An example would be custom-written and desktop published family histories. This service is not yet as well accepted as is the group photograph that many families arrange for on a regular basis. Families need to be told about this new service and convinced that they need and can afford it. Customized storybooks for children with the child's name, hometown, school, or pets worked into the story, pose a similar challenge. If your service falls into this category, plan on extra marketing with heavy emphasis on publicity that will explain the need you plan to fill.

## Research the competition

While you have your information resources in hand, make a separate search for names and any details you can find about your competition. Additional sources of information about competitors are creative services directories, clients, imaging service bureaus, art supply stores, printers, communications and graphics associations, and computer users groups. Find out what you can about your competitors' specialties and reputations and how long they have been in business.

## Economic and demographic projections

To gather information on the economic and demographic outlook for an industry or region, turn again to your library or chamber of commerce. Government census and business data as well as regional economic reports will reveal trends that can affect your business plans. Business publications also provide such information—both by region and by industry.

## Credit-worthiness

For credit-worthiness, you must evaluate each client individually, but industry statistics (and common sense) will suggest which types of clients are more reliable, which are less. You need not pass up clients with shaky or unknown credit. But you should insist on a big down payment, and the balance on delivery.

## The guerrilla marketer takes over

At this point, you have enough information to begin learning, in depth, what kinds of writing and desktop publishing the clients you are concerned with buy, who they buy it from, and what they are paying. Gathering this information will be less straightforward, and the distinction between marketing and sales will become blurred. In every sales contact, for example, you will be trying to collect these valuable nuggets—from your initial call for an appointment, during your sales presentation, and in all the rest of your encounters with that client. Even though many firms have policies against revealing exactly what they paid for a job, questions about price ranges may bring you an answer.

Vendors such as imaging bureaus and printers may also provide information—especially about who is doing what for whom. And of course, there are your competitors themselves. It might be crude to ask, "How much did you charge for that job?" But you might find out. Or a friend or family member with a writing or desktop publishing project might solicit bids from some of your competitors.

Marketing research tells you who's buying, or might buy what. It also gets you into the ballpark on price. In Chapter Nine, you will learn about pricing issues in detail.

# Marketing Strategies and Positioning

Developing strategies gives you an edge over the competition and helps you position yourself.

That was what Rob, the desktop publisher, did when he decided to present himself as a specialist in sports graphics and go after sports-related accounts. That was what I did when I decided to pare away some of my less-profitable, nonrepeating business and began concentrating on newsletter jobs.

If you are in the early stages of establishing your business, don't worry if the words "strategy" and "positioning" create a mental blur. You need some marketplace experience in order to form strategies. You need to find out which jobs are profitable and professionally satisfying and which are not. And finally, you need to discover how clients perceive you, versus how you want to be perceived.

# Working Toward a Business Plan

## BUSINESS SUCCESS WORKSHEET THIRTEEN

Concept: *Understand your market and position yourself strategically.*

*Research your potential customers and competitors; then combine your capabilities with existing or forthcoming market opportunities to give yourself a competitive advantage. What sources will you use to obtain the following information?*

- Who are the actual clients in the industries you plan to serve? What specific writing and desktop publishing services are they buying now?

- What are the going rates of payment—high, low, average? Where do you fit in? How creditworthy are your prospects?

- Who are your competitors? What are their qualifications? How long have they been in business?

- Look for niches that are not currently being filled. Can the industries you have selected accommodate more vendors?

- Examine the general economic and demographic outlook for the industries you want to serve. What are the market trends and opportunities?

- Do you plan to offer a service for which a new market will have to be created?

- What are the best ways to reach your potential clients and sell to them?

- To answer the above questions, use creativity techniques such as brainstorming (coming up with as many solutions to a problem as possible within a limited time—no evaluations or judgments allowed). Do free-associational right-brain thinking. Float over the situation mentally, looking for new patterns and approaches.

- In addition to your skills, experience, and equipment, be aware that your personality, personal history, age, and other unique characteristics can help you carve out a market position that is credible and appealing.

- Involve others. Seek feedback from clients and associates.

- Consider using a marketing consultant. Independent marketers are available at an hourly rate or by assignment. Give any consultant you hire a full and open hearing, and follow their advice when you feel comfortable with it at gut level.

- Discuss your strategies and positioning plans with trusted associates. Monitor their reactions and apply what fits.

- Remember that as the marketplace and your capabilities change, so should your strategies. Stay open minded.

# Determining and Presenting Your Image

Since you work at home, clients may never come to your office—though it's important to have a presentable space in your home with table and chairs where you can sit down with a client if necessary. In most cases, the image your business presents will be based on your business name; your logo, letterhead, business card; your marketing materials; and, of course, on your own personal appearance and demeanor and your professional reputation.

## Your business name

Your business name is a very important part of your business image. If you find, after a period of time, that the name you selected and licensed yourself under does not describe what you are selling as effectively as another name would, go ahead and make a change. You can do this either gradually, with a minor change in emphasis and the same or similar graphics on your business materials. Or—if you think the situation warrants a new identity—make a total change with a completely new name and new graphics. Either way, it's wise to make sure your business is registered under the correct business name, even if it involves additional fees.

## Designing your logo

I believe logos are very important—and not just because I used to design them. Throughout my independent writing and designing career, I have used a pen-and-ink portrait of myself at my drawing board. (Fortunately a drawing doesn't age as fast as a photo.) When I first put the drawing on my letterhead and stationery, I thought it might seem pushy or conceited, but I have received nothing but positive response. People see my logo, remember it, and often comment on it. I have even gotten business solely on the basis of my card!

But don't delay starting your business until you have the perfect logo. A real entrepreneur goes to the instant print shop and gets something, anything, printed in order to get started right away and then develops a good logo within the first six months.

Your logo can be registered as a trademark or service mark with your state or the federal government. (See the Source Directory.) For most of us—especially if our own name is part of our business name, obtaining a registered service mark is probably not necessary. But for certain names in certain markets (the trademark-sensitive computer industry, for example) it could be a wise move. Having to reprint all of your materials and redo your business licenses because someone has already registered the name you chose would take time and money, while damaging the image you have established.

## Your image on your printed materials

The printed materials that represent you are very important and should have a graphic unity that grows from, or is compatible with, your logo design. This includes your business card, letterhead, envelopes, labels, fax cover sheet, forms, invoices, brochures—whatever bears your business name and message.

Everything does not have to match precisely, but as you develop each piece, lay your materials side by side and make sure they work together. Having a unified graphic theme makes your business more memorable—and it suggests good planning and organization.

## Your personal appearance

You thought you were getting away from business dress codes by starting your own home business! Well, yes and no. In your office, of course, you can wear what you like. One designer told me she makes it a point to get dressed every day—as opposed, apparently, to working in robe and pajamas. It never occurred to me not to get dressed before going into my home office, but I often do battle with myself about what is the least "dressed" I can be when I zap over to a client's office. I'm talking about just picking up some copy or dropping off a proof—not making a sales call. For a sales call or serious business conference, I always dress to fit the marketplace. And you should do the same.

A corporate editor I have worked for recalls referring a writer friend, a newly minted freelancer, to a colleague in her firm. To my client's dismay, the writer arrived for her first appointment in sweats, carrying her baby. "She'll never get another referral from me!" said the editor. Corporate people have to wear collars and ties or heels and hose all day, every day (except for an occasional "dress-down Friday"), and they expect you to be equally professional. Clients in other environments have distinctive dress codes or guidelines, and you should observe them. It shows awareness and respect.

## Your phone and office image

Make sure your phone is answered professionally during business hours and that messages are taken reliably when you are out. Your promptness (or the lack of it) in returning calls also forms an image in the minds of callers. If clients or vendors will come to your home office, make sure that public areas are presentable.

# Publicizing Yourself and Your Services

Many marketing people look on publicity as "free advertising." On the plus side, having someone else talk about you builds credibility (as opposed to talking about yourself). On the minus side, you can't be sure you will get coverage, and you can't control what will be said. And, of course, you have to provide something worth saying.

## Maximum return for minimum cost

In spite of being impossible to control, publicity in all its forms is a very good way to market a home-based writing or desktop publishing business. It can provide maximum return for minimum cost. The impact of publicity is cumulative; over time, having your name associated with your industry in a positive way establishes you as an authority and an industry leader. On the sales side, including reprints of selected clippings can strengthen your business biography or sales presentation. Reprints of a significant article (say, your views on writing effective business letters) can form the basis of an inexpensive, friendly, yet authoritative special mailing to solicit new business.

## Getting it done

The main problem with publicity is doing it—planning where you will send business news about yourself, making sure your media names and addresses are current, tailoring releases to each outlet, getting a supply of good quality photos (if appropriate), and sending everything out while the item is still news. If doing publicity is part of your client services, doing publicity about yourself should be easy. An established writer or desktop publisher might find it worthwhile to buy services from a home-based associate who specializes in publicity. Just starting out, you'll probably have to do it for yourself.

Remember that the rule about marketing in general applies to publicity as well—make it part of your routine, and do it on a regular basis.

## Two types of publicity

Publicity falls into two general categories: The first is the simple media release that announces some news about you or your business. You send it out and hope it will be used. After mailing a release to newspapers, magazines, radio and TV stations, and news services, many publicists phone them all to try to assure coverage. But this procedure may annoy, rather than ingratiate. Call only if you have a reason for calling. For example: "If you think you might use the story, I can supply pictures." "If you're planning to attend my lecture, I can arrange free parking for you."

The second publicity category is engineered coverage—something set up in advance with the cooperation of editors or reporters. Engineered coverage might be a newspaper profile of you as a successful home entrepreneur; it might be an article written by you in a trade journal; it might be you participating in a radio or TV business show, discussing ways to improve business communication. If business reporters are aware of you from receiving useful press releases in the past, they may call on you for a quote relating to another story. Always be available. It pays off.

## Preparing and submitting news releases

Media releases should be double-spaced and error free, preferably in black ink on white 8½x11 paper. Multiple pages should be stapled. Photos must have captions attached and will not be returned. A covering letter is not necessary. Releases are usually written in journalistic style, covering "who, what, when, where, why, and how." A brief headline may be used above the text to summarize the story. Keep copy as short as possible. If detailed additional information is relevant, include it as a separate fact sheet on which the editor may draw.

A release should include a heading that identifies its source, the name and phone number of someone to contact for more information, an origination date, and the words "RELEASE AFTER (DATE)" or "FOR IMMEDIATE RELEASE." The end of the release should be marked with some designation, such as ###. If the information runs more than one page, write "MORE" at the bottom of each continuing page, and make sure every page is clearly numbered and identified. When sending a release to broadcast media, it is best to rewrite it in a briefer form, designed to be read aloud. Broadcast material is often typed in capital letters for the convenience of announcers.

Releases may be mailed or faxed—your preference. Obviously, to enclose a photo you must use the mail, so allow time for delivery.

"Media kits" are used by professional publicists to generate interest in celebrities and major events. A media kit consists of a folder containing one or more releases, biographical information, photos, reprints of clippings, and any other pertinent material. When might *you* need a media kit? Perhaps before doing a series of lectures, after publishing a book—or when spearheading a group in some significant community effort. The start of a new business could be an occasion for a media kit, but most home-based freelancers start on too small a scale to warrant major media attention. A news release announcing your start-up would be more appropriate.

More important than any wording or form of presentation is selecting media that might be interested in your release—media that you know carry the type of information you are supplying. Next in importance to selecting the right media is getting the material to them at the right time—neither too early, nor too late. For daily and weekly publications and local broadcast media, allow two weeks. For monthly publications, lead time varies widely, so check with editors.

## What's worthy of publicity?

Activities that can bring you publicity include winning an award; landing a major new client; adding a new business service or a new associate; taking office on the board of a professional organization; publishing a business-related article or book; serving on a business-related committee; and teaching a class or seminar, giving a lecture, or serving on a panel on a business-related topic.

## Volunteer to help

Here is a more subtle way to gain publicity, while doing some good at the same time. Volunteer for a community agency or project in a way that will draw the attention of prospective clients to your business—and then make sure you get credit for your services. Writing or designing the program for a charity event supported by the local business community would be an ideal example. Be on the lookout for service opportunities that fit both your business goals and your charitable interests. But beware of doing too many free projects in hopes of gaining attention! A designer friend volunteered for our United Way's communications committee—a select group that included many potential clients—but so over-committed himself with free work that he could barely serve the clients he already had. Be selective!

## Where will your publicity be used?

Major outlets for business publicity are local daily and weekly newspapers; local and regional business publications; local, regional, and national trade publications that deal with communications or an industry you serve; and—very important—the newsletters and magazines published by your networking organizations. Other media possibilities include talk shows and community calendars on local radio and TV (including cable TV). Inaccessible mysteries to some people, but essential resources to others, are business-related computer bulletin boards and ongoing computer network discussions.

Finally, don't overlook the value of listings. Being listed as a new officer in a professional association puts you in good company. Being listed as the instructor for a course on writing speeches offered by a local community college puts your name in front of thousands of people who might not take your class but are nevertheless potential customers for your speech-writing service. Of course, those who take your class are all potential clients.

## Selecting media

Aim your publicity efforts at media that can reach potential clients or individuals who may give you referrals. Just by thinking about it, you can come up with the names of several media that potential clients may see, but racking your brains won't do the whole job. Lists of media, including the names of reporters and editors specializing in various topics, are provided in annual media directories. Several standard media guides are listed in the Bibliography. These directories are costly, but current editions may be available in your library.

Your most useful guide, however, will probably be the one covering your local media. Most communities have local media directories. If you don't know whether yours has one, check with your library or inquire in the public relations office of a local corporation, college, or hospital.

If you receive good coverage that will not be seen by potential clients or by individuals who may give you referrals (for example, a local newspaper report on a seminar you presented at an out-of-town conference), incorporate clippings or transcripts of this coverage in your promotional materials to help create interest in your business.

## Do some of the work in advance

Busy writers and desktop publishers often miss out on publicity opportunities because getting a release out can be time-consuming. To circumvent this problem, have your supplies ready. Tools for business publicity include:

- An updated biography of yourself in narrative format, typewritten and double-spaced, drafted in at least two versions (one no more than half a page, the other no more than two pages). Be sure to mention any prestigious clients.

- A good, professionally photographed business portrait of yourself. (If it was shot in color, have a supply of black and white prints made for publicity use.)

- A basic description of your business, perhaps in brochure format.

- A current list of local and other pertinent news media on a computer data base or on labels.

- A planning calendar.

# Advertising Your Services

Advertising costs money, and home-based freelancers must be cautious about commitments that may produce limited results. Make it standard procedure to find out how every inquiry from a new prospect as well as every referral came about so that you will know which marketing efforts are paying off.

Forms of advertising you might consider include display advertising, broadcast time, classified advertising, cooperative advertising, Yellow Pages, other directories, direct mail, newsletters, and imprinted novelty gifts. One form of advertising that is free is posting your business card in art and office supply stores, copy shops, and other locations. Check to see if a bulletin board is supplied for that purpose—and use it!

## Display advertising

Display ads make sense for you only in low-cost publications that reach a very targeted audience. Normally, a small ad repeated on a regular basis will be more effective than a single large ad. Rates come down when ads are repeated, so negotiate.

## Broadcast time

Radio or TV time is not a cost-effective buy for you unless an extremely targeted, low-cost slot is available.

## Classified advertising

Local and regional business publications often carry classified service directories in their back pages. Your daily newspaper's business section may do so as well. If you can afford it, test such an ad, and repeat periodically if it pulls.

## Cooperative advertising

Normally, "cooperative advertising" refers to ads jointly promoting manufacturers and retailers, but you may be able to arrange your own coop ads, exchanging some business service for a mention in a display ad paid for by another advertiser. It's worth considering.

## Yellow Pages

Never underestimate the power of the Yellow Pages. Some enterprises derive virtually all their business from them. These ads, including simple one-line listings, are billed every month and cannot be stopped until the following year, so consider the commitment carefully. Since both consumer and business-to-business Yellow Pages may carry listings for writers and desktop publishing, consider which directories will be most profitable for you, including suburban directories if you're in a large urban region. Consider other listings, such as "advertising," "artists-commercial," "marketing consultants," and "public relations."

## Other directories

In general, being in directories that reach potential clients or referral sources is a very cost-effective strategy. Some large communities have creative directories designed for clients in advertising, public relations, and marketing. Professional associations to which you belong may sell display ads in their annual directories. Buy what you can afford and track the results.

## Direct mail

Here is another technique that makes sense for home-based writers and desktop publishers. Even though postage and printing costs continue to climb, you can target your mailing precisely and spread costs over several months by mailing to one small segment of your list at a time—the number that you can follow up with phone calls within the next week or ten days. Be careful about faxing to a large list of prospects unless what you are faxing is very useful information. Most people hate to receive ads on their fax machines.

## Newsletters

No form of advertising is more appropriate for a writer or a desktop publisher than a newsletter. While introducing you as an authority, showcasing your abilities, and conveying some sense of your personality, a newsletter provides your clients and prospects with useful information about your specialty. People pass good newsletters around and keep them on file—assuring that your name and number will be handy when a writer or desktop publisher is needed! One continuous source of high-interest newsletter copy is client profiles, wherein you show how a client has profited from projects you have done for them. A four-page newsletter is plenty long. Two pages will do. And quarterly is a good plan for publication—often enough to make an impact, but infrequent enough for you to produce and pay for it.

## Imprinted novelty gifts

An imprinted novelty gift, especially one that will sit on a desk or win some other lasting spot in the work environment, is a great idea and well worth the money. An imprinted gift can get you in the door to see a prospect—and it can build loyalty in a regular client. If you can tie in some play on words or symbolism relating to your company name or business specialty, so much the better. Keep you eyes open for truly distinctive items. Advertising novelty firms offer many excellent ideas, but since imprinting can be purchased separately, you are not limited to their selections. Buy what you can afford, and keep the gifts on hand for times when you believe they will make an impact.

## Marketing message on your phone

Having a custom marketing message played while callers are on hold is not for all writers and desktop publishers, but it might be a good move for some. It suggests size and professionalism at surprisingly low cost. You can have a message made and installed commercially—or devices are available to play a tape you make yourself.

# Keeping Records to Evaluate and Update Your Marketing Plan

Marketing is a process, and as such it is always evolving. Keep a record of where your inquiries and new clients come from. This data—when correlated with management data on the amount and the profitability of business from each client—will tell you what works best for the least effort and expense, what brings you the most desirable clients, and what brings you no business at all. Adapt your efforts, based on what you learn. Some programs, like publicity and newsletters, will take a year or more to have an effect, so allow time for such marketing to work.

When a brochure, an ad, a directory listing, or any other marketing effort brings you profitable business, keep using it until results start to diminish. When an effort doesn't work, try something else.

## Working Toward a Business Plan

### BUSINESS SUCCESS WORKSHEET FOURTEEN

Concept: *Market through image, publicity, advertising, and evaluation.*

*Establishing an appropriate business image, obtaining favorable publicity, and doing selective advertising will help you market your business. Continuous evaluation will keep your marketing on track.*

- What will you name your business? What title will you use for yourself?

- What are your plans for obtaining a business logo and for producing coordinated business cards, letterhead, and other materials?

- What personal appearance standards will you follow when meeting with clients?

- How can you obtain publicity that will lead to more business? What media will you use?

- Will you maintain an ongoing business publicity plan? How?
- What kinds advertising will you do? Do you have an annual advertising budget and plan?
- Would a newsletter be useful in marketing your business? How will you produce it? Where will you circulate it?
- How can you tell where your new business is coming from?
- What procedures will you use to evaluate and update your marketing program?

---

## Jan Franck
### *Frank Communications, West Des Moines, Iowa*

### Positioning for Profit

After a few years in business, Jan Franck went from calling herself a "freelance writer" to a "marketing consultant" and everything changed.

With an undergraduate degree in advertising and a master's in mass communications, Franck was "ready to conquer the world" in 1981 with her new degree. But Des Moines was in recession at the time, and the only job offers she received were to build business for advertising agencies. Since she had minimal financial pressure at the time and two small children to care for, she decided, "I could do that for myself."

Franck began knocking on doors, taking any communications job she could find, from trade show booths to brochures to press releases, and was profitable within six months. But something was wrong. She was defining her business as a "cottage industry" and found it sounded like "kitchen table" to her mostly male clients. "Freelance writer" sounded like "side income, pin money." And her strategy of "since I'm home-based, I can do it for less" was perceived, not as a benefit, but a compromise with quality.

"I erased all that from my presentation," she says, "and came on as a professional, customized service, and things really started to click."

Today, Franck Communications provides a combination of research, marketing plans, and marketing materials. Handling sales, client strategy, and most of the writing herself, she calls on some fifteen subcontractors—research specialists, designers, illustrators, and photographers. "I get the best creative services for the project," she says. "Too many agencies hire a generalist and hope he or she can do whatever comes in the door."

Franck pays her subs and printers and handles all client billing. "I manage the project," she explains, "that makes clients come back to me."

Initially expecting that she would have to lure jobs away from established agencies, Franck says she was surprised to find "how much work is out there." She reports "I've always been able to find a niche where I can provide something that is too specialized or too small for the client's agency or too expensive to do at agency rates."

Franck is involved in such groups as the International Association of Business Communicators, the National Association of Women Business Owners, and the Marketing Association of America. As a networker, she knows "someone at every agency in town" and does an annual rate survey of Des Moines-area advertising agencies. She says that getting "even a ballpark figure" helps her stay both profitable and competitive.

In another successful marketing activity, Franck teaches free seminars on "how to start your own business" for the Small Business Administration and passes out cards entitling new entrepreneurs to a free hour of consulting. "I'm seeding the field for the future," she says, "and sometimes I hit a business that's ready to grow now."

Referrals are an important "and cost-effective" component to Franck's marketing plan. "At the end of a project, I always say, 'Thanks for the business, and now that we've worked together and you know what I can do, is there anyone else you can refer me to?'"

What's ahead for this dynamic midwesterner? "Agencies in general are reinventing themselves," Franck says. "They're finding new market niches and seeking new ways to relate to each other. I'd like to combine with some other person or group for mental and professional stimulation. Maybe we could create a non-traditional but very effective way to serve clients."

# 8

# Selling Your Services

## Prospects Are Just People

Selling is everything you do to make direct contact with prospects and close sales. And the most important thing to remember about selling is that even a Fortune 500 corporation is just people solving problems and meeting deadlines. The same goes for the rest of your prospects—they're men and women you might meet at a chamber of commerce breakfast or on a telephone prospecting call—people with hobbies and families, priorities and preferences. Above all, they're people with emotions—because, no matter why they *think* they buy, people base buying decisions on what they *feel*.

As a salesperson, it's your job to identity these people and find out what they need and how you can help them. If you are offering competent help, a certain percentage of these people will want to know about it.  Actually, it's their job to know about it! They will keep your card or brochure. They will listen to your presentation. And of that group, a certain percentage will buy your services.

Cross my heart. Trust me. It's true!

It's often been said that nothing happens until somebody sells something. Sales people like this saying, and they like to think of themselves as the most important people in the business cycle. Incomes tend to bear this out because some top sales people earn more than their CEOs.

"But selling can't be as important as producing a product," you protest. "The product or service is what matters. Sales people just inflate their egos to to make up for the rejection they have to face."

I don't think so.

I love the writing and designing process, and I enjoy sitting at my computer being creative. But that moment when a deal is set, when an enthusiastic client says "yes!" and starts to anticipate the job I am going to do, is matched only by the moment when I deliver a good, creative job—on schedule and within budget—to a happy, satisfied client. Those are the times when I feel really great about my life as a freelance writer and graphic designer. And those are times when selling is taking place. They are sales opportunities—because the very best time to solicit more business is when your client is happy with the work you have already done!

# The Benefits of Selling— and of Sales Training

Fortunately for us, the same basic methods used in selling most products and services are also appropriate for selling writing and desktop publishing to prospects in business firms, retail stores, professional groups, hospitals, government agencies, and universities, among others.

We may not think of ourselves as fortunate to have to sell our services over and over, compared with a novelist, screenwriter, or illustrator, who is represented by an agent and doesn't have to pound on the doors of her publishers, producers, or advertisers. But remember that at least 15 percent of everything she earns goes to that agent, who may or may not be worth it.

We, on the other hand, are mastering our own survival skills, learning every day to keep our fingers on the market pulse. And to help us, we have a vast storehouse of motivational and technical sales training—offered in virtually every city and town—along with enough books and tapes on selling to keep us closing deals for the rest of our lives and then some.

When I was working in higher education, I tended to scorn what I thought of as the "rah-rah" self-motivation and self-improvement of the marketplace. From Napoleon Hill to Anthony Robbins, I thought it was corny and commercial. But that was before I became an outside salesperson living solely on commission! I became humble in a hurry when I found that listening to a tape in my car before a difficult sales call gave me the confidence to sail through my presentation and an evening spent in a training seminar would translate into more calls, more proposals, and more sales.

I even changed my mind about the "positive thinking" so central to sales training when I saw what a few days of negative thinking could do to my sales performance. I no longer derided it as superficial.  In fact, I realized that attitude lies at the very core of meaning and survival in our lives.

In his book, *Successful Cold Call Selling* (1983), sales trainer Lee Boyan reminds his readers of the work of Viktor Frankl, the renowned Austrian psychiatrist who survived the Nazi concentration camps and described his experiences in his famous book, *Man's Search for Meaning* (English translation, 1959). According to Boyan, Frankl "observed that everything can be taken away from human beings except what he called the last of the human freedoms. And that is freedom to choose one's attitude in any given situation."

We are not faced with the life-and-death circumstances of a concentration camp, but as Boyan points out, we are "faced with situations where ... inner decision will determine our circumstances, our relationships with other people, and how we're going to feel."

So be glad your work requires you to sell—and to choose the positive way.

When you offer your services, it's true that you will meet rejection. But what is rejection? Isn't it getting past those who currently have no need or interest? Much rejection is no more than that—the

# PROSPECT INFORMATION FORM

Company/Organization _____

Name of Prospect _____

Title _____

Address _____

City _____ State _____ Zip code _____

Phone (_____)_____ Ext. _____ Fax (_____)_____

E-mail, pager, other _____

Is this person the decision-maker?  Yes ____  No ____

If not, who is?  Name/s, title/s _____

_____

Source of referral _____

Referral thanks (if appropriate)  Date _____

---

**Personal/Professional Info** (prospect's interests, background, birthday, etc.)

---

**Types of Services Purchased**

Probability of repeat business   High _____ Avg _____ Low _____

Probability of reliable payment  High _____ Avg _____ Low _____

Current suppliers (if known) _____

_____

---

**Sales Angles** (upcoming needs, problems with current suppliers, special interests)

---

# FOLLOW-UP

Date _____ Contact: Phone ___ In person ___ Other_____

**Comments**




Outcome _____

Continue following? Yes ____ No ____ Scheduled follow-up date _____

Date _____ Contact: Phone ___ In person ___ Other_____

**Comments**




Outcome _____

Continue following? Yes ____ No ____ Scheduled follow-up date _____

Date _____ Contact: Phone ___ In person ___ Other_____

**Comments**




Outcome _____

Continue following? Yes ____ No ____ Scheduled follow-up date _____ prospect doesn't need your services *at this point in time.* He may buy later, or he may not. Either way, if you stay focused on the benefits of your services and your desire to help your clients, you will start connecting with people who do want what you have to offer.

The material presented in this chapter is just a taste of the resources available to help you sell. Among the many nonbillable activities required to run your business, I urge you to devote time to sales motivation and sales techniques. Unfortunately, reading one book or attending one class won't be enough. You need to keep reading books and articles, listening to tapes, and attending lectures and seminars—frequently at first, and later on an occasional repeating basis. You'll be able to measure the results!

# The Value of a Prospect List

Your good prospects and eventually your buyers will emerge out of your prospect list. I had an object lesson in the value of such a list a few years ago, working with the Direct Marketing Association of Orange County, for whom I do a newsletter. Ever since its founding, this organization had wanted to build a relationship with the higher education community, but they had made virtually no progress. I knew why, having worked for colleges and universities for years. That environment is hard to penetrate if you don't know your way around.

Then one day, shortly before a major West Coast direct marketing conference, a two-year-old list of marketing educators fell into the hands of the new education committee. Now they knew what to do! Giving a direct marketer a list is like giving a case of lobster to a chef. Never mind that the list was old and didn't include every school in the region. The committee mailed out letters offering several free (magic direct-marketing word) admissions to the conference.

Instant response! Faculty were vying for the privilege of attending. As a result, one instructor developed a new course in direct marketing. Others invited professionals to address their classes. Students began coming to the group's monthly meetings as the guests of member firms. And a major university opened discussions about a direct-marketing certificate program.

What can we learn from this in terms of building our own businesses? If your list has even a few names that fit your client profile, start calling. Refine your list as you go. Don't wait for the complete and perfect list, or you'll be out of business before you finish assembling it.

# Qualifying Prospects

Your marketing research helps you develop an initial list of people likely to buy your services, but once you are in business, you will continue adding to your prospect list. As you gather names, don't clutter your list with those you have no intention of following up on. Instead, develop a quick test for qualifying your prospects, based on what you do and for whom. Here are some questions to ask:

- Do they have an ongoing need for my services? (One-time clients are much less profitable than repeat clients.)
- Can they afford my services?
- Is their credit reliable?
- Will I be credible to them in terms of the quality of my work and my experience?
- Who makes the buying decisions, and how can I get to that person?
- Do I want to work with this client?

For some prospects, your general knowledge will provide most of the answers. In other cases, you will have to phone the prospect or do some library or on-line research. Always look for the names and titles of those who do the buying. Qualifying a prospect includes not only finding out if there is a fit, but finding out who makes the purchasing decisions. One of the most frustrating mistakes in sales is to spend time selling a "prospect" who just loves your service but turns out not to have the authority to buy.

# Sources of Prospects

In addition to directories and commercial lists, here are some ongoing sources of prospect names.

## Media and conversations

Since your marketing research has identified the categories of clients you are looking for, make it a habit to watch for prospects as you read newspapers and business journals. Pick up names from news media. Watch for news of appointments, business start-ups, and reorganizations as well as new contracts and projects. Clip articles, make notes, and add the names to your database.

## Networking

One of the oldest sayings in sales is that people buy from people they know. And it's true. Meeting people at business organizations has brought me at least 75 percent of my freelance clients. I enjoy meeting people and learning about their interests—and, of course, I collect their business cards. I concentrate on communications organizations, such as the International Association of Business Communicators and Women in Communications, Inc. You should research the groups available in your community and see what works for you, based on the services you offer and the clients you are seeking.

Sales authorities will tell you that without a referral or previous contact, it can take five to ten sales approaches (such as a mailing or a phone call) to get a face-to-face meeting with a buyer, even when that buyer has a potential need for what you're selling. I find that having had lunch with a buyer in a friendly environment can get me an appointment with just one or two phone calls. Of course, the buyer must have been favorably impressed at our initial meeting and have some need for writing or design services.

Another way to use networking as a prospecting tool is to keep track of awards given by advertising, public relations, and other communications and marketing groups in your community. Collect the names of winning clients and those who did the creative work and the production. Then select for follow-up those who appear to fit your services. In some cases, this may be a two-step process. For example, you might want to use an award-winning printer or photographer for some of your own projects, or you might refer them some business. The printer or photographer, in turn, might become a source of referrals for you. And, of course, you may want to start calling on the award-winning client with some creative ideas of your own.

My personal view about networking is this: *don't be a tourist!* Pick a few organizations you care about and work for them. Be a contributor. Of course, you can visit other groups occasionally—perhaps to hear a special speaker, or just to check them out. But the business butterfly flitting through a premeeting reception, scattering and collecting business cards, often makes a negative impression.

Experts on networking suggest that you

- Set a few goals before the meeting.
- Have a supply of business cards conveniently at hand.
- Put out samples or brochures if appropriate.
- Prepare a short description of your business in case public introductions are called for. Be sure to include something listeners will remember.
- Avoid talking or sitting only with people you know.
- Spend enough time with each person you meet to learn something about that individual.
- Follow up good prospects within a week.

While you may get more direct assignments for writing and desktop publishing through networking in business, industry, or professional groups, don't overlook your own trade groups—organizations for writers or desktop publishers. In addition to current information about your craft, you'll have a chance to learn about local rates of payment and business customs and build a network of referrals for jobs. For example, it was by serving on the board of the Independent Writers of Southern California that I met the editor who asked me to write this book.

## Referrals

Asking for referrals is one of the very best ways to obtain prospects. Yet few of us do it often enough or consistently enough. Clients are usually your best sources of referrals. When you are serving a large firm, a client referral may be to another department within the same organization. For example, if you're already doing a good job for human resources, the marketing department is more likely to be interested in your services than if you had never served the firm. Salespeople call this "penetrating" an account.

Other important sources of referrals are business associates (including vendors) and personal associates. If you belong to a business and social organization such as a country club or tennis club, take advantage of it and make your personal contacts extra productive.

The value of a referral is that it gets you in the door. You can say, "Joe Smith suggested I call you." If you know Joe well enough, ask him to pave the way by telling the prospect you will be calling. That's even more persuasive—and it forces you into following up. You don't want to hear Joe say, "Hey, my friend at the ad agency said you never called her."

Make it a habit to ask for and follow up on referrals.

## Inquiry tracking

Whenever you get an inquiry, make it a point to ask how the prospect heard about you. This is essential information if you are to evaluate the effectiveness of your marketing and sales efforts. I suspect that most writers and desktop publishers keep this kind of information in their heads, but I urge you to set up a tracking device for your leads—if no more than a sheet of paper listing inquiries chronologically and indicating the source of each lead. In six months or a year, you will have a clear idea of where your new business is coming from.

## Referral courtesies

When you receive a referral from an associate, it's an important point of business etiquette to thank that person. This is just common courtesy, but it also keeps the wheels of your marketing operation turning smoothly. A note or phone call is the usual method. Sometimes your thanks can be more elaborate, taking the form of a luncheon or a small gift—or even a referral fee.

Referral fees fall close to some ethically gray areas. When does a referral fee become a kickback? When I was selling printing, a local public relations man asked us to build in a referral fee of 10 percent whenever he requested a quote for his client. The client never knew about this fee. When the bill was paid, my firm sent the public relations man a check. This practice is not illegal and may be very common in certain industries, but I was never especially comfortable with it. On the other hand, if the public relations man had handled payment for the printing, he would naturally be expected to mark up the bill when passing it on to his client.

Use your networking contacts to find out whether referral fees are accepted (or even expected) in your community and the industries you serve.

## Advertising and public relations

These topics were discussed under marketing techniques in the previous chapter. For our purposes here, I'm lumping together all of your efforts to put your name in front of prospective buyers—whether it's through a display or classified ad, a direct mail campaign, a directory listing, an ad in a postcard deck, your card on a bulletin board, your name in the paper for having won an award or on a committee for a community event, your face on a business talk show, a display of your work, or you in person, giving a lecture or teaching a class. The result is the same: A prospective buyer learns about and contacts you.

What do you do? Of course, you fulfill any specific request promptly, whether the prospect has requested a copy of an article you wrote or asked to see your samples and brochure. After that, if the prospect is qualified, you add his or her name to your database for further cultivation. If the prospect doesn't need or can't afford your type of services but is impressed with your work, ask for some referrals.

## Trade shows and conferences

I met my oldest and one of my best clients through a trade show. I swapped some writing services for a booth in a desktop publishing exhibition, and through that event I was introduced to a client whose newsletter I've produced for over five years. Many trade shows will be too costly for you to exhibit in, but if an event is targeted and affordable, put together an interesting display and give it a try. Make sure you have a good device for capturing names while you're busy talking to other visitors in your booth. Collecting business cards for a drawing is a tried and true method.

Even without being an exhibitor, a trade show or conference provides a good opportunity to meet prospects, since many people with similar interests are gathered in one place. Be aware, too, that conference planners sometimes designate an area where attendees may display their literature. To be on the safe side, bring a supply of literature along.

## Take-one boxes

Putting a box of your literature in a place where prospects are likely to see it is a technique that might be suitable for certain writers and desktop publishers—such as a resume writer or a designer specializing in business stationery. If you work with a quick printer, for example, ask if you can put your literature on the counter.

## Seizing the moment

People who are extremely difficult to reach will usually talk with you when they are on public view—when they are giving a lecture, teaching a class, or just attending a public event. Your goal is to get a card and an invitation to call—or a referral to the appropriate person in the VIP's organization. (Then you can legitimately say, "I met Mr. VIP when he spoke at our trade association recently, and he suggested I call you.") But don't push too hard. Crude use of this technique can backfire. I watched a promoter trap an internationally known executive in a hotel elevator once. The executive had to listen, since the promoter was holding the door open—but I'm not sure he appreciated it.

# Telemarketing for Prospecting and Follow-up

Telemarketing involves calling lists of people with a standardized message and objective. This is a vast topic and one that is becoming increasingly important in the business world. As the cost of making in-person sales calls rises, phone selling grows ever more attractive—and that is just as true for you and me as it is for a multi-billion-dollar corporation.

Telemarketing will be useful for

- Qualifying prospects—and seeking an appointment or a chance to bid.
- Follow-up—again seeking an appointment or a chance to bid.
- Soliciting business from past clients.

What I am defining as telemarketing, however, is what we freelancers congenitally put off whenever we possibly can: the time when we must sit down to call a list of names—be they new prospects, old prospects, those in a certain industry, or past clients we haven't heard from recently.

Telemarketing can help you identify new prospects who might use your type of service, let existing prospects know about a new service you have added, or see if prospects or clients have any jobs available.

Recently I heard a presentation on telephone selling by a smart young sales trainer named John Klymshyn of Palmdale, California. With his permission, I'm going to share some of his ideas—what he calls the Klymshyn Method. At the same time, let me stress that his approach is just one of many.

Klymshyn advises making calls in twenty-call bursts. Making twenty calls at a time keeps you focused, he says. Since not all calls will be completed, you must follow up later. Start the call by identifying yourself, your company, and the purpose of your call. "What I do is . . ."

Follow that with such open-ended questions as: "Who makes decisions about this type of service?" "How familiar are you with this type of service?" Develop several open-ended questions and avoid any that can be answered with a yes or no. Know what you want to accomplish with the call and stay on track.

Since many people consider a phone call an intrusion, Klymshyn tells his students "Go in with the idea that what you are presenting has value." You have information that can benefit the person you're calling. As the caller responds, take notes for your database. Next time you call, you can bring up specifics, and the prospect will be impressed by your interest and knowledge of his firm.

In Klymshyn's view, whether you're selling on the phone or in person, you must identify a need, create interest, and get out. "Don't bang your head against the wall," says Klymshyn. "Most salespeople don't know when to shut up."

Is the prospect away from her desk? Leave a message. Klymshyn views voice mail as a sales opportunity. Your message can create interest by suggesting a benefit and can show you're proud of the service you provide.

The Klymshyn Method identifies eight requirements for effective telemarketing:

1. Imagination. "People buy on the basis of emotion. Imagine your customer enjoying the benefits of your product or service."

2. Organization. "Who are you going to call? What result do you want? Why should the prospect buy?"

3. Discipline. "Don't make fewer than twenty calls at a time. At about the seventh call, you'll start to make the contacts you need. It will begin to feel natural for you to be on the phone selling."

4. Perspective. "If your calls go well, it's great! If your calls go badly, the phone seems like a monster. Step back from both good and bad calls. Remember, it's persistent effort that pays off."

5. Enthusiasm. "Enthusiasm is contagious. Do you know what IASM means? It means, 'I Am Sold Myself.'"

6. Strong Communication Skills. "It's the old eighty–twenty rule. Eighty percent of our job is to shut up and listen. If you can get the customer to talk, you stay in control. There's only one issue in a sales call—the customer. And the customer is interested in WIIFM—'What's In It For Me?'"

7. Product Knowledge. "Without this, our entire presentation can fail. Buyers lose confidence if a salesperson can't answer their questions." (Fortunately for writers and desktop publishers, we know the product since we're selling ourselves.)

8. Clear Objectives. Every sales call should have five objectives, says Klymshyn:
   • To sell.
   • To gather information.
   • To share information.
   • To establish a relationship.
   • To maintain a relationship.

But even with the best technique, no telemarketer completes all of his or her calls. How many times should you work through a list, trying to reach those you previously missed? "You want to try a minimum of three times to get to the decision maker," says Klymshyn. "After that, it's a judgment call based on what you feel is worthwhile. Valuable information can be gained by treating the decision maker's secretary as an equal. If you don't feel you have a shot, move on."

# Organizing Your Database

It's essential that you put information about your prospects in some unified and accessible form. A card file or pages in a loose-leaf notebook will work, and many salespeople still use these simple tools. But since you are already computer based, why not take advantage of one of the many contact-management–mailing-list programs available? Such programs are not difficult to learn and can boost your productivity enormously!

If you could produce a set of labels for, say, all the real estate brokers on your prospect list by simply hitting a few keys on your computer, guess what? You might send out a quick post-card promotion that would bring you in some nice business. But if you had to go through all your prospect files, including folders stuffed with newspaper clippings and boxes full of business cards, to pick out the real estate brokers, and then if you had to type up several dozen individual envelopes, would you do it?

Incidentally, the work of building and maintaining your database can be shared by family members or occasional paid workers. It will get done if you line up others to do it. Sure, you may be interrupted to answer questions as the data is entered, but consider the alternatives—doing it yourself or not doing it at all.

Contact-management–address programs usually allow you to record the prospect's full name, title, company, department, address, phone, fax, even birthday. Categories for grouping and sorting can be assigned to each record—such as client, top prospect, secondary prospect, prospect in a specific industry, and so on. You determine the categories. Most programs provide a free-form field for background information, such as the prospect's needs, interests, tastes, current suppliers, and the like. Data can usually be formatted and printed out in various ways, such as on mailing labels, in an address book to carry with you, or on a flat list. The program may also be able to dial the phone for you.

# Managing Your Contacts

The goal of a contact-management program is to keep track of each contact you have with a prospect as well as the outcome of that contact. You make a plan for your next contact and remind yourself with a tickler method, such as a computer calendar, pocket calendar, or monthly file folders.

Usually you are the one who must decide what and when the next contact will be. For example, you might want to call an editor on the first of the month because he told you that was when he normally assigns articles. To a list of fifteen instant printers you got from a business directory, you might decide to send a series of three mailings, one every other month, followed by phone calls. For a restaurant that occasionally requires menu design, you might decide to call the owner every six months.

Sometimes it is the prospect who establishes a contact date. "I don't need anything now," she may say. "Call me next month." Or, "I may need a proposal written in September. Call me then." Such an invitation from a prospect is very valuable! Treat it with respect and follow up religiously. Be sure to remind the prospect that he or she asked you to call back. Being able to say that Ms. Jones asked you to call is also useful in getting past her secretary.

As long as you see evidence that the prospect needs and can afford your services, it's not unusual for a writer or desktop publisher to make such follow-up contacts for months or even years before making a sale. Veteran sales reps will tell you that such dogged persistence pays off. It builds confidence and respect. The prospect is convinced that you are interested and that you keep your word.

# Follow-up Techniques

The purpose of the follow-up phase is to get to know the prospect and increase the prospect's interest. Stay focused on benefits to the client and on the sales progression you need to make—

- a presentation
- an invitation to bid
- awarding of a job
- awarding of future jobs

Somehow, gathering the names of prospects seems to be a lot more appealing than following up on those names. As a result, many of us have files bulging with names we haven't gotten around to calling. Not to mention the piles of cards from people we don't call because we're embarrassed to say, "Hi, I'm Bob Stone, the writer you met at the advertising luncheon a year ago. I said I'd call you." I think the solution to this dilemma is to gather fewer names or separate the names we gather into "real" prospects and "whenever" prospects. Such preliminary sorting will make your data manageable.

Follow-up, also euphemistically described as "cultivation," can be a long process, but it is your best form of business insurance. We're all tempted to forget prospecting and drop everything for the wonder client who appears out of nowhere and gives us a series of profitable jobs. But that client can disappear just as suddenly—and then what? A solid prospecting base with a number of good potential clients who are aware of your work can always be counted on to produce some new jobs.

This chapter has already suggested several types of follow-up. Here's a quick overview.

## Networking contacts

For your initial follow-up on a networking contact (someone you met at a professional event), send a note and then make a phone call. Or just make a call. Try to learn more about the prospect's role in the professional group, as well as about his need for your kind of services. If possible, offer some useful information, along with some background about what you do. If the prospect seems interested, suggest a meeting. If not, schedule him for follow-up. Appearing too pushy when contacting a buyer you have met at a professional meeting will be resented. Buyers from high-profile organizations have told me horror stories about vampire vendors descending on them the day after the meeting.

## Phone calls

One of your most basic selling techniques, already covered, thanks to trainer John Klymshyn.

## Sales letters

This is another huge field about which much has been written and said. If you're a writer who can craft successful sales letters, you can make very, very good money! If you're a writer or a desktop publisher seeking to interest prospects with your own sales letter, here are some tips.

Open with something that will arouse interest in your service. It could be an example of how another client has benefited or a way for the reader to solve a problem or save money. Stay in the "you" viewpoint. When you're finished writing, count the number of times "you" has been used, versus "I" or "we." If necessary, rewrite to put the focus on "you."

In the body of the letter, present your most powerful selling point, emphasizing how it benefits the reader. Provide evidence to support your claims. Avoid "stoppers"—anything the reader might find confusing or disagree with. A poorly worded sentence can be a stopper. So can words that may unwittingly offend, such as "mailman" (substitute "mail carrier").

In closing, state the action you want the reader to take. Provide an incentive for responding (such as a free informational brochure or a free consultation). Make it easy to respond (with a business reply card, phone number, or fax number). Sales letters have no fixed length. In fact, they can be quite long if they are well written and brimming with benefits. Finally, research shows that a post script (P.S.) scores high readership, so include one. It's your last chance to motivate action.

Try your sales letter out on test readers representative of your intended audience, and study their responses. If you are doing a large mailing and want your marketing to be effective, you must record and measure the response you receive. Studying responses allows you to learn from both success and failure. Consider testing your mail package by varying one element (usually the letter itself or the offer) for part of your list. Measure and compare the response.

If a sales letter pulls, use it again.

## Samples

Samples are your most important sales tool. Be sure to keep samples of every job. (This is especially important for desktop publishers.) Organize your samples in a way that will protect them, make them easy to find, and assure you of an adequate supply. If you are using your last copy of a clipping, make more copies now—not a month from now when you're in a hurry and can't remember why you can't find the blankety-blank clipping.

Why do you need many different kinds of samples? Why not just keep copies of your very best work? Because of a human quirk that every experienced salesperson has learned to anticipate. No matter how good the writing or how elegant the design, buyers will respond much more strongly to samples (and also to lists of clients) in fields related to their own.

## Testimonials

Testimonials are effective because a third-party endorsement is automatically more convincing than what you say about yourself. Keep copies of complimentary letters from clients. If a client praises you in a significant way, don't hesitate to ask him or her to put it in writing, and explain why. If you want to establish your expertise in a certain area, request a client to write a "to whom it may concern" testimonial letter about a job you have done. Make sure all such letters are on your client's letterhead. I keep original testimonial letters in my client files, but I keep extra copies with my samples, where I can find and use them as needed.

## Sales literature

Your sales literature may include one or more brochures about your services; your resumé, client list, and business cards; a custom

Rolodex card with your name and sales message; your own newsletter, articles you have written, reprints of articles about you; and custom presentation folders. Keep your sales literature organized, accessible, and current. If you run out of an item, update it if necessary. Then reorder promptly. If you can't easily locate want you need when you need it, you will be tempted to put off following up on requests for information and presentations. And that's death!

Keeping samples and sales literature organized and up-to-date represents an area where a family member or occasional worker can make an enormous contribution. It's an investment that will pay for itself many times over.

## Other mailing pieces

In addition to your own material, you may find it useful to send prospects information of interest to their specific industry or specialty. Make sure the material won't backfire, such as an essay on a controversial issue or far-out humor that might be misunderstood.

## Specialty items

Advertising specialty catalogs are full of clever and useful items that can be imprinted with your name and business message. Such items may be a good investment. They're ice breakers, and can often get you an appointment. For example, Claudia Miller, a California-based desktop publisher profiled in this book, swears by her "cookie."

"If you're going to do a mailing in the creative business, you'd better be creative," Miller says. "I have this cookie notepad. It's looks like an Oreo cookie 6 inches in diameter, and inside is a round notepad. On the inside of the lid is my message—telling what a sharp cookie I am! I send my cookie in a box, and people wonder what it is. They're curious and they have to open it. Then it sits on a desk, where others see it. When they open the lid, they read my message, and I reach even more people that way."

Miller often sends the cookie as her first contact with a good prospect, following it up with a phone call. "My cookie," she says, "almost always gets me in the door!"

## Getting past purchasing departments

When you sell creative services to large organizations, your actual buyer is usually not the purchasing department—but don't offend these folks by trying to go around them if company policy says they must be in the loop. The purchasing director may be happy to pass you along to the communications director once he has qualified you as a vendor. Or maybe he won't. If you have also built a relationship with the person who will actually use your writing or design—most likely someone in marketing, or corporate communications, or human resources—then that person may tell purchasing you're the vendor he or she wants.

## Getting around a turndown

"We're happy with the freelancers we're using." When you hear this, a good answer is, "I respect your loyalty. I'm loyal to the people I work with, too. But if you ever have an overload or a crisis project when your regular people can't help you, please give me a call." Usually this response will have a calming effect, and the prospect may accept your literature. Although such a client is currently a poor prospect, don't delete her. If she uses freelancers, many things could change. A freelancer could mess up a job, leave the area, or be unable to meet a deadline. Or company staff members could change, creating a whole new ballgame.

## Making friends with the prospect's staff

View whoever works with your prospects—assistants, secretaries, receptionists, security guards—as your allies. Ask and remember their names. Take time to learn something about them. Be friendly—but also show that you respect their bosses' time. It's amazing how well this tactic works! You'll hear (music to your ears!), "Oh, I think he can find time to see *you*." Another benefit to this approach (aside from its obvious human kindness) is that your prospect may leave, and his assistant (already your friend) may be promoted. Or your prospect may leave and the receptionist (still your friend) may tell his replacement what a great person you are.

## Following up at events

When I see prospects at professional meetings or other events, I make it a point to speak with them and exchange news. Often I learn about bidding opportunities that way. ("The vice president wants me to start a newsletter for our dealers in the fall. I don't know how I'm going to find time for another publication!") It also gives me a chance to share something of interest about my own recent work. Having spoken with the prospect, of course, provides yet another contact opportunity. When I send a note or call her, saying how good it was to see her, I can add, "If you need help writing or designing your dealer newsletter, I've had a lot of experience with that kind of publication. I think we could work something out that would be cost-effective."

## Do an "incomparable"

Years ago, I took my first class in printing sales from a tough veteran saleswoman. Her advice for dealing with prospects and clients surprised me. "Do an 'incomparable,'" she told us. "Do something they don't expect, something they appreciate, something no one else would do." Claudia Miller's oversized Oreo cookie is a good example. For my part, I try to listen carefully to the special interests of prospects and clients and provide them with information when I can—nothing expensive, perhaps a newspaper clipping or a magazine article—just a thoughtful gesture that makes me stand out from the crowd. I can't tell you what your "incomparable" would be. But look for it.

## Gifts and entertainment

As freelancers, we don't have much money to spend on gifts and entertainment, and in my experience, it's not really expected. If the topic is of interest, you might bring a prospect or client to a professional meeting as your guest. Or you might suggest lunch to discuss a project and pick up the tab. In December I deliver small gifts, such as dried fruit, to my clients and their staffs to wish them holiday cheer. (I stopped bringing boxes of chocolate creams when an overweight client received my chocolates with painful groans of obvious dismay. For the same reason, I never give alcohol as a gift.) Be aware that in many business settings, accepting even token gifts or entertainment is prohibited. If you're not sure, ask what the policy is.

# The Steps Toward Buying

Classic sales theory holds that a prospect follows a simple progression toward becoming a buyer:

- Attention
- Interest
- Conviction
- Desire

You cannot rush these steps, and you cannot take them out of order. For example, offering a deeply discounted price to a buyer who has never heard of you will probably not produce a sale—and it may tarnish your reputation.

Until you have the prospect's *attention,* selling cannot take place. Until the prospect is *interested,* has the idea that your services may be useful to him, he will not sit still to learn about their features and benefits.

Now it gets more complicated. The process of *conviction* begins as the prospect learns about the benefits of using your services. (And remember that features and benefits are not the same thing. A feature of your service is that you meet your deadlines. The benefit, however, is that the buyer will have peace of mind.) Until the prospect has seen some proof, however, both features and benefits remain merely claims. Let's say you show him several testimonial letters from other clients, thanking you for meeting deadlines so efficiently. With proof, the prospect becomes *convinced.*

Even when a prospect is convinced that you can do the job, he may not buy from you. Since he can buy from any number of qualified vendors, he must have a *desire* to buy from you. Perhaps he visualizes how much easier his work will be with your help or how much credit he will get when your materials produce results.

Perhaps he begins to like and trust you and to think of how much he would enjoy working with you. Perhaps he fears his competitors and believes that the brochure you have suggested will strengthen his position in the market. Now he feels he must have that brochure!

Now he is ready to buy.

# Making a Sales Presentation

The presentation, with its numerous methods for overcoming objections and equally numerous techniques for closing the sale, has been the subject of many seminars, books, and tapes. Don't let that scare you. Read up and take some training when you can—and in the meantime, apply these basic pointers to your selling experiences.

I should point out that in the classic sales scenario, the salesperson makes his or her presentation, asks for the order, and closes or fails to close the sale in a single session. In our kind of selling, that's not likely to happen. Your first presentation will probably be quite smooth, as you show your best samples and describe the best features of your services. Your "close" will be to ask for a job to quote, but you may not get one right away. When you are given a request for a proposal, you may go in again to discuss the job requirements. At yet another meeting, either in person or on the phone, you will discuss your proposal. If you're lucky, you'll get a simple go ahead. Otherwise, you may have to answer objections and negotiate specific issues.

## A presentation may not be necessary

If the client starts talking about her project from the moment you arrive, she may already be sold on you. Keep her talking! Forget the presentation you practiced and the samples you prepared, and find out how you can help her.

## Use samples to shape your presentation

Writers and desktop publishers usually find that their presentations are structured by the samples they have brought. You talk

your way through your samples, bringing out features and benefits. Select samples appropriate to the prospect, and arrange them
according to the points you want to make, based on your understanding of the prospect's needs. Include appropriate testimonials
and copies of your own sales literature. It may seem overwhelming to think of custom-tailoring each and every presentation, but
soon you will do it automatically.

## Bring material for the prospect's files

Be sure to bring something you can leave with the prospect—usually your brochure, resumé, and client list, along with your
business card and some samples (or copies of samples if you can't
leave the originals). Putting these in an imprinted folder—or just
in a plain file folder with your name already lettered on the tab—
is a nice touch. The folder encourages your prospect to put your
material in the vertical file—rather than the round one.

## Avoid "stoppers"

"Stoppers" during a sales presentation are points the prospect may
disagree with, be offended by, or not understand. I'll never forget the
artist who called on me when I was a university publications director during the antiwar seventies. He attacked the military with every
other word, and obviously had not taken the trouble to learn that
our institution depended heavily on military students. He did not get
my business, even though I agreed with some of his sentiments.

You may be a person with strong opinions, but why risk
offending with controversial political and social views? You can
also offend by attacking a writing or design style the prospect happens to like or speaking in computer jargon that the prospect
doesn't understand. People make up their minds about others very,
very quickly.

## Never bad-mouth a competitor

It just isn't professional to attack or criticize a competitor—you will
come out the loser. On the other hand, you can attack unspecified

competitors by noting, "Very few writers have the background to do this job." Or you might say, "My price is a little higher because my quality is, quite frankly, above average among desktop publishers." (Then go on to explain what you do to provide better quality.)

But if you are asked directly about a competitor, either be noncommittal or vaguely complimentary. "Mary Williams is a good designer," you might say, "and I'm sure she could do the job, but (again bring in a benefit of your services)."

## Assume the sale

From the beginning, take a "we" attitude that implies you are part of the prospect's team, a helpful and dependable resource. Convey that you are interested in the prospect's goals and concerned with his success. This is a good position to take because it's true. You can naturally assume that the prospect will do business with you. But use good judgment. Assuming the sale too aggressively or too soon can backfire and you'll hear, "Now wait just a minute! We're talking to several writers about this manual. We haven't made a decision."

## Present features in terms of advantages and benefits

I suggest you do some writing to prepare this part of your presentation, even though it should appear to be extemporaneous to the prospect. List the features of your service. For every feature, identify the advantages it represents and the benefits the client will experience. Be sure to define benefits in terms of feelings and emotions. For example—

- Feature: "I can take disks in almost any format and convert them for desktop publishing for a nominal fee."

- Advantages: "My disk conversion service saves you money and time. The alternative would be to pay a service bureau a higher fee for disk conversion, or to have someone rekey your data, with the possibility of errors."

- Benefits: "You can relax. You don't have to worry about data formats. Everything will be taken care of."

When you make each presentation, you will be able to choose from the prepared material in your head the appropriate features and benefits to address.

## Have proof to back up your claims

For every feature of your service, be prepared to offer some proof. Often you will not need to present it, but in some situations testimonial letters, price comparisons, industry statistics, and the like can turn doubt to conviction so that you can get on with the sale.

## Handling objections

Veteran sales trainers will tell you that the best way to handle objections is to anticipate them. As you work with prospects, you will begin to recognize areas where objections may arise. Stressing points like "at no extra cost," "with your approval," and "at your convenience" assure prospects that they will be in control and have no unpleasant surprises. But since no presentation is perfect, you will encounter objections. To handle them, here are some tips:

- When the prospect presents an objection, keep him talking to find out what he or she is really objecting to. Since objections are generally emotional in nature, look for hidden feelings, especially factors that might cause the client to feel worried, overburdened, or vulnerable to criticism.

- Don't contradict a prospect even if his objection reveals misunderstanding or lack of information. If the prospect says, "This catalog is too complex to produce with desktop publishing," a good response would begin, "I can understand how you might think that, but . . . " Contradictions are "stoppers" because the client feels he is under attack and must defend himself.

- Don't try to suppress objections, because unanswered objections create more objections. Instead, answer promptly. An objection is like a loop that takes you back into your presentation to cover a point more fully.

- What appears to be an objection may only be a stall, meaning that the prospect's desire to buy is not yet strong enough.

- Price objections show lack of perceived value. Build more value into the project. (More about that in the next chapter.)

- If possible, convert objections into questions. Suppose the client says, "Four weeks is too long to produce this newsletter." Assuming the sale, you answer the prospect's implied question about timing: "How can we plan the job differently to get it out faster?" But suppose you encounter an even more difficult objection when the prospect announces, "We got a very similar price from your competitor, and she says she can do the job in three weeks." Now you segue to the question: "What are the steps involved in producing a really good newsletter?" And without bad-mouthing your competitor, you try to plant seeds of doubt about a fast job, while showing that your approach will produce a quality product, one that will accomplish its objectives. And so it goes. Some you win. And some you don't.

- If an objection is real and unavoidable, try the "other than that" approach. Often it will clarify key points and reopen negotiations. For example: "I like your writing style, but we have to have a writer who can also shoot photos." "If photos were not an issue," you reply, "would you want me to write this monthly column?" "Yes, but we must have photos. That's why we pay a higher rate for this column." "How many photos do you need?" you ask. "We need at least three photos of the topic store each month—an exterior, an interior, and a close-up of the manager in action."

  "What if I guarantee to provide you professional photos at the same price?" you ask. You're gambling on several things—that a photographer you sometimes work with will help you out for a few months while you improve your photo skills and that each store profiled will buy prints of what he shoots, helping to cover costs while you make up the difference. Later that day, you check with the photographer, and the next morning you close the deal. The worst that can happen, if you can't get your photography up to par, is that you continue to accept a lesser fee or resign the account. Either option represents a strong incentive to succeed. After all, we're risk takers or we wouldn't be in this business.

## The trial close

Closing scares many salespeople because it is the moment when they may be told no. But closing is actually a continuous part of the sales process. You do it all along as you assume the sale through simple comments like: "When can I get the information from you?" "Would you like to me proofread the copy or will someone on your staff do it?" You are getting the prospect on the same wavelength with you, assuming you will work together. From this position, it's a small step to a "trial close."

A trial close is a question that contains an implied purchasing decision, such as, "Shall I start interviewing your people next week or would two weeks from now be better?" Or you might ask "Is that price within your budget?" A trial close can be used to flush out hidden objections. It also makes it easier for you to ask for the order. This is something you must eventually do, although, believe it or not, some salespeople are so afraid of being told no that they never really ask that crucial question. Instead, they allow the purchasing decision to be deferred to another day, greatly weakening their position.

Remember, no sale is closed until you have the order in hand—establishing full agreement on services, terms, and timing. Some sales trainers use the memory device "ABC"—Always Be Closing—to help salespeople make full use of closing as a powerful sales tool.

## Silence

Don't be afraid to be silent after you have presented your proposal. Salespeople often think they must fill an important moment like that with rapid chatter. Wrong. Silence can be a greater pressure on the prospect than words. It keeps you in control.

# Keeping Your Prospect/ Client List Active

If you have not yet been invited to bid, or if you have presented one or several bids and been rejected, you would normally continue to follow a prospect—if you believe business is there for you—until you begin making sales. But just how long you follow each prospect is a judgment call.

Some salespeople will question a prospect on this point, especially if they feel they are being used to provide comparative bids with no real chance of being selected. The approach would be friendly, but concerned: "I've been calling on the Mid-City Corporation for X months now, and I've given you prices on several jobs. You've seen the kind of work I do, and I know my prices are competitive. I'd very much like to work with you here at Mid-City. Do I have a chance of getting an assignment?" You may or may not get a straight answer, but the move is a professional one and will be respected. It could even produce some jobs.

More typicallly, you will get a clear message when your calls are not accepted or returned and you are never asked to bid. Unless you can find another point of entry, there's no business here.

## When a client stops buying

A similar, but more serious close-out can occur when you stop getting jobs. Don't ignore this situation. A frank conversation with the buyer may reveal a problem that can be solved. If the client has decided to take the work in-house, use someone else, or discontinue the project, put your efforts elsewhere.

## Disposition of prospects

The final step in a contact management program is to dispose of unproductive or inactive prospects and clients. If a name is in your active file, you should be contacting that individual or organization periodically with the expectation of getting work. That's what active means. If you do not feel further contacts will be productive, the name should be moved to an inactive file or deleted.

# Soliciting Additional Business

Once you have served a client, having a good contact management program will help you stay in touch to obtain additional assignments. Don't expect the client to call you, even though he may have been delighted with the work you did last month or last year. Many clients give new jobs or bidding opportunities to any qualified vendor who phones or walks in the door. They're not disloyal customers exactly, just busy ones. Work hard to develop repeat business. All studies show that serving existing clients is much more cost-effective than developing new ones—though both kinds of business are necessary, since old clients will eventually drop away.

## Working Toward a Business Plan

### BUSINESS SUCCESS WORKSHEET FIFTEEN

Concept: *A consistent sales program will keep your business vital.*

*When you go out into the marketplace to sell, you master your own survival skills. You learn every day to keep your finger on the market pulse. Use sales training and other aids to stay positive and strong.*

- What techniques will you use to provide yourself with training in prospecting and selling? How will you keep a positive attitude?
- Do you have a list of prospects? If not, how will you develop one?
- What criteria will you use to qualify prospects?
- What ongoing prospecting techniques will you use?
- How will you integrate telemarketing into your sales program?
- How will you organize your prospect database?
- What is your plan for contact management?

- What follow-up techniques will you use?
- Have you written out the major points in your presentation—the most compelling features of your services, including advantages, benefits, and proof? Have you studied these points so that you can present them spontaneously? Are you focusing on benefits?
- How will you organize your sample and literature files?
- What will you leave with clients following a presentation?

## Ken R. Alford
### Arts & Graphs, Clewiston, Florida

### Making Friends and Making Sales

Ken R. Alford has two business "partners" who account for a large part of the work that comes into his six-year-old desktop publishing firm, but he's not "in business" with either one.

Alford established Arts & Graphs in Clewiston, a remote town of 5,000 in south central Florida, when he became burned-out after twenty years in solo practice as a nurse anesthetist. Since the introduction of the Macintosh in 1984, he had been a Mac enthusiast, eventually designing many of the forms for his hospital along with materials for the medical staff as a hobby. Leaving the medical field, he opened two Subway sandwich shops and a desktop publishing business "to see which one would take off." He's still running all three.

Alford got to know a local printer whose old Compugraphic equipment limited his typesetting capabilities. The printer began referring work to Alford, and Alford, in turn, brought work to him—each giving the other a 20 percent discount.

"He's the only print shop in town, and I'm the only desktop publisher," says Alford. "When he has a job they can't do in-house, he marks it 'ECR'—extra creativity required—and the clerks know they're supposed to call me."

Another "bit of serendipity" was Alford's meeting with the local high school art teacher/football coach, who runs a thriving silk-screen printing business on the side.

"He and his partner have a big six-color press, and they needed special typesetting for a graduation T-shirt," Alford recalls. "The job was referred to me, and now I'm doing layouts for them regularly with the same 20 percent discount arrangement."

Putting in sixty- to seventy-hour weeks, Alford uses a 1000 dpi LaserMaster printer and has upgraded his Mac IIx to 20 MB of RAM. He has a scanner, an 88-megabyte cartridge drive, CD ROM, tape backup system, and a vast collection of electronic clip art. A businesslike studio in his house has its own client entrance.

Alford says his two "workhorses" are Adobe Illustrator and Manhattan Graphics' Ready, Set, Go! He swears the little-known page layout program can match PageMaker and Quark XPress at half the price with outstanding technical support.

Getting much of his work through referrals, Alford has done little advertising but says membership in two local chambers of commerce and the National Association of Desktop Publishers has been "very advantageous." Designing a newsletter for a nearby corporation has opened up a promising new avenue of business.

Alford prints his own brochures on his LaserMaster and displays them at the print shop. When writing is needed, he does it himself. He doesn't use contracts. "People in this town would be offended by that," he observes.

Crediting much of his success to his printer "partner," who taught him about "grippers, traps, and registration," Alford confides, "It feels good when somebody picks up a job and says, 'Wow! Does that look great!' Especially when they brought in something awful. To make a silk purse out of a sow's ear—that's the most gratifying."

# 9

# How to Charge and How to Collect

## Deciding What to Charge

"What shall I charge?" is the question I am most frequently asked by would-be or fledgling freelancers. Arriving at the right answers is complicated but essential to your business success. In this chapter, we will examine rates and payment from several different perspectives:

- What others charge
- How to arrive at your own rates
- Determining what work is profitable for your business—your profit zone
- The psychology of setting a price
- The bidding and negotiating process
- Terms of payment and credit approval

- Additional job expenses and the final bill
- Getting paid

# What Do others Charge?

Research pertaining to this question falls under two categories— industrywide pricing and local or industry-specific pricing. You should study both, although the second category is the most important in helping you win assignments.

National or regional surveys are a good place to begin your own research. These surveys publish averages or bottom–top ranges for various kinds of writing and desktop publishing. You can buy most of this information in book form or borrow it from libraries (see below). But in some cases, you must belong to the organization or subscribe to the publication that conducted the survey to read the results. Since new surveys come out periodically, keep this information current if you are using it in pricing.

Your second source of information is your own ongoing research about what clients like yours are paying writers or desktop publishers in your community (or in whatever market you serve).

Collect all the industrywide information you can. Start asking speakers at lectures and seminars how much the jobs under discussion cost and how much time it should take to do each phase of the job. Talk over issues relating to costs and time with your mentors. Consult with colleagues at professional meetings. Discuss pricing with vendors.

Numerous books and trade journals provide information on *how* to do different kinds of jobs, but rarely do they tell us *how long* each phase of the work should take or how much was paid for the project under discussion. We should start asking trade journal editors to include time factors as part of their "how-to" coverage, along with more information on pricing.

## National and regional rate studies for writers

*Books.* Each year, the *Writer's Market* (see Bibliography) includes a section listing current rates for various kinds of writing, along with advice on how to arrive at an hourly rate. The 1993 edition offers nine tightly packed pages listing rates for jobs in the following ten categories: books; magazines and trade journals; newspapers; business and technical writing; advertising, copywriting, and public relations; audiovisual and electronic communications; educational and literary services; editorial and design packages; and miscellaneous.

Here are some sample rates:

Book review: $50–$300

Research: $12-$20 per hour

Company newsletters and in-house publications: writing and editing 2–4 pages, $200–$500; 4–8 pages, $500–$1,000; 12–48 pages, $1,000–$2,500; writing $20–$60 per hour; editing $15–$40 per hour.

Sales letter for business or industry: $350–$1,000 for one or two pages

Many writers buy a copy of *Writer's Market* annually or at least every few years. But my guess is that few really take time to discover what a treasure-house of information this venerable resource really is! It offers advice on such topics as research, manuscript formats, contracts, and copyright, as well as nearly nine hundred pages listing book publishers, magazines (including the trade, technical, and professional journals dealt with in this book), script writing contacts, syndicates, greeting card companies, and writing contests and awards.

*Writer's Market* is mainly addressed to writers who want to sell fiction or nonfiction to book publishers and magazines, but in the section on what to charge, the editors give a knowing nod to the hidden market for writers who want to make a dependable living at their craft. This is the meat-and-potatoes market we have been discussing throughout this book. Going through the rate listings will give you many ideas for practical jobs you can do in your own community. It's as though the editors were saying under their breaths, "Look, we're devoting this book to the glamorous side of writing, but if you really want to survive, go after jobs like these."

In his popular book, *Secrets of A Freelance Writer: How to Make $85,000 A Year* (1988), Robert W. Bly lists a few "typical fees for commercial freelance writing projects," including an hourly rate for freelance writers of $35–$150 and up (see Bibliography). Bly's is one of the few writing guides to provide any actual figures. The reason, I am sure, is that fees vary widely according to the region, industry, writer's expertise, and type of writing involved. Fees also vary with the condition of the local economy.

*Magazines.* When writers' magazines such as *The Writer* and *The Writer's Digest* (see Bibliography) report on markets (usually that means magazines) they normally list rates of payment. This can be useful information, but not always for the obvious reasons.

I was feeling noble, accepting an hourly rate far below what I am paid by corporations to write for a regional religious publication (even though I greatly enjoyed the assignment), when a friend told me she was assigned to contribute to a cover story for *People Magazine* at a dollar less per hour than the denominational tabloid was paying me! See what I mean about glamour? Unless you have a name that can command big bucks, even altruism pays better.

*Organizations.* Some writers' organizations conduct periodic rate surveys. One example is the Independent Writers of Southern California, to which I belong. IWOSC does a rate survey each year, mailing results to members only. Check with your local writers groups. A list of writers' organizations is provided in the Source Directory.

Incidentally, you'll find that writers' organizations fall into several categories, including amateur or professional and literary or commercial. You'll get more help in setting fees from a group that is concerned with giving writers business advice.

## National and regional rate studies for desktop publishers

Although as an industry desktop publishing is new, graphic design, typesetting, illustration, and prepress production (pasteup and film work) have been around for a long time. In the early stages of the industry, some desktop publishers drew on the graphic design tradition—as I did when I got started. Others approached their work from the point of view of the quick printer, focusing on the low costs and fast turnaround made possible by new technologies. A third group came out of the computer industry and often brought with them a consulting or training orientation. Thus, prices varied enormously—as did the skills of practitioners. To some extent, that's still true.

Today desktop publishing is evolving its own traditions, as reflected in a growing number of publications, addressed both to in-house and independent desktop publishers. These publications are helping to stratify and clarify a field that is becoming more and more technically sophisticated.

*Pricing Guide for Desktop Publishing Services.* Robert C. Brenner (profiled in Chapter Ten) is a desktop publisher who saw the confusion and rapid growth in this emerging field as an opportunity. Since he is also a writer and an independent book publisher, he built a database and undertook research to find out what desktop publishers are charging for various kinds of services throughout the United States and Canada.

The first edition of Brenner Information Group's *Pricing Guide for Desktop Publishing Services* came out in 1992, based on approximately 250 responses from over 500 desktop publishers. (Brenner had personally interviewed many of these entrepreneurs.) The 1993 edition was based on the responses of over 11 percent of the 14,000 desktop publishers who received confidential questionnaires in the mail. The 372-page loose-leaf book sells for $49 plus shipping and handling (see Bibliography).

Brenner's *Pricing Guide* has more in common with estimating methods in the printing industry than in the world of graphic design. But whatever your orientation, I recommend you buy a copy and study it. In addition to pricing information, as a bonus, you will get a state-of-the-art overview of what services are being offered by desktop publishers nationwide, along with terminology for describing them.

The first 148 pages of the *Pricing Guide* comprise a small textbook on pricing, entitled "Street Smart Pricing for the Small Business Entrepreneur." It includes theories of market demand;

pricing strategies; and techniques for estimating, bidding, and negotiating.

The heart of the book presents price tables for seven regions of the United States, plus one section for Canada. Types of work described are

- file conversion
- text creation (a desktop publisher's term for writing!)
- data input and manipulation
- image processing
- graphic design
- document design and layout
- special services
- prepress services
- printing services
- imaging services

Under each category, prices are shown for individual jobs, such as indexing, text scanning (OCR), typography (spreadsheets and tables), black and white photo scanning, logo design, technical illustration, annual report design, certificate and award design, form design, changes and alterations—and many, many more. For each specific job, the book supplies average and typical prices and often a maximum price for a given region and compares them with prices in the rest of the United States and Canada. Here's an example:

## Invitation Design

| MIDWEST | | | U.S. and CANADA | | |
|---|---|---|---|---|---|
| AVG. | TYP. | OTHER | AVG. | TYP. | OTHER |
| $27.50 ea | $28 ea | $30 ea max | $45.56 ea | $35 ea | $150 ea max |
| $52.22/hr | $60/hr | $75/hr max | $43.01/hr | $40/hr | $80/hr max |

Most prices are figured either by the hour or by the page (or unit), and they vary dramatically. In the 1993 survey, for example, typography ranged from a low of $10 an hour to a high of $100, while hourly rates for graphic design ranged from $15 to $175.

Brenner's survey for the 1993 edition turned up some interesting statistics:

- Desktop publishers working in home offices reported annual gross sales as high as $5 million.

- About one-fourth of all desktop publishers reported annual incomes of $100,000 or more.

- In California, earnings of full-time female owner–operators averaged $2,458 a month—32 percent less than the $3,599 that full-time male owner-operators were earning. This figure bears a clear correlation to the 1991 statistices provided by the U.S. Department of Labor's Women's Bureau, which showed that nearly thirty years after the 1963 Equal Pay Act was signed into law by President Kennedy, women workers still earned an average of 30 percent less than their male counterparts. As a woman entrepreneur, however, what I find most startling about the California figures is that they are based on the fees women set for our own work *and the salaries we pay to ourselves!*

*Magazines.* A number of publications have arisen to serve the desktop publishing industry (see Bibliography), but most emphasize equipment and techniques, rather than how to run a desktop publishing business. *In-House Graphics*, a newsletter aimed primarily at desktop publishers who are not self-employed, publishes an annual salary survey. The January 1993 report was based on 592 respondents, covering salaries paid to men, women, and overall in 13 categories. Women averaged $31,894; men averaged $39,738.

Since these publications are new and still evolving, I believe reader response could have a big impact on what they cover. If you want price rates or income averages reported on in the publications you read, let the editors know.

*Organizations.* According to the Brenner study, the most popular organizations for desktop publishers (next to local networking groups, chambers of commerce, and special interest groups) are the National Association of Desktop Publishers, Typographers

International Association, Ventura Professional Users Group, and Printing Industries of America. Check with these and other organizations (see Source Directory) to see what pricing assistance they may provide.

## Getting local price information

Determining local prices paid by the kinds of clients you want to serve for the kinds of services you want to provide is part of your marketing research (see Chapter Seven). By the time you are actually pricing jobs, you should have some good local guidelines, but a single research effort will not be enough to keep your prices on target for long.

Make it a habit to gather price information whenever you have the chance. Whenever a client, a prospect, or a colleague discusses a job with you, ask about the price. Some people won't divulge price information, but many others will. Or at least you can get a range, such as "over $2,500" or "between $300 and $500."

When a competitor is selected for a job you have bid on, always try to find out why, probing for price among other factors. Some buyers are prohibited by organizational policy from divulging such information, but many will share it if you make it clear that you understand your competitor has been selected for the job and you have no problem with this. You are not trying to persuade the client to change anything; you simply want some guidance for your future marketing efforts. What were the deciding factors that made your competitor's proposal more attractive?

Vendors such as service bureaus and printers are another good source of price information. Call an advertising or public relations firm to see what they charge for what you do. (The figure will probably reflect their high overhead costs.) You might even have a friend obtain bids on a real or bogus job.

# Deciding How to Price Your Services

Setting your prices is an important process. It determines your personal income. It is a factor in establishing your image in the marketplace. And it helps to decide whether or not you get a specific job and whether your business will survive.

From the client's point of view, the *way* you present your price is also important. Here are some options:

- By the hour: a very common approach for many jobs.
- By the full or half day: usually for on-site work, especially consulting.
- By the head: one way to charge for training or presentations.
- By the word: typical of magazines and newspapers.
- By use: typical of illustrators and some writers. Price depends on how widely or how often work will be used.
- By the project: popular with clients because they feel secure knowing costs in advance.
- Flat rate: the same charge for a repeating job.
- Retainer fee: an agreement that the client will buy X hours of your time each month.

## Hourly rates

Regardless of how you present your price to the client, the hourly rate is your real yardstick. I like getting agreement up front with the client that my time is worth, say, $50 or $60 an hour. It's surprising how readily clients will nod in agreement when you tell them your hourly rate. You are establishing yourself as a valued professional—and you are also flushing out clients who can't possibly afford you. This saves time and misunderstandings. Once your rate has been agreed upon, you need only show that each part of the job will take so many hours.

Rarely, however, does a new client agree to an open-ended purchasing decision, authorizing you to work for an unlimited number of hours for a certain hourly fee. Normally, you will be asked to estimate how many hours the job (or each phase of the job) will take. To give yourself latitude, you might say, "This job will take me 10–14 hours at $X per hour."

Some writers and desktop publishers use the marketing strategy

of offering lower rates for nonprofit clients or for jobs that automatically repeat. As a marketing strategy, there's nothing wrong
with this—as long as the numbers work out. In other words, your
gross income must be sufficient to meet your expenses and produce a profit. If you get more work at the lower rates, you may be
able to keep your numbers up—but beware! You may also end up
working sixty- and seventy-hour weeks to turn out low-profit or
no-profit jobs.

## Different hourly rates for different tasks and different workers

Since the marketplace rewards creative and managerial work at
higher rates than, say, proofreading, transcribing a tape-recorded
interview, or keying in text, you will need to estimate your own
time—or that of your employees or subcontractors—at different
rates, depending on the job. Furthermore, one creative worker
commands a higher rate per hour than another, depending on his
or her experience and reputation. Your client may be willing to
pay more when you are doing the writing or designing than when
it is handled by your assistant. If you chose to, you may be able to
sidestep this issue by assuring your clients that all creative work is
done under your supervision.

A common trap for creative workers is to start charging less
when they themselves are doing less skilled work. Let me illustrate
this trap with an example from my own experience.

As a writer, I formerly tape-recorded all interviews for my corporate clients, transcribing them myself. This tedious work took
me hours, but when I finished the transcription, I was in a good
place mentally to write the article—if I wasn't too exhausted. I
invested $250 in a transcription machine, which helped a little, but
the job was still tedious. I could not charge $50 or $60 an hour for
transcribing tapes, and it was a moot point whether I could charge
for transcriptions at all, since my clients usually did not instruct me
to tape record their interviews.

Initially I handled the problem by overcharging slightly on my
writing hours and not mentioning transcription in my bills. In

other words, I was working for less. I have now developed a technique of taking abbreviated notes on my computer, either on my desktop at home, when I am interviewing by phone, or using my PowerBook in the field. With this method, I have close to a verbatim account of each interview printed out clearly and instantly ready for me to start writing—though some of the spelling is bizarre! This is a much more satisfactory arrangement for many interviews, and while it slows them down a little, I can legitimately charge for that. Furthermore, subjects seem to like knowing I am doing my best to quote them correctly.

What can you learn from this example? The lesson is *don't work for less*. It's a bad business practice, since all you have to sell is your time. Find a way out! If you can get away with it, you might raise your hourly rates enough to cover the time you're doing low-skilled work. You might use a subcontractor and bill for his or her time at a lower rate, plus your markup, of course. Or you might change your procedures, as I did, in order to avoid doing low-paid work.

## Charging by the full or half day

Corporations and government agencies are used to this approach—typical of consulting and training services. Figure your rate on a seven- or eight-hour day with a premium for overtime. If preparation time is required prior to your visit, be sure to include it in your estimate.

## Charging by the head

Teaching a seminar or a class involving several meetings is often compensated by the head—the number of students who enroll or attend. To protect yourself, you should specify a minimum number of enrollments required for you to teach the class—or a minimum fee you will accept. If attracting the public is a factor in enrollment, you may want permission to do your own publicity since a school district or local college or agency may not do enough promotion to attract the crowd you need.

## By the word

This time-honored approach is very familiar to writers who write for national and regional magazines—but is less familiar to those of us who do corporate writing. I recently received my first payment-by-the-word assignment in eight years of freelancing from a national medical news publication. At 50 cents a word, I was pleased to find the compensation comparable to my corporate projects. Writer colleagues tell me that editors will often negotiate with you for payment above the publication's stated rates if you can show why you're worth it.

## By use

Most of the writing and desktop publishing discussed in this book is custom-tailored to a client's specific needs, so the issue of "use" rarely comes up. Unless you specify otherwise, your business clients will assume that they are buying all rights to the work you agree to do. Some large firms require work-for-hire agreements stating that you are selling all rights to the creative work done under the agreement.

Some illustrators, photographers, and writers stand their ground, however, insisting that the work belongs to them and that the use made of the work should determine its worth to the client. Widespread use, such as a cover illustration in a national magazine, or repeated use should be compensated at a higher rate, they maintain. Writers similarly believe they should be compensated for reprint rights when their work is reused in a new context.

Issues surrounding the rights to intellectual property are very complex, regulations are difficult to establish and enforce, and infractions are hard to police. Electronic data transmission and the development of quality, high-speed duplicating equipment have added to the problem, which is certainly beyond the scope of this book.

- Stay informed on accepted rates for various uses and on copyright laws. A good, brief discussion of copyright is given in the *Writer's Market*. The *Designer's Guide to Making Money*

*with Your Desktop Computer* (see Bibliography) also deals
with this issue.

- Work with your industry organizations. Many of them are
  doing battle on your behalf to establish industry codes and
  legislation that will provide creative workers with fair compensation. For example, the Independent Writers of Southern
  California is working with other writers' groups to establish
  payment policies regarding the placing of articles on electronic
  databases.

- If your name is to appear on your work, establish with your
  client in advance your right to approve cuts or alterations.
  You can back off from this if a client is adamant, or if relin-
  quishing your right to approve alterations becomes a point in
  price negotiations. But it is important to protect your reputation. Of course, as in all business, earned trust and a
  reasonable understanding between respected colleagues is the
  basis for most of what happens.

- Help your clients see your point of view—and listen to theirs.
  I once hired an artist to do a simple, one-color illustration for
  a newsletter I produced for a corporate client. The project
  turned into a nightmare. The client was furious at the artist's
  rate, which was high because the artist understood the
  newsletter received national distribution. Furthermore, my
  client wanted the right to use the illustration again if he chose
  to, while the artist specified one-time use only and demanded
  that his original art be returned. We finally dropped the artist
  and found another one who was easier to get along with.

## By the project

This method is popular with clients because they know what they
are committing themselves to. Writers and desktop publishers like
it when they feel the price is advantageous to them. They need not
disclose how they arrived at the amount nor how many hours they
actually put in. Project pricing also forces you to be efficient—to
find ways of doing good work for minimum effort—and to keep

track of your time and costs so that you will be on target with future estimates. Project pricing allows you to tailor your work to the project budget. If you quote $1,000 for a brochure, for example, and the client tells you he has a maximum of $800 to spend, you can negotiate what you will provide for that amount. Finally, with project pricing it's easier to charge more when you know you will be dealing with a difficult client and less when you expect smooth sailing.

## Charging a flat rate

A flat rate can be advantageous for both you and the client on projects that repeat, such as newsletters, flyers such as those describing real estate properties, or programs for repeating events. The flat rate makes it easy for the client to plan his budget. It may give you an edge in getting the business, and it contributes to your "nut"—that portion of your monthly gross income that you can count on. If arrived at fairly, a flat rate will average out, with more work one time and less work the next, so that you receive profitable compensation. You may or may not have a formal agreement with the client to do, say, a year's newsletters for $X per issue. Get an agreement if you can.

## Charging a retainer fee

Here's another opportunity to increase the monthly income you can plan on. Public relations services are often contracted for on the basis of a retainer fee—usually monthly. Since there is no limit to the amount of promotion that could be done for the client, you agree to set aside a certain number of hours each month and do what can be done within that time frame. It's vital that you plan the work, clear appropriate time for it, and keep the client informed, so that he feels he is getting his money's worth. Otherwise, your retainer might be an easy item to trim off a tight budget.

If a major project, such as a special event, requires more than the allotted time, discuss with the client whether you will bill extra that month or work fewer hours for the next few months. Try to sell your client on the former, since public relations efforts are cumulative: The same amount of work brings a better response when done consistently than when done occasionally.

## Is an estimate always required?

Once you have established a relationship with a client, you may not be expected to estimate every job. This is how I work with a regional publication for which I do a variety of tasks, including research, writing, photography, editing, and occasional page design and production. I bill these services at the same rate and the editor and I both know approximately how long various tasks will take. If, for example, a story should run into many more interviews than anticipated, I would call the editor to discuss the mounting charges and consider alternative ways of handling the story.

In my experience, corporate assignments often take this semi-open-ended form—and for me it has been a very profitable approach. For example, I might be asked to write an article of 1,500 words on the launching of a new monitoring device at $50 an hour, not to exceed $700.

# How to Arrive at Your Basic Hourly Rate

First of all, you need to know how much money you must bring in to survive. This means the monthly costs of operating your business—such costs as the portion of your housing expenses, including utilities and maintenance, that you charge to your business; taxes; insurance; equipment depreciation; supplies; services; memberships; subscriptions; and salaries paid to any employees. It also means your profits—the money you pay yourself to cover monthly family expenses, including insurance, savings for retirement, and Social Security and income taxes, as well as the surplus income that will enable you to grow your business and eventually improve your family's lifestyle. From these figures you can arrive at your monthly gross income goal and your annual goal.

---

### EXAMPLE

| | |
|---|---:|
| Monthly cost of business operation | $1,100 |
| Monthly family expenses | 3,100 |
| Surplus | 500 |
| Total | $4,700 |

$4,700 x 12 = $56,400 — your annual gross income goal

---

## Basing your hourly rate on your gross income goal

Your annual gross income goal will help you establish your hourly rate, recognizing that only a certain percentage of your working hours are billable. One authority suggests you figure five billable hours a day for yourself and six for any employees. In his *Pricing Guide for Desktop Publishing,* Brenner proposes a 30-60-10 rule, which states that typical desktop publishers spend 30 percent of their time marketing, 60 percent performing the work, and 10 percent handling administrative details. Since 60 percent of eight hours a day is four hours and forty-eight minutes, this correlates well with the previous estimate.

Let's work this out using weekly figures. Give yourself two weeks' vacation (you'll need it, though you may not wind up taking it!). Now you have

---

### EXAMPLE

50 weeks x 25 billable hours per week
= 1,250 billable hours a year

$56,400 annual gross income required ÷ 1,250 billable hours a year
= $45.12 per hour

---

There's a temptation to use the salary you received when you were employed to arrive at your hourly rate. Resist it, or you'll start out thinking too low. If your salary before you opened your business was the amount you now feel you need to survive—$3,100 a month, or $37,200 a year—dividing that by 2,000 hours (40 hours a week x 50) gives you an hourly rate of $18.60.

## Basing your hourly rate on the salaries paid to others

But suppose salaried people who do the kind of work your business provides actually earn about what you were earning on your last job—$18.60 an hour. A formula suggested by The National Writers Club in their book, *The Professional Writers Guide* (1990), instructs you to double the typical hourly wage to cover your direct and overhead costs as an entrepreneur. This gives you what the editors call a "gross hourly rate," which, they advise, you must increase by 25 percent "to cover overhead time." The final rate they describe as your "billing rate."

### EXAMPLE

$18.60 per hour x 2 = $37.20 gross hourly rate

$37.20 gross hourly rate x 1.25 (a 25 percent increase)
= $46.50 per hour
—very close to the $45.12 arrived at by the previous formula!

Once you have an hourly rate you are confident of—say $50 an hour—the rest of the calculations become fairly simple. Will the proposal take ten hours to write? Then you need to charge $500. How much for a day of your time? Seven hours x $50 = $350—plus preparation time. Will you be paid $15 each for ten students enrolled in a seminar that takes you three hours to prepare and three hours to teach? No way! You'll earn only $150. But you could teach the same seminar profitably with twenty students bringing you $300.

As has been pointed out, you may not be able to bill $50 an hour for every service you provide, such as proofreading or transcribing. In that case, you will need to build in some other costs or increase the total hours to come up with the $50 an hour that you need to make. But what if padding your estimate prices you out of the market? That could happen. If you do a lot of jobs that involve less skilled work, you would be better off hiring someone at $10 or $15 an hour to do work that you can bill out at $20 or $25 an hour. Or you would be better off not doing the job.

# Finding Your Profit Zone

As you analyze your price structure and gather data on prices charged by others, you will discover that some types of work are not profitable for you. This may be obvious as soon as you hear what the going rates are. Or you may have to do several jobs and run time/profit analyses on them before a pattern begins to emerge.

Perhaps your quality standards make your price prohibitive, but when you drop your price to get such jobs, you put in long, unpaid hours. Be aware that certain work is better done by writers or desktop publishers who are willing and organized to just "knock it out." Perhaps you are unfamiliar with the material you are writing or designing and your client is not willing to compensate you for the time you must spend to complete an assignment. Perhaps you lack equipment, such as a scanner, and must buy out part of a job, while competitors can do the whole job in-house. Whatever the reasons may be, search for your own profit zone—the jobs you do well at prices that allow you to make money. Then look for more of those jobs.

Remember, one of the rewards of being in business for yourself is the option of declining jobs you don't want to do.

# The Psychology of Setting a Price

As necessary as an hourly rate is to your estimating process, don't become fixed on it, or you will stay at or below that rate for the rest of your freelance career. If that happens, you will lose many opportunities for personal and professional growth. What we're about to discuss here is something you won't be able to master until you have some experience as an entrepreneur—the psychology of setting a price.

Joy Mieko White's firm, InfoTeam, in El Toro, California, sets up partnering agreements with writers and desktop publishers to produce technical materials for industry and government. (Joy is profiled in chapter four.) Her experience in pricing psychology makes the point better than I could.

"I follow the marketing strategy established by Gerry Foster, a marketing consultant who works with service-based, rather than product-based businesses," says White. "It's difficult to sell something as intangible as writing and design, and that's what Gerry specializes in—intangibles. I ran into him in 1990 and quickly latched onto his ideas."

White was attending a conference put on by the City of Long Beach on how to do business with the city, and Foster gave a workshop on finding the real prospects in your prospect list. Foster conducts his business, Foster Marketing Resources, out of his home in Laguna Beach, California.

"Through attending Gerry's workshops and seminars, I learned that I was approaching marketing like a used-car salesman," White says. "I was going after price. In a recession, I was trying to hawk our low prices because we didn't have a high overhead. A lot of clients got turned off on that. They thought the product must be cheap if the price was cheap.

"Through Gerry I learned how to remarket myself and to provide added value," White continues. "In fact, I finally understood what 'added value' is. I learned that prospects will buy your service—even if you have the highest price—if they feel that they will get something spectacular for their money. I learned to walk away from those prospects who only want the best price, and I learned to feel sorry for those who take them on."

White concludes: "We had a prospect who had haggled over price come back to us recently and say, 'You were right. Let's start over!'"

## Set a high value on your services

Scrambling to cut corners and save pennies for your client is a self-defeating trap. Your service appears to be worth little, and your client—far from appreciating a bargain—may even be unhappy with the budget price you have agreed to, while you toil resentfully, doing less than your best because "that's all this cheapskate deserves."

You may not always get the price you want, but if you think of yourself as a valuable, high-quality supplier, you will be treated that way!

## Bring a strategy to the pricing situation

To get an idea of what I mean, consider buying "How to Get Paid What You Are Worth," a videotape by Maria Piscopo, a California-based creative services consultant. It sells for $29.95 and is one of four marketing videotapes Piscopo has produced for those who sell their own creative services (see Source Directory).

Since creative types find it difficult to talk about themselves and about money at the same time, Piscopo suggests techniques for "taking yourself out of the pricing picture." For example, instead of talking about "what you charge," she advises you to talk about "what it costs." She also offers techniques for creating a win–win pricing situation, "where you get what you want and the client gets what they want." If this intrigues you, buy and study Piscopo's tape. For now, I'll just summarize a few points.

- As your business grows and your prices rise, accept the fact that you may not be able to take old clients with you. You will need to find new ones.

- Think of your work as your property. As Piscopo puts it, "You own it and someone wants to use it." (This strategy does not apply to a "work for hire" situation.)

- When someone asks "What do you charge?" turn that around and ask what they need. Answers to several key questions give you the information you need to price strategically.

- Piscopo suggests a two-step bidding process. First you offer a verbal estimate to get a sense of the budget and other factors. "Writing a policy manual of that type," you tell the prospect, "would probably cost $3,000 to $4,000." If the prospect says, "Oh, we can't possibly pay that much!" you have not taken yourself out of the bidding, but can discuss what price range the client can afford and what you can do for that price. The verbal estimate is followed by a detailed written proposal complete with your sales materials. For most writers and desktop publishers, a two-step bidding process would be especially applicable to major jobs or new clients.

- "If the client wants to pay less," says Piscopo, "either you should get more or you should provide less." Be prepared to negotiate—and have your negotiating chips ready in advance. You could get more time to do the job, more sample copies, or a credit line. You could get the guarantee of a series of similar jobs. (You can expect to be more efficient as you become familiar with the work. You will also save time by not having to sell the subsequent projects. Both of these cost-saving factors can be passed on to the client, while you still make money.) If you can't get more, try providing less—perhaps the client will scale back the job, calling for less copy or fewer pages.

## Working Toward a Business Plan

### BUSINESS SUCCESS WORKSHEET SIXTEEN

Concept: *Know what your basic hourly rate must be and earn it five hours a day.*

*Your prices must be based on research, both outside and inside your business. While you may use various pricing strategies, setting and getting your basic hourly rate will be the key to your success as a home-based writer or desktop publisher. Approximately 60 percent of your time should be billable.*

- What research will you do to help you answer the question, "What shall I charge"?

National or regional rate studies available through books, periodicals, and organizations

Local pricing information

- How will you charge for various services? What is your rationale for selecting certain methods of payment?

  By the hour

  By the full or half day

  By the head

  By the word

  By use

  By the project

  Flat rate

  Retainer fee

- How will you avoid the trap of working for less than your normal rates—either in doing low-skill jobs or cut-rate jobs?

- Will the laws and customs surrounding intellectual property in your specialties have an impact on you? How will you inform yourself and stay current on such topics as

  Work for hire

  One-time or multiple use of intellectual property

  Copyright laws

  What rights you retain

  Issues surrounding electronic data

  Right to approve alterations in your work

- How will you arrive at your basic hourly rate? What will your basic hourly rate be?

- Do you have systems in place to gather information about time and costs on jobs, and to compare this information with the actual income from the jobs? Will you analyze the results to help you price jobs accurately? Will you also use this information to find your profit zone—those jobs that are most profitable for you?

- Do you understand the psychology of setting a price? Once you are established in business, will you concentrate on setting a high value on your services and bringing a strategy to the pricing situation? Are you prepared to lose some clients and replace them with new ones as your business grows?

# The Bidding and Negotiating Process

Establishing your basic hourly rate takes you a long way toward successfully pricing your work. But it's far from the whole story. Here are some additional points on bidding and negotiating.

## Taking specifications

Take accurate specifications when you are asked to bid. If possible, meet personally with the prospect. For example, does the client want a newsletter? If so, what is the budget? What is the audience? If readers are older, is type size a factor? What impression does the client want to make? How many pages are they thinking about? What page size? How much copy? How many photos? Any drawings or charts? How many colors? Is there an existing design, or must a new nameplate and format be developed? Is there a company logo or "corporate look" the newsletter must relate to? What materials will the newsletter be used with? How will it be mailed? Will it be folded?

Writers, too, collect "specs," though they may not use that term. A company or trade magazine editor asks you to write an article. What is the topic? How many words? When is the piece due? Who are the readers? What is their reading level? What slant or focus does the editor want? What is the budget and how much research will it cover? Can the editor provide you with background material? Interview suggestions? Any individuals who must be interviewed? Their names and numbers? Will photos be needed? Does the editor want photo ideas? Who will provide the photos? Will you need to write captions? If the material lends itself to sidebars, should you handle it that way? How should the article be delivered—hard copy, modem, disk, fax? If rewrites are needed, do you and the editor agree on time and costs? (One set of revisions is usual for many kinds of writing.)

Discussing the job in detail accomplishes several things. First of all, you will know that you are basing your price on what the prospect really wants. Your probing may also reveal client "hot buttons" that will help you sell the job, such as a very tight deadline, or a desire to win an award. Knowing these concerns will help you shape your proposal and your presentation. I recommend you develop a simple request-for-estimate form. It should cover

- Client name, address, phone, fax, modem
- Job name
- Job description (spelled out as specifically possible)
- Date due (and dates when portions of job are due)
- Delivery instructions
- Any special requirements or instructions
- The budget (Ask, even though many clients won't tell you.)
- Any related jobs (A promise of more related work could be a pricing factor.)

## Deal with the decision maker

When you gather information about the job, make sure you are getting it from an authoritative source, preferably the final decision maker. If you sense confusion about specifications—perhaps from a very inexperienced buyer—offer to help the buyer put the specifications in writing. This will help assure that you and your competitors will be bidding on the same thing. But don't suggest that the buyer obtain competitive bids. Inexperienced buyers often accept an initial price without negotiations or comparisons—if they feel comfortable with the vendor. Experienced buyers will also appreciate your efforts to get accurate information about the job. That way they know they are comparing apples with apples when they evaluate the bids.

## Determine time required and hourly rates for the work you do

Good estimating requires data—not only an accurate description of the job to be done, but a clear idea of all your costs for the various kinds of work you do. Collect information on the time required to do various jobs and use that data to determine your rates for various tasks. As you develop this information, your estimating and your billing will go hand-in-hand. Keep track of your time spent on each part of each job for billing purposes. Then find a way to summarize this data so that you can analyze it and build your own rate structure. If you are currently employed doing work similar to what you plan to do as a home-based writer or desktop publisher, start keeping track now of how long various tasks take. Ask yourself how much you would be willing to pay an outside vendor to do these tasks. Compare the time you take to do various jobs with the information you have collected on typical job prices. As an entrepreneur, you will view efficiency with more urgency than you do as an employee, and you may find that you need to become more efficient at certain tasks. If you are asked to bid on work you have never done before, try to equate it with jobs you have done previously and consult colleagues for advice.

## Direct costs

In addition to the time the job will require, you need to know what other costs you will incur to do the job. Such costs include consumable supplies needed for the job and regular employees you will have to pay to work on the job. Direct costs also include "buy-outs," such as equipment you will have to lease or rent, consultants or other professionals you will have to hire, service bureau time, photo processing, off-site duplicating, and printing. When you prepare your estimate, put a markup on all buy-outs. This could range from 15 percent up to whatever the traffic will bear. It's one of the areas where you can "sharpen your pencil" when it comes to negotiating the price, but be aware that if you put no markup on a buy-out, you are losing money because it costs you something to handle every purchase.

## Reimbursable expenses

Normally, expenses incurred in doing a job, such as phone and fax costs, postage, mileage, meals (especially if related to an interview), and parking are reimbursable. You keep track of these expenses (with documentation) and include them as separate items in your final bill. However, reimbursable expenses may figure in the estimating process if your prospect asks what you think these costs will total. In another possible scenario, your prospect may not be willing to cover all these costs, in which case you will need to make sure that they are covered elsewhere in your price.

## Hidden costs

Many writers and desktop publishers consider "it took me longer than I thought it would" to be a hidden cost. In a way, it is—but you could also call it "poor estimating." Watch out for unanticipated time spent in client meetings. Watch travel time. What should take one hour will take two in heavy traffic. Getting material for a job in small batches instead of all at once wastes time. So do interruptions. You may encounter unexpected costs in doing research. Checking printing jobs on the press may be unexpectedly time-consuming. If you're late in delivering a job, sending a messenger across town will be an unanticipated cost. Build a contingency fee into your estimate, if you can. Remember that if you do not have your seller's permit on file with your vendors, you pay sales tax on your buy-outs. Long-term storage may also represent a hidden cost on certain jobs.

Many hidden costs fall under Murphy's Law: If anything can go wrong, it will. Over time, you do get better at anticipating problems and faster at solving them. But if an unavoidable disaster skyrockets costs on a job, discuss it with your client. You shouldn't have to eat it all.

In my experience, the biggest hidden cost is probably the difficult client. After you've completed your research and started writing the brochure, this client calls to say she needs a new feature of her business covered and tells you to call her partner for details—but, of course, she still needs the copy by Friday and is already paying you "more than your competitor would have charged" so she can't afford to pay you more. Difficult clients usually don't know what they want, but they do know what they don't want. For example, you may have planned to show one set of proofs on an employee handbook, but the client makes repeated changes, demanding three more sets of proofs—which you must take to his office personally, since he wants to discuss them. Loaded for bear when you bring up extra costs, he doesn't want to pay you for any of this, since you "couldn't get it right."

You can fight to get paid for these extras and risk losing the client, but another approach is to build an "x-plus factor" into subsequent prices—by adding time to each step or by marking up the total. If the client objects to your estimate, the simple fact is, you probably can't afford to serve this client.

## Special job requirements

In order to do the job, you may need to purchase a special piece of equipment or software, a specific publication, or some other resource. How you should cover such costs is debatable. If you are likely to use the item for future clients, you probably cannot charge it to the job. Such a purchase is part of your cost of doing business. However, if the item is specific to the client (an unusual typeface, for example), you should discuss the matter with the client. Possible arrangements include the client lending you the needed item or the client reimbursing you for the needed item—either paying the full cost at one time or paying for it through markups on several jobs. In the latter case, the client might own the item but let you house it in order to do future jobs for them, or you might own the item.

## Develop one or more estimating forms

Develop a form to help you produce estimates quickly and accurately. If you do several kinds of work that are significantly different, you may need more than one form. (See sample estimating form on pages 246–47) If you don't want to develop an actual form with spaces to fill in data and numbers, at least develop a check-list for yourself to make sure you are covering everything. Here's what your worksheet or form should include.

- Labor

  List the steps involved in producing and delivering the job. Estimate the time required for each step and multiply by your hourly rate (or the rate you charge for that task).

- Materials

  List the materials you think will be required. Estimate the costs of materials, including your markup.

- Buy-outs

  Estimate any outside labor costs from subcontractors who work with you—writers, desktop publishers, artists, photographers, or others—and include your markup. You will probably have to contact them to get this information and must allow time for that step in your estimating process. Estimate the cost of other buy-outs, including your markup (for example—research services, special clip art, high-quality output from your service bureau, printing). Again, it may take extra time to get these prices.

- Shipping or delivery costs, if applicable.

- Out-of-pocket costs

  (Needed only if the client has asked for an estimate.) List the out-of-pocket expenses you think will be required, such as phone, postage, mileage, and parking. Estimate the out-of-pocket costs.

- Other costs

  Storage comes to mind as a billable charge that occasionally comes up. Watch for others that may be unique to the job.

The truth is, you probably will not do such detailed estimating on most jobs after you are established in business. You will develop a "feel" for the work, and you will be doing repeat jobs for which you have a financial track record. But never let yourself get too far from ground zero, where you predict what a job will cost and then compare what you made on the job with what it actually did cost, including any expenses entailed in collecting the money. Losing sight of this central business reality has meant the difference between success and failure for many, many entrepreneurs.

## Your presentation

Presenting your price to a client could be as informal as a phone call in which you say, "Hello. Harry? That flyer we discussed will run about $200. Is that OK?" Or it might be a package containing your detailed written estimate along with your resumé, client list, samples of your work, and even testimonials from clients—presented by you, and possibly your associates, at a meeting with the client's entire project group. For each presentation, you should analyze what it will take to get the assignment. Don't invest more than necessary. Overkill could be counterproductive. But don't shortchange yourself or appear too casual. Clients need to know that you take their work seriously, that you are bidding on correct specifications, that this is a fair price, that you are ready to start work and can deliver on time, and that you want to do the job.

## Negotiating

As has been suggested, you should have your negotiating chips ready when you present a price. One key chip is the lowest price you are willing to accept. When I was selling printing, a firm I represented gave its salespeople a range of prices to present to clients—from the desired price to the lowest acceptable price. And our commission rate was structured to keep us from immediately offering the lowest price, since we made a much higher commission on the profit portion than on the basic costs of the job.

When you're willing to cut your price to get a job, conveying this willingness can be a delicate matter—because you don't want to hear an exasperated prospect demanding, "Why didn't you give me that price to start with? Are you trying to cheat me?"

One technique is to use the salesperson's tried and true phrase for handling objections—"Other than that . . ." (See Chapter Eight.) Suppose your prospect says, "I like your approach to this brochure, but we can't afford $2,000."

"Other than that," you reply, "if price were not an issue, would you want me to do the job?" "I think so," says the prospect (a major victory for you!) "but price *is* an issue." "What were you thinking of spending on the brochure?" you ask innocently. "We're budgeted for $1,500 maximum," the prospect replies.

Now you have a new negotiating position. You can cut your price, risking a loss of credibility if the cut is large—in this case 25 percent. Or you can offer a smaller cut and see if the prospect will split the difference. If you do drop your price significantly, justify it. For example, "I recently had a big job fall through, so I have some extra time." Or, "I'm trying to get more clients in your industry." Avoid admitting that you are simply lowballing the prospect to get his business. Such an admission puts a client on guard against a big jump in your prices next time around.

Another approach is to tell the prospect what you can do for $1,500 and try to get the project redefined. Or you might offer to include some extra services in order to get your price. Or perhaps you could do the job for less if the client gave you more time, using the work to fill in slow spots. There are many negotiating positions that keep both you and the prospect in a win–win position.

But what if your bid will be examined and the decision made when you are not present? Here's a technique that may keep the door open. Call the prospect to make sure he has received your estimate. Offer to answer any questions, and tell him, "I feel $2,000 is a fair price for this job, but I'm willing to discuss it. I think (mention a key benefit of your services) would be very helpful to you on this job, so if price is a problem, call me before you make a decision. Will you do that?" If the client says, "No, that's against company policy," you can reduce your price now, on the phone, or take your chances in the bidding process.

In the last analysis, you don't want to do jobs you can't make money on. So if the prospect will not pay your bottom price, let the job go and look for other business.

# Getting Paid

## Terms of payment and credit approval

It's important to remember that you, the seller, are entitled to set the terms of payment—though you should make sure your client agrees to your terms—and you are also entitled to check a client's credit record before extending credit. This is normal business procedure. You state your terms on your invoice. If you have any doubt about getting paid, you should state them in your estimate or proposal as well and ask for credit references prior to starting the job.

You may think that appearing to doubt your client's creditworthiness will seem rude and be resented, but like many other customs in business, a vendor's cautiousness about credit and payment is not something experienced business people take personally. I remember doing a small rush desktop publishing job for an international corporation. The printer I selected because of his good prices and fast turnaround demanded payment in advance from all new clients. Period. It was a bother for me to arrange to have the check cut in advance and run to corporate headquarters to pick it up and take it to the printer, so I built those extra steps into my bill. But nobody resented the printer's policy.

## Credit checks

By "credit" I mean the period of time you have to wait for your money after you have done the work. When you wait, you are extending credit.

When dealing with large corporations, government offices, and large nonprofit agencies over the years, I have not checked the client's credit or asked for partial payment in advance unless the job was of long duration. And I have never been stiffed by such clients. If you have any doubts, large credit services, such as Dun and Bradstreet, can check your client's credit quickly for a fee. For a small businessperson dealing with other small businesses or organizations, a more typical way of checking credit would be to ask for three credit references—firms that have recently extended

Estimate # _____          Estimate due on _____

# ESTIMATING FORM

Client _____ Phone _____

Job name _____ Date _____

Date project is due _____ Production time available _____

Rush job? Yes ____ No ____  Will client pay rush charges?  Yes ____  No ____

Client budget (if known) $ _____

## PROJECT DESCRIPTION

*Design this space to fit your needs. Writers might want blanks for sections, length, number of interviews, research requirements, photos, tables, reader level. Desktop publishers might want blanks for number of pages, dimensions, amount of copy, photos, illustrations, charts, scanning and imaging requirements, paper type and color, ink colors, bindery instructions.*

Special instructions _____

Is this a repeat job?  Yes ____  No ____

Are related jobs available?  Yes ____  No ____

## LABOR (including preliminary proposals, client meetings, travel)

Task _____

　　No. of hours _____      @ Hourly rate $ _____  $ _____

Task _____

　　No. of hours _____      @ Hourly rate $ _____  $ _____

Task _____

　　No. of hours _____      @ Hourly rate $ _____  $ _____

## MATERIALS

Item _____

　　Quantity _____          Price ea. $ _____  $ _____

Item _____

　　Quantity _____          Price ea. $ _____  $ _____

Item _____

　　Quantity _____          Price ea. $ _____  $ _____

**BUY OUTS** (labor/materials)

Task _____

    Vendor _____

    No. of hours _____ @ Hourly rate $ _____

    Estimated cost $_____ x ____% markup    $ _____

Item _____

    Vendor _____

    Quantity _____ Cost ea. $ _____

    Estimated cost $_____ x ____% markup    $ _____

Shipping/delivery (describe)_____

    Method _____

    Estimated cost $_____ x ____% markup    $ _____


**OUT-OF-POCKET COSTS** (omit if billlable to client later)

Item _____

    Quantity _____ Cost ea. $ _____ $ _____

Item _____

    Quantity _____ Cost ea. $ _____ $ _____

SUBTOTAL  $ _____

Subtotal $_____ x ____% overhead/profit  $ _____

Rush charge (if applicable)  $ _____

**TOTAL PROJECT COST**  $ _____


**OPTIONS FOR NEGOTIATION**

Lowest acceptable price as described    $ _____

Possible changes to job description or delivery schedule

_____ Est. saving  $ _____

_____ Est. saving  $ _____

credit to your client. You then send a standard credit reference form (available from stationers) to the firms whose names your client has supplied. Such a form asks how much credit the firm has extended to your client, how recently, and how promptly your client paid. Often you will have to call to get this information after mailing or faxing the form, but in most cases you will get it. Small businesses are used to helping each other this way.

## Terms of payment options

The standard for payment in most business and nonprofit settings is thirty days from date of invoice. Here are some other options you may prefer, depending on the situation

- Payment on delivery.

- Payment due on receipt of invoice.

- Payment due in seven days or fourteen days from date of invoice.

- Discount of 2 percent or so for payment in ten or fifteen days, net amount due in thirty days.

- Charge of ____ percent added for payment after thirty days. This might vary with the industry. Find out what is customary, bearing in mind that a slow-paying client may or may not pay your late-payment fee, and you may make enemies if you try to collect it.

- Payment due one-half in advance and one-half on delivery—or one-third in advance, one-third halfway through, and one-third on delivery (or in thirty days). A wide variety of arrangements is possible. The point is to get something up front to protect yourself with an unfamiliar client, or when the job is likely to take several months to complete. When you have confidence in the client, you will probably drop the advance payment request unless you need it to even out your cash flow over an extended period. Insisting on payment in advance or at least prior to delivery is wise, however, when dealing with a financially questionable client, no matter how often you have served them.

In general, finding out what is customary is a good idea when establishing your payment terms. You do not have to follow the local or industry customs, though. Your terms are an individual matter, and if you do good work at good prices, your clients will probably accept them. Clients who refuse to make advance payments or require ninety days to pay will just have to find another vendor.

## Billing policies and methods

*Recording your time, and the ethics of hourly billing.* As in all other dealings with your clients, you must be ethical in billing. To do this, you and your staff must keep good records on a daily basis. There are many ways to keep such records—from computer programs that help you charge time to various clients at various rates, to mechanical timekeeping devices sometimes used in ad agencies, to simple paper-based timekeepers, such as the popular Daytimer system. Be sure that whatever system you use will allow you to extract the information for periodic use in analyzing your pricing strategies and your productivity.

*Additional job expenses.* When, as a college publications director, I was a buyer of graphic services, I really hated being nickel-and-dimed. I would agree with a vendor to do a job. The job would be completed, with some changes in the process, but no discussion about them. Then I would get a bill for considerably more than the original estimate. When I called to complain, I would hear an annoying litany of what seemed to me minuscule details for which I was being gouged. This threw budgets out of balance and made me look bad with the college departments and offices that I served.

When I became a printing salesperson, I saw the matter in a different light. I learned that some vendors watch in silent glee while inexperienced buyers call for costly changes, and I realized that some of my own "minuscule" changes had involved major adjustments. My boss, the owner of the printing firm, was not about to "eat" such charges—and since I knew my clients would *and should* be charged for them, I resolved that whenever changes were made, I would explain to my clients what was involved and approximately what it would cost.

As a home-based writer and desktop publisher, I follow the same policy, though I probably err toward staying with the estimate and keeping my clients happy—leaving money on the table in the process. But when a client calls for a significant change in either a writing or a desktop publishing job, I do not hesitate to charge for it—making it a point to let the client know at the time the change is made that what he or she has asked for will cost extra.

It's good policy to keep a written record of all job changes as you go along since a simple hourly record of the time you and your staff or subcontractors spent on the job may not highlight such changes. Suppose you promised one set of proofs, but in fact you showed three; suppose you had estimated five interviews would be required, but in fact you had to do seven; suppose you did not expect to have to spend an extra two hours designing a three-dimensional pie chart. In order to charge your client fairly, you will need this data, and, of course, you may also need it to justify charges if your clients question them. If you learned from my example, however, your clients won't question added charges because they will have been forewarned!

*When a job comes in under budget.* What if a job costs less to do than you originally estimated? Following a policy of charging for every extra expense would, it seems to me, obligate you to pass the savings along to your clients when the job turns out to be less costly to produce. But again, it's up to you. My impression is that few of us do pass such savings along, unless they are significant and the client is likely to ask about them. ("You bid on a forty-eight-page instruction manual and what we actually produced was a twelve-page booklet. How come you didn't charge me any less?")

*The final invoice.* Establish a special format for your invoices, even if it's just the word "invoice" added to your letterhead. It's preferable, especially when dealing with large corporations, to give each invoice a number. I don't do this, although every year I promise myself I will. When I did a series of newsletters for Kaiser Permanente, their accounts payable people called and told me they required a number, so I started a series of "K" invoices just for them.

Your invoice must show the name of the client, the client's purchase order number, if applicable (very important when dealing with large organizations), a brief description of the job, and the amount due. You might also include the date the job was delivered. Any variations from the original estimate should be detailed. If you do not state your terms, most clients will assume your terms are "net thirty"—meaning the full amount is due in thirty days.

*Bill promptly.* No matter how busy you are, make it a rule to bill as soon as you deliver the job—or according to whatever payment schedule has been agreed upon. This is probably the most vital part of your office paperwork routine because, obviously, if you don't bill, you won't get paid. But it's more subtle than that. If you don't bill promptly, your client will assume you don't care about being paid promptly, and your bill may go on the bottom of the pile. Furthermore, if you don't bill promptly, both you and your client will forget about details of the job, which may lead to your receiving less than you deserve or to disagreements with your client about what you do deserve.

## Getting paid on time

I am often surprised to discover that some seemingly aggressive writers and desktop publishers are reluctant to go after their money when they are not paid on time. As a commissioned printing salesperson, I was expected to collect late payments in order to get paid myself—which was a very strong motivation. As a result, I never hesitate to call about my freelance invoices. No invoice should be allowed to go unpaid for more than thirty days without action on your part.

*Is your invoice in order?* It may help you to know that checking on payment is a standard business procedure and if you call to "make sure everything is in order," no one takes offense and the vast majority of your payment problems can be solved. Calling when the invoice has been out about three weeks is a reasonable procedure. Your bill may have gone astray. Some documentation may be missing. Your client may have been holding your invoice because she had a question. Or she may have simply forgotten to submit your invoice for payment. From a psychological perspective, politely showing that you are concerned about payment has the effect of moving your invoice toward the top of the pile.

*Accounts Payable Departments.* In large organizations your client probably has nothing to do with payment. You will need to make yourself known to the Accounts Payable Department, which often organizes vendors alphabetically. When I check on payment from large hospitals and corporations, I find myself asking to speak to "the person who handles the P's." Even in small companies, it's usually not your client, but the bookkeeper, who writes the checks. Treat these bill-paying folks with friendliness and respect. Cooperate with them and try to help them do their jobs. Asking for an immediate check is not helpful since it interrupts their routines. If you need extremely fast payment, call in advance to see if a "handmade" check can be arranged.

*When payment is late.* In the small percentage of cases where the client's intention is to put you off, polite persistence, not rudeness, is the best approach. Once you have determined that everything about your invoice is in order, send regular reminders. When one institution of higher education where I worked hit hard times, bills started going 90 and 120 days and even longer—and vendors were becoming frantic. What I learned from the besieged business office was that the abusive vendors were the very last to get paid.

If possible, try to work out a payment plan with a client who is experiencing financial difficulties. Consider offering to accept in-kind payment if that would be an option. Know the laws regarding collection procedures in your area and be prepared to take further action if the amount justifies it and you have some chance of collecting. Just sending a letter on your attorney's letterhead may result in a check.

# Working Toward a Business Plan

## BUSINESS SUCCESS WORKSHEET SEVENTEEN

**Concept:** *Estimate accurately, bill promptly, and make sure all your costs are covered.*

*Estimating and billing go hand-in-hand. Accurate information helps you bid competitively and allows you to get all that is coming to you on every job. Always bill promptly, and follow up until payment is received.*

- Do you have a good method for obtaining all the information needed to produce accurate, competitive estimates?

    A specifications form or worksheet

    Assurance that you are dealing with the decision maker

    Analysis of direct costs, including buy-outs

    Analysis of special job requirements

    Analysis of reimbursable expenses

- Will you develop an estimating form or worksheet for various types of jobs, breaking each step of the job down by time and materials required and buy-outs?

- Do you have several negotiating strategies in mind when you present a price to help you win the job? Are you ready to walk away from the job if you cannot get your bottom price?

- Do you have methods for determining the creditworthiness of your clients?

- What terms of payment do you plan to use

    Payment due on delivery

    Payment due on receipt of invoice

    Net seven days, fifteen days, thirty days

    Discount for prompt payment

    Percentage charged for late payment

    Arrangements for partial payments in advance or during the job

- How will you record your time and that of employees or sub-contractors for billing purposes? How will you keep track of other job costs?

- How will you keep track of billable changes or additions to jobs? Will you regularly pass such costs on to your customers?

- When a job takes less time or materials than estimated, will you pass savings along to your clients?

- Do you have systems in place to assure prompt billing and regular follow-up until each invoice is paid?

## Ilene A. Schneider

*Schnieder the Writer, Irvine, California*

### Combining Business and Family

Ilene A. Schneider had always thought of freelancing in terms of staying home to be a mom. It took a terrifying medical experience to show her how much she really wanted to be a home-based writer.

After college, Schneider had worked in Cleveland as an editor for *TV Guide,* then spent six years with a Cleveland trade magazine where she learned technical writing. Moving to California with her husband, she went to work as a public relations representative for Beckman Instruments, a large medical and scientific equipment firm.

Schneider enjoyed her work and stayed at Beckman for seven years, but she and her husband were becoming concerned about starting their family.

"I went in for surgery in December of 1984 to find out why I wasn't getting pregnant," Schneider recalls, "and for a time we thought I had a life-threatening condition. I asked myself what I wanted to do with my life and got motivated to make changes."

Her experience prompted her to act quickly, and she decided to leave Beckman in 1985, after a second operation.

Then, while recuperating, she started thinking business. "From bed I was contacting future clients so I could make money from day one," she said. She dubbed her firm Schneider the Writer.

Schneider's initial idea was to find "a lot of little Beckmans" that would not have in-house public relations capabilities. Today most of her clients are large corporations, including Beckman, which continues as a major customer. Nonetheless, her favorite account is a small, private school "that is making a difference in people's lives."

Her services range from press releases and articles to full-blown public relations programs and trade shows and include a growing number of newsletters. She often works fourteen-hour days and frequently asks for—and gets—50 percent payment up front.

Nine months and one week from the day she started her business, Schneider's daughter was born—and she has never used day care.

It was because of her role as a mother-entrepreneur that she became friends with Joy Mieko White (profiled in Chapter Four). Schneider was president and White was president-elect of the Orange County chapter of Women in Communications, Inc., when White, who had just started her own business, came to Schneider for advice on how to combine a career with motherhood. It was a significant meeting.

Schneider had been looking for a colleague who could provide desktop publishing, and the two began collaborating despite Schneider's early concerns about doing business with a friend. In 1989, when White began assembling her communications consortium, InfoTeam, Schneider asked, "Do you have someone for PR?"

As an InfoTeam member, Schneider says, "I find that with 'teaming' power, there are more services I can offer. Plus, Joy keeps me organized and does mailings and cold calling."

Motherhood impacted Schneider's career again in 1992, when her daughter entered first grade. "With more time for my clients, I began calling myself a consultant rather than a freelance writer," she explains. "It's made a real difference in how people view me."

Shortly after the "transformation," Schneider was approached about a fulltime job. "I gave them a figure, thinking, 'I could make that much money in my own business, on my own terms.' At the end of the year, I was amazed. I had made almost twice as much!"

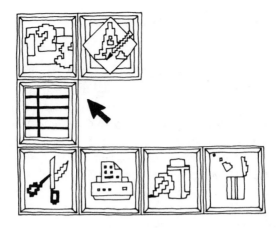

# 10

# Tips for Managing Your Business (*and Yourself*) and Writing Your Business Plan

## What Else Is Involved in Running Your Business?

The nine chapters you have just completed cover what you need to know to *open* your home-based writing and desktop publishing business—and much of what you need to know to *operate* it. You've analyzed marketing and selling, pricing and bidding, billing and collecting, and finding the jobs most profitable for you. In my own experience and that of many people I have talked with in researching this book, these are the operational activities that will most concern you during your first months in business. The topics we will touch on in this chapter will seem less urgent initially, but they are no less important.

Several legal issues may concern you on a continual basis. You may want to protect yourself from liability with business insurance. If you hire help, you will encounter management issues as well as numerous state and federal requirements. Taxes will always be a major concern.

To keep your business solvent, you must manage your cash flow, do regular income projections, and deal with other financial issues. The organization of your business, your procedure and policies, and on-going systems analysis can significantly impact your profitability.

Another concern will be the set-up and maintenance of your records. You will need to establish methods for purchasing, controlling inventory, and maintaining your equipment and facilities. Your computer system will require administration. The security of your entire operation, especially your computer system, is important, too.

Many personal issues also affect your business performance—issues such as goal setting; time management; your management style; staying current with knowledge and skills; issues of stress, attitude, and motivation; retirement planning and investing; and the ongoing impact of your business on your family.

My purpose here is to share a few tips that may get you thinking about these important topics.

# Legal Issues

*On-going legal issues.* Setting up your business involves certain legal issues, discussed in Chapter Four, but your ongoing business operations involve others, among them issues of liability, contracts, collection problems, and rights to intellectual property. Regulations concerning employees represent another important legal area, dealt with later in this chapter.

Many successful home-based writers and desktop publishers give little thought to legal matters, but don't you take that chance. Consider these issues and, at minimum, know an attorney you can turn to for occasional business-related advice.

## Will your home owner's policy cover it?

If a business visitor is injured on your property, you are liable, and your home owner's insurance is not likely to cover it unless you have broadened the policy to do so—or obtained separate coverage. If your computer or copier is stolen or destroyed in a fire, the situation is the same. Home owner's policies are not likely to cover business equipment. I believe most home-based entrepreneurs realize this potential risk, and many of them make sure their home owner's coverage is extended.

## Covering general liability

But what if you damage something in a client's office? What if a subject is injured during a photo shoot you are supervising? What if a client sustains a loss because of an inaccuracy in work you have written or produced? General liability insurance will protect you in such situations, and it's something you should consider.

I must admit that sometimes the whole idea seems far-fetched to me. *Moi?* How could I ever be found liable for some business injury? Then I remember the harrowing experience of a close writer friend. My friend had interviewed a patient and written an article for a hospital publication. The patient had read the article, and it was my friend's understanding that the patient had approved it, but a release was never signed. My friend had kept her client informed, so the hospital knew there was no release. After the material was published, the patient sued both the hospital and my friend, claiming that the article was damaging. My friend was fortunate that the hospital backed her up and covered her court costs.

While the best insurance against such an experience is to scrupulously cover all bases, liability insurance is also a good idea.

## Contracts

Most of the writers and desktop publishers I interviewed for this book said they did not deal much with contracts. Those setting up agreements involving the work of others were the exception—along with ghostwriters and others who do major, long-term projects.

Your verbal or written estimate or proposal to do a job is also a form of contract, however. And, of course, a written agreement is safer for both parties. At minimum, this "contract" should include

- A description of the job
- The production schedule
- Delivery instructions
- The amount and terms of payment

Advertising and public relations agencies usually ask clients to return a signed copy of such a proposal before beginning the work—and so can you. If major changes occur during the job, put them in writing and send a copy to the client.

## Collections

Collections were discussed briefly in the last chapter. The best way to avoid collection problems is to stay on top of all your outstanding invoices and stay away from clients with questionable credit. Very often, when a colleague has told me how he or she got stiffed, I hear such comments as, "I had my doubts about them from the beginning." Or, "I should have gotten some money up front, but it was a big rush job." Know the small-claims court procedures in your community, and discuss serious collection problems with your attorney.

## Copyright

United States copyright law unequivocally recognizes the creator of a work as its owner unless the work was done "for hire" or you otherwise signed away specific rights. Your work, therefore, is copyrighted whether or not you register it with the Copyright Office, a division of the United States Library of Congress (see Source Directory). The Library of Congress does not require you to register each work individually. You can, in fact, register several works in one large group. Although there are some requirements you must follow when submitting groups of work, there is no limit on the number of works that can be included in a group.

Laws governing the use of intellectual property are complex, but read up on this subject regularly if it relates to your work. Since most of the assignments discussed in this book would be considered work for hire, you are selling all rights. Bear in mind, however, that you can establish a different agreement with a client, perhaps arranging to make a noncompetitive use of the material. If you want to do this, it's wise to do it in advance.

Copyright laws could also affect you if you engage in copyright infringement, including illegal copying of software. In October 1992, federal law made it a felony for anyone to steal ten copies of a program or more than $2,500 worth of software—with a maximum penalty of five years in prison and $250,000 in fines. Unauthorized use of copyrighted graphic or written material could also land you—and your client—in trouble. Good copyright-free clip art and stock photos are widely available. If that won't do, it's often surprisingly easy—and inexpensive or free—to get permission to use copyrighted material. Before approaching the copyright holder, think of some way to benefit them, such as giving a generous credit. Major publications and publishers have staffers responsible for handling such requests, but it may take time to track down other sources.

# Issues Concerning Employees

## Paying federal taxes

In the aftermath of President Clinton's withdrawal of several proposed appointments in 1993 because the appointees had not paid federal taxes on domestic employees, millions of Americans took a second look at their casual employment practices. IRS rules say that if you pay an "employee" more than $50 in any calendar quarter, you are supposed to obtain an employer identification number (apply using Form SS-4) and fill out at least two employer tax forms. If you pay an individual more than $1,000 a quarter, additional forms are required, and state rules may apply as well. How closely you adhere to these regulations is your decision.

## Independent contractor vs. employee

The federal government—including the IRS, the Department of Labor, and the Immigration and Naturalization Service—and most states have specific, but differing, definitions for "independent contractors" and "employees." One important point on which they do agree is that the employee has a continuing relationship with the employer, and an independent contractor does not.

Among other goals, federal and state agencies want to prevent employers from defining employees as independent contractors so they can avoid paying withholding taxes and benefits—thus depriving state and federal governments of revenues and employees of their rights. If you hire independent contractors, know your state's rules.

Technical writers and designers frequently fall into a gray area, carrying out long-term, full-time assignments for a single client. If you handle such assignments, consider the impact of employee versus independent contractor status on your income, business, and taxes, and make sure you are protected.

The IRS's free publication, *Circular E-Employer's Tax Guide*, explains the definition of an employee. The IRS will evaluate your individual situation if you file Form #SS-8.

## Full-time employees

Adding a full-time employee is a very serious step for a home-based entrepreneur. It will greatly increase your paperwork, and, of course, you will need to sustain a larger volume of business. Signing regular salary checks without jobs to cover them can be a terrifying drain. Nevertheless, the right employee could be well worth it if he or she provides a vital skill you lack or frees you to do more profitable tasks.

Federal and state regulation governing employees vary according to size and type of business, but in general employers are responsible for federal and state withholding taxes, including Social Security; state disability insurance and unemployment taxes; workers' compensation insurance; health and other benefits; and regulations covering minimum wages, maximum hours to be worked, health and safety, and fair employment practices. Whew!

Check with the IRS and state agencies or your local Small Business Administration (SBA) office to find out which requirements apply to your situation.

Having several employees can qualify you for health insurance plans not available to individuals. A group health insurance plan could benefit you and your family as well as your employees. Since health insurance may soon be affected by federal legislation, check with your insurer or local SBA office for more information.

## Part-time workers

Hiring part-time help is a typical solution to a home-based writer or desktop publisher's labor problems. You have less financial drain and can hire various workers for the skills you need. But unless you and your employee are willing to risk becoming part of the underground cash economy, you cannot escape the basic employer responsibilities of withholding taxes and complying with minimum employment regulations.

## Temporary workers

If you have an occasional need for clerical, desktop publishing, or other help, a temporary agency may provide the answer. The cost will be considerably more than you would pay to the worker directly, but workers are prescreened, they are there when you need them, and you have no employer responsibilities.

## Occasional labor

The occasional worker fills in for a few hours on an irregular basis. For example, I've used crews of my daughter's friends to stuff envelopes and stick on labels, paying the workers with checks or cash—and usually pizza—and passing the cost on to my client as labor.

# Taxes

The good news is that if you're used to filling out "the long form," paying your income taxes as a home-based entrepreneur will not be much more complex. If you're a sole proprietor, you will deduct your business costs from your gross income, treating what's left as personal income, just as you did before you were self-employed. The bad news is that since no employer is withholding your taxes, you are responsible for making quarterly advance payments of your estimated federal and state income taxes. These payments must also include both the employer's and the employee's portions of your estimated Social Security tax. Payments are due on April 15, June 15, September 15, and January 15, using Form 1040-ES. At the end of the year, you will file a final Form 1040 and a Schedule C—the form on which self-employed individuals report the costs of running their business.

## Home office deductions

One of the benefits of working at home is that you can deduct a percentage of your utility, maintenance, and rental costs on Schedule C. If you own your home, you can also depreciate a portion of it (the value of the house times the percent used for your business, divided by the anticipated years of life of the house). But beware! If you sell your house, you could wind up paying capital-gains taxes on the portion you call your office, instead of deferring all gains into your next house, as is usually done with a residence.

Home office deductions have become a hot issue, so check with your tax consultant for the latest rulings. While the IRS denies it, tax authorities say that an individual who takes a home-office deduction has a better-than-average chance of being audited, and some home-based entrepreneurs prefer to avoid potential problems by not taking the deduction. I have always taken such a deduction, however—and so have most home-based writers and desktop publishers I interviewed for this book.

The goal of the Internal Revenue Service, of course, is not to keep you from claiming legitimate business expenses, but to stop tax evasion by those who may have a home office, but earn little or nothing from it. Unfortunately, many legitimate businesspeople who work *out of* (rather than *in*) their homes were caught in a January 1993, U.S. Supreme Court ruling that struck down an anesthesiologist's homeoffice deduction because he did not spend the bulk of his workdays there. Home-business advocates immediately began fighting back, claiming that the ruling creates a double standard since other businesses are not required to prove their offices are *where* their revenues are generated. Reading *Home Office Computing* or other publications for home entrepreneurs will help you stay informed on this important issue. And if you can influence laws or regulations, your help will be welcomed.

If you decide to take a home-office deduction, here are some things you can do to protect yourself.

- Make sure your home office is used exclusively for business, not for other purposes.

- Install a separate phone for your business. Otherwise, you may be required to produce records showing which calls on your home phone were business calls.

- Make sure your office serves as your place of business at least 50 percent of the time. If this might be an issue for you, keep a log of the hours you spend there as opposed to time you may spend working in your client's office or at other off-site locations.

- Do everything you can to strengthen your status as an independent contractor, if this might be an issue. Avoid working for just one client. Get a written contract for each job.

- If you're still moonlighting and haven't gone full-time with your business yet, take care. Unless your home-based business supplies "a significant portion" (some say half) of your income, tax specialists advise you not to take the deduction. Be aware also that the IRS considers an enterprise to be a hobby if it does not show a profit in three out of five years. In other words, to qualify for deductions, your business should be showing a profit by the third year. Discuss current regulations with your tax consultant.

## Deducting other business expenses

Like any businessperson, you are entitled to deduct the costs of doing business. Such expenditures include

- Depreciation on major equipment and furniture

- Supplies and materials
- Labor and employee benefits
- Commissions and referral fees
- Consultant fees (sometimes a touchy area, document carefully)
- Professional services (legal, tax preparation, etc.)
- Advertising and promotion
- Postage, shipping, and messenger services
- Electronic mail and other on-line services
- Mileage or a portion of your auto expenses
- Business travel, meals, and lodging (at present, 100 percent of lodging but only 50 percent of meals apply)
- Lobbying
- Gifts (up to $25 per recipient per year)
- Entertainment (strictly regulated, so, again, know the rules)
- Copyright costs
- Training and professional memberships
- Professional information and research
- Business insurance (including a portion of your home owner's policy)
- Taxes (including 50 percent of your Social Security taxes)
- Bad debts and losses from theft or disaster
- Any other costs directly associated with your work

## Sales tax

Obtaining a reseller's permit was discussed in Chapter Four. Having one doesn't require you to collect tax on every job or even on most jobs, but it does require you to file reports and pay the tax you have collected several times a year (or annually if the amount is small) to your state tax department.

Must you collect sales tax? Yes, if you are delivering a product; generally no, if you are delivering a service. States vary, however, in how they define these categories. Get information from your local SBA office or state tax department. Discuss the matter with your mentors and colleagues. Being required to pay the state a large sum for taxes you failed to collect could be an unpleasant experience. A gray area that is important to desktop publishers is camera-ready art or film. Is prepress material considered a product in *your* state?

If you are charging sales tax, you do not have to pay sales tax on the supplies you use to produce the job. Your vendors will ask you to fill out a resale card, and they will keep your resale number on file. If you normally collect sales tax on your work and are selling to a client who charges a sales tax—such as a book publisher—you will do the same.

# Cash-flow, Income Projection, and Other Financial Issues

## Setting up your books

You can ask your accountant or bookkeeper to help you set up a chart of accounts. Or you can set up your books yourself. Your accounting system will need to cover income and expenses and reveal how much you are spending in various categories and how much you are receiving from various sources. For example, you may want to know how much you are making on different types of jobs, as well as how much you are earning from each client. If you design a system yourself, it's wise to get your accountant's feedback on it.

Stationery stores offer a variety of simple bookkeeping systems for small businesses—or you can opt for a software program. While it may be more trouble to learn and set up a computer system, software offers the enormous benefit of generating instant reports and producing the information you need at tax time, totalled in appropriate categories. The system will probably write checks for you and may even include an invoicing capability.

The important thing is to establish a reliable system for keeping track of all the money you spend for your business and all the money you take in—and to establish it right away. What we're talking about is called single-entry bookkeeping, which is probably all you need unless your accountant thinks otherwise.

## Business vs. personal funds

Not every home entrepreneur sets up a separate business banking account, but all authorities advise it. Keeping business and personal funds separate is important, not only for tax purposes, but to let you see clearly where your business stands. The same thing applies to credit cards. You don't have to apply for a new business credit card unless you want to. Use one of your personal cards exclusively for business expenses.

## Using financial information

Financial information lets you know how you're doing. It allows you to record and project your monthly income, cash flow, profit, and loss. Financial information also keeps track of jobs for billing and estimating purposes. It tells you which jobs and clients are most profitable (very important!) and how much you can afford to pay yourself each month. Failing to stay on top of these numbers is like driving without a road map.

Past financial information is normally the basis for both short- and long-range business planning, and it helps you enter realistic figures when doing "what if" business modeling. "What if I bought another computer and hired an assistant?" "What if I stopped writing trade journal articles and concentrated on writing advertising copy?"

At tax time, your financial records provide the information you need to prepare tax forms and take advantage of legitimate deductions. If you're audited by the IRS, your records will provide back-up data.

Some types of clients require financial information about vendors in order to qualify them before awarding work. Lenders making business loan decisions will require even more data, including a summary of your business' assets, liabilities, and net worth (assets minus liabilities). If your figures are clear, accurate, and complete, lenders will be favorably impressed. The same is true of a potential partner or a person who might be interested in buying your business. The first thing they will want to see will be the books.

## Cash flow

A simple way of thinking about cash flow is, "Collect everything that's owed you as soon as you can, and hold onto cash as long as you can." Within the usual 30-day period, you can pay bills at the best time for you. That may include taking advantage of a cash discount for prompt payment, if one is offered. You can also use short-term credit with a business credit card. A business credit card allows you to make 800-number purchases, and it will even out monthly cash flow—but keep it paid up. A cash reserve is a prudent safeguard.

## Income projection

What's coming in? There are two ways to keep track of income— cash and accrual. A cash system counts the money you have actually received. An accrual system keeps track of receivables— what you are owed. Obviously, in our work we need to be on top of both. But I'd like to suggest that you take income projection a little further.

Try this:

Each month, review your ongoing jobs, the bids you have presented, the jobs you have discussed with clients, and any other immediate business you have pending or planned. Then, *in writing*, project what you will sell over the next three months—month by month, job by job. Put an estimated amount and a completion date on each project.

If three months is too long, forecast for two months or even one. But give it a serious try and see how helpful it can be.

This income projection exercise can be tremendously motivating. You are hoping to get these jobs. In fact, the numbers show you *need* these jobs. But you have not sold them yet. Better make sure you do sell them! And better make sure you can get them done. If all the jobs in the pipeline are more than you can handle in the next three months, now is the time to work with clients or subcontractors to make sure all deadlines can be met.

# Policies and Procedures

## An organization chart for a home-based business?

If employees or other family members are involved in your business, their roles and responsibilities need to be defined. How much responsibility and authority do they have? Who is empowered to make what kinds of decisions? You probably don't need an organization chart, but you do need a clear understanding by all concerned. And thinking it through will help you determine the best arrangement.

## Think it through and write it down

It's a good idea to have important policies and procedures written down—especially if family members or employees help you in your business. Writing down procedures helps you clarify them and make a mental commitment to observe them.

Here are some of the day-to-day business questions that your policies and procedures can quickly answer.

- Which tasks take priority?
- Which clients take priority?
- When and in what priority are bills paid each month?
- How often are machines serviced?
- What forms do you use and how are they filled out?

## Quality

One of your most important policies involves quality. How important is quality to you? How do you maintain quality? The truth is, quality varies widely in our work since not all clients want or need the same levels of quality. Within your own business framework, however, you must establish and maintain certain quality standards. Systems analysis, discussed below, can help you make sure quality is built into every step of your work.

## Professionalism

*Hello? Is anyone home?* In researching this book, I have been astonished at how often the phones of home-based writers and desktop publishers go unanswered or are answered by a casual "Hello." How much does it cost to put in an answering machine? How hard is it to train a spouse or child to give a business salutation? Some of my interview subjects have told me of successfully training even small children to sound professional on the phone. If I were setting up policies and procedures for a home-based business, the first rule I would establish would be: "Make sure the phone is always professionally answered during business hours."

## Government requirements

Your state or local regulations may require written policies and procedures covering such topics as employees, safety, and the handling of hazardous materials. Rarely does a business your size have to produce such documents, but thinking through the issues can't hurt.

## Systems? What systems?

What steps do you take as you perform specific business tasks? In what order? What tools do you use? Could processes be simplified, combined, eliminated? Who is the best person to do various jobs?

Analyze your systems periodically and try to improve them in terms of both efficiency and quality. For example, even if you have no employees, you may find that buying out certain services, such as bookkeeping or deliveries, makes sense. Or you may decide to hire an employee. Realizing the hourly value of his consulting time, one young home entrepreneur decided to stop doing things like researching personal and business matters on the phone, writing checks, even putting gas in his car. Instead, he hired a student from a nearby university as a personal and business assistant.

Studying your systems in detail will also show you where errors are creeping in.

# Record Keeping

## Planning your files

Applying systems analysis to the way you organize your records is especially important for writers, since our stock-in-trade is information. But being able to locate what we need and deciding how long to keep various documents is important for all of us.

Make a list of the kinds of information you keep and analyze it. Can any groups of records be combined? What cross-referencing is needed? How do you basically want to organize things? By client? Subject matter? Type of job? Individual job? Do you use titles or numbers to identify jobs? How and where will your paper data be stored? Your electronic data? Can you computerize material and discard the paper version?

## Tracking jobs

How do you keep track of jobs? Consider assigning each job a number that will stay with it through invoicing and storage. Will your job number contain a code for the year? Month? Client? Type of job?

## How long to keep it?

The sensible answer is keep documents as long as applicable with regard to your information, job, and client files, that's entirely up to you, based on the kinds of jobs you do and your clients' needs. As a former buyer of writing and graphics services, my suggestion is that before you discard materials relating to client projects—such as art boards or research documents—offer them to the client.

If you are discarding electronic data from your hard disk on a regular basis, be sure to inform clients of your policy in advance or before you delete the last copies of their files. Today's color graphics with their gigabyte appetites will force you to set up a policy on this matter. A solution might be to keep a backup file on a low-cost medium, such as tape for several years. File compression programs can also help. If you routinely dump client files after a certain period of time, inform your clients of this policy.

As for business-related and personal files, most people keep far more records than they need. While a few records are permanent, most should eventually be discarded.

You can discard copies of your tax return and supporting documents six years after filing, unless the IRS has begun an audit. (Check with your accountant to make sure this is still the current ruling.) Other records in the "as long as applicable" category include business financial records not needed for tax purposes, partnership agreements, corporation papers, employee records, Keogh statements, nondeductible IRA records, insurance policies, brokerage and fund transactions, stock and bond certificates, certificates of deposit, stock-option agreements, loan records, membership records, warranties and receipts for major purchases, and operating instructions for equipment. Also in this category are vehicle documents and real estate records, including deeds, title insurance policies, and documentation of major property improvements.

Not worth saving once you're satisfied they're accurate are credit card bills, bank statements, and cancelled checks (unless needed for tax purposes). You should also toss out receipts for everyday or small purchases unless you need them for tax documentation.

## New solutions

Look for new record-keeping solutions. Caere Corporation of Los Gatos, California, the optical character recognition software firm, has a new PC product called PageKeeper—available in individual and networked versions also selling for about $600. Check it out—especially if you're a writer who needs to access a wide range of information. Used with a scanner, PageKeeper scans pages of copy, newspaper and magazine clippings, whatever—automatically storing the material in compressed files that can be edited and that you don't even need to title: PageKeeper does that for you, selecting the three most frequently used words in the document. Retrieval is PageKeeper's real strength. Type in a few related words and PageKeeper will quickly search your entire hard disk, producing an organized, weighted list of documents for you to review.

Not to be outdone, Xerox, the all-time paper consumption champ, has a new product called PaperWorks for about $250. It's a Windows program that uses a stand-alone fax machine to input data on paper into your personal computer through a fax modem. Instructions are given to PaperWorks via special forms you fax along with the data. A PaperWorks template even lets you build your own forms for activities such as reporting expenses and updating prices. Fill out the form, fax it to your PC, and your PC will follow PaperWorks' instructions.

## Comments on Master Job Log

In this log, the date is the controlling factor. The log would be filled in chronologically as you receive your jobs. You might not even assign numbers to your jobs and invoices, although I strongly recommend that you do. You could also make the job number the controlling factor. A series of job numbers might be assigned to a long-range project even though all the individual jobs were not yet in hand.

A master job log can be designed to record any important information. If, for example, you have partners or employees, you will want to know who is in charge of each job. If you do multiple-part jobs, you may want to log in the parts rather than giving each part its own job number, since they will not be separately invoiced. If you invoice a large job in parts (for example, one-third in advance, one-third halfway through, one-third on delivery), you may need room for several invoice numbers.

Keep your log simple. Its purpose is to help you check on or locate a job or invoice, to help you gather and analyze data such as volume of business and client activity, and to provide quick answers to questions like "When did I do that job?" or "What was the job we did for Smith & Smith last year?" For specific details on a job, you will go to the job control form.

This log, as shown, is designed to serve a writer or desktop publisher who normally receives an assignment before starting a project. Writers who submit finished articles to publications might create a log with such headings as "Date," "Title," "Job Number," "Sold to," "Date of Sale," and "Date Paid."

# MASTER JOB LOG FORM

| Date | Job. # | Client | Job Name | Invoice # |
|------|--------|--------|----------|-----------|
|      |        |        |          |           |
|      |        |        |          |           |
|      |        |        |          |           |
|      |        |        |          |           |
|      |        |        |          |           |
|      |        |        |          |           |
|      |        |        |          |           |
|      |        |        |          |           |
|      |        |        |          |           |
|      |        |        |          |           |
|      |        |        |          |           |
|      |        |        |          |           |
|      |        |        |          |           |
|      |        |        |          |           |

If you are a writer who often re-writes the same material for different markets, you might add a heading such as "Re-write of Job # _____." If you sell reprint rights to published articles, you might add a heading to record additional sales. If you normally query editors before starting an article, a separate log might help you keep track of queries.

# Purchasing and Inventory Control

## Establish business credit

Early on, set up credit with several vendors, such as a stationer or desktop publishing service bureau. Establishing business credit will help your general business profile, especially when you need credit in the future. Credit with your major vendors will also help you even out your cash flow over a thirty-day period.

## Pay on time

Regardless of what your personal credit history has been, it's important to maintain good business credit. Don't let bills go unpaid over thirty days. If you have a cash-flow problem, discuss it promptly with your vendor.

## Try for business discounts

When dealing with firms that serve the general public, such as art supply and stationery stores, ask for a business discount. Many will comply.

## Value vendor relationships

Build good relationships with key vendors. You may save money at a giant discount store, but the owner won't stay open for you when you realize a few minutes before closing that you need some supplies. And the young guy indifferently putting up stock along the endless warehouse rows can't solve your technical problem and doesn't care to try.

# JOB CONTROL FORM

*Printing this form on the outside of a large envelope or attaching it to a manilla folder can facilitate handling a job. The envelope or folder contains working materials for the job and will eventually hold the documentation and a few job samples that will be kept on file—usually by job number or name of client.*

Job name _____ Job. # _____

Client _____

Address _____

City _____ State _____ Zipcode _____

Contact _____

Title _____

Phone (____)_____ Ext. _____ Fax (_____)_____

Bill to _____ P.O. #_____

Address if different _____

Ship to _____ Attn._____

Address if different _____

Via _____

## PRODUCTION SCHEDULE

Job received _____ Date due _____ Date delivered _____

*Allow space below for dates due and actual completion dates of major steps in production, including client approvals. Briefly describe the steps.*

Step 1 _____ Step 2 _____ Step 3 _____

Date due _____ Date due _____ Date due _____

Completed _____ Completed _____ Completed _____

## JOB DESCRIPTION

*Design this space to fit your needs. Writers might want blanks for sections, length, and reader level. Desktop publishers might want blanks for number of pages, dimensions, halftone screen line specifications, paper type and color, ink colors, finishing and bindery instructions. This job description can be less detailed than the Estimating Form job description, but be sure that final choices on such points as paper and ink are recorded for future reference.*

Special instructions _____

continued on next page

## RECORD OF COSTS

| Date | Task/Item | Source (if buy-out) | No. hrs./ Qty. | Rate/ Price ea. | Amount |
|------|-----------|---------------------|-----------------|------------------|--------|
| _____ | _____ | _____ | _____ | _____ | $_____ |
| _____ | _____ | _____ | _____ | _____ | _____ |
| _____ | _____ | _____ | _____ | _____ | _____ |
| _____ | _____ | _____ | _____ | _____ | _____ |
| _____ | _____ | _____ | _____ | _____ | _____ |
| _____ | _____ | _____ | _____ | _____ | _____ |
| _____ | _____ | _____ | _____ | _____ | _____ |
| _____ | _____ | _____ | _____ | _____ | _____ |
| _____ | _____ | _____ | _____ | _____ | _____ |
| _____ | _____ | _____ | _____ | _____ | _____ |
| _____ | _____ | _____ | _____ | _____ | _____ |
| _____ | _____ | _____ | _____ | _____ | _____ |
| _____ | _____ | _____ | _____ | _____ | _____ |
| _____ | _____ | _____ | _____ | _____ | _____ |
| _____ | _____ | _____ | _____ | _____ | _____ |
| _____ | _____ | _____ | _____ | _____ | _____ |
| _____ | _____ | _____ | _____ | _____ | _____ |
| _____ | _____ | _____ | _____ | _____ | _____ |
| _____ | _____ | _____ | _____ | _____ | _____ |
| _____ | _____ | _____ | _____ | _____ | _____ |

## BILLING

Original estimate  $ _____  Changes to estimate  _____

_____

Sales tax _____% Applies to _____

Invoice # _____  Date _____  Amount $ _____

Payment received date _____

Payment received date _____

## Respond to all bids

When you have requested a bid, perhaps from a printer or a designer, extend the same courtesy you would like from your own clients. Bids take effort to prepare, and the vendor may even be tentatively reserving time to do your work. As soon as you have made a decision, let each bidder know whether that firm did or did not get the job. Rarely will you be harangued to change your mind. Rather, your courtesy will be appreciated.

## Control your inventory

Be aware of the supplies you use regularly and develop a method for reminding yourself to buy more when your stock gets low. Losing production time because you were out of materials is money out of your pocket—since the lost time can't be regained.

*Beware of bargains.* "Conserve cash" is good advice in the early years of any business, so if you see a bargain on supplies or equipment, balance any savings you might achieve with the usefulness of ready cash. Stock up only when you can afford it—and when you have room to store it.

# Maintenance of Equipment and Facilities

## Using business services

Just because you're working at home doesn't mean you can't have business services to maintain your equipment. I keep a service contract on my Sharp copier (currently $280 per 20,000 copies), and the repairman is at my office within one to three hours whenever I have a problem—just like in a "real" office. I've replaced the drum once in four and a half years, and the quality I get from this machine is still as good as from a new machine. Equally valuable to me is the peace of mind I get from knowing I can avoid lost productivity following a copier breakdown. Similarly, the firm that delivers laser printer cartridges to my home office provides prompt printer repairs. Look for such services for small businesspeople in your community.

## Keeping clutter at bay

What about office maintenance—keeping your work space clean, neat, and in repair? If you were a clean-desk person when you were employed outside your home, chances are you'll remain one, but my guess is that many of us are clutterers. (I base this impression on the long list of anti-clutter books offered by both the Writer's Digest Book Club and the Graphic Artist's Book Club—not, of course, on visits to the offices of writer and designer friends.)

In the interest of making a good impression on business visitors, finding materials when you need them, and maintaining your own sanity, I suggest you have some plan for regular cleaning, straightening, and repairs in your home office. This is something another family member might help you with to make sure it gets done. In my own case, I find myself having to "clean up for the cleaning people" every other week.

# Computer System Administration and Security

## Saving and backing up documents

Save your documents regularly as you work. Do it automatically, without fail. Back up your hard drive on a regular schedule, using whatever media you choose—floppies, removable cartridges, rewritable optical disks, another hard drive, or tape.

If you have very important documents, keep current copies of the disks (or other electronic media) in a separate location so that they can survive whatever disaster might, heaven forbid, befall your office.

## System administration

Allow regular time in your schedule—and in your pricing structure—for computer system administration. Solving problems and installing new equipment and software need to be done when there's time to do it properly, not under crisis conditions. If the installations and troubleshooting are beyond you, get help.

## Getting help

Build a computer support network before you need it. This should include a reliable computer repair service (possibly a maintenance contract on key items like your computer and printer), a consultant for occasional heavy-duty service and advice, and some knowledgeable colleagues on whom you can call for quick troubleshooting. Your local PC or Mac user group may be a valuable resource. Desktop publishers may get free or low-cost advice from their service bureaus. The National Association of Desktop Publishers has a member helpline network staffed by member volunteers

Have a contingency plan that will let you continue working if your computer goes down for an extended period. You might have a second computer on your premises—or know of one you can borrow or rent. Some large copy centers rent Macs and PCs by the hour—a possible emergency solution.

## Computer security

Do you need to keep others out of your system or to secure certain documents? Do your clients require security safeguards? Working at home, we're likely to overlook issues of computer security (unless young computer users are a problem). But think about it. Unix has built in security provisions, but DOS, Windows, and the Macintosh operating system don't, unless you add passwords to protect certain files.

# Security for Everything Else

You have some valuable equipment in your home office and you certainly don't want the loss and work disruption that a security problem could cause. Do what you can in advance to keep your property secure.

When guarding against theft, experts say the best security is the *appearance* of security. Any home can be broken into, but thieves will pass by homes where windows and doors are closed and properly locked (especially sliding patio doors), lights are on in the evening, people are seen coming and going, mail and newspapers are picked up, the yard is tended, and security night lights are installed. A dog that barks at strangers can help, too.

Since we work out of our homes, we have an advantage over our neighbors, but be aware that in "safe" suburban neighborhoods, many break-ins are carried out by kids skipping school and sometimes high on drugs. Such kids are often willfully destructive and can be unpredictable. Don't let your residence appear inviting.

## Do a safety audit

Fire and water damage pose dangers. Once a year, look over your facilities with security in mind. How would you evacuate your office in an emergency? Do stored materials or temporary electric wiring pose fire hazards? Could water leak in? As I write this, I realize that since I rearranged my basement office, my computer is directly under the washing machine. Water leaking through the floor following an overflow could be bad news. Home safety experts tell us never to leave the house with the washing machine on, but how many of us pay attention? Guess I'd better start!

## Working Toward a Business Plan

### BUSINESS SUCCESS WORKSHEET EIGHTEEN

Concept: *Systems solve management problems.*

*Knowledge and advance planning will help you establish systems and policies to keep your business running smoothly.*

- Legal issues and business insurance

  Do you have insurance to cover injury theft, fire, or other disaster in your home office? To cover general liability? Do you view job agreements as contracts? If you joint venture with other vendors, how are all parties protected? How do you handle collections? Is copyright an issue for you? If so, how do you stay informed on copyright regulations? Do you ever infringe on the copyrights of others?

- **Issues concerning employees**

  Do you know the difference between an employee and an independent contractor? Do you hire independent contractors, and can you prove it? Could this be an issue in your own dealings with clients? If you hire employees, do you know and follow federal and state regulations? What kinds of employees do you hire? Full-time? Part-time? Temporary? Occasional labor?

- **Taxes**

  Are you set up to pay your income and Social Security taxes quarterly? Do you take your home office as a deduction? Do you keep good records to identify and substantiate other legal deductions? How will you handle sales tax?

- **Cash flow, income projection, and other financial issues**

  How will you set-up your books? On paper or computer? Will you use professional help? Will you keep business and personal funds separate? How? Can you get the financial information you need from the records you keep? How do you handle cash flow? Income projection?

- **Organization, policies and procedures, and systems analysis**

  If others are involved in your business, what authority and responsibilities do they have? Do you have written policies and procedures to define priorities and keep routine matters running smoothly? How do you define and maintain quality? Have you analyzed the steps involved in various processes?

- **Record keeping**

  Have you established record-keeping systems to meet your needs? Do you have a reliable method for tracking jobs, invoicing, and storing or returning client materials? Do you have a plan for retaining and discarding records and electronic data? Are you on the lookout for new systems and solutions?

- **Purchasing and inventory control**

  How will you establish business credit and develop vendor relationships? How will you assure that business bills are paid on time—and do you think that's important? How do you maintain inventory control?

- **Maintenance of equipment and facilities**

  Do you plan to use professional services to maintain key office equipment? Do you have a regular system for keeping your office clean, neat, and in repair?

- **Computer system administration and security**

  Do you save documents frequently? Do you back up your hard drive regularly? Do you store current copies of vital electronic data in a separate location? Do you have a method for regular system administration? What will you do if your computer fails? Can you assure security for sensitive documents?

- **Security for everything else**

  Do you have a security plan covering theft, fire, and other disasters?

# Goal Setting

I was well along in my professional career before I fully realized that personal and business goals should be aligned with each other—and with daily behavior. I got this message by listening to a series of tapes called *Time Power* by the time-management expert, Charles R. Hobbs. Hobbs maintains that goals grow out of our underlying personal values—what he calls "unifying principles"—and that the whole personal management process is one of self-unification.

## Success is based on goals

Hobbs's system is one of many good programs that will teach you what should be self-evident, but often isn't: "Success is based upon goals." Goals guide the way you organize your time, the projects you undertake, the purchases you make, the training you seek, the people you associate with. And if you have no goals, that, too, is a choice. But you wouldn't be starting a business if you didn't have goals. And perhaps your most important long-range business goal is "growth."

Many of your key business decisions will be based on the goals you set for the growth of your business. But what is your definition of business growth? Will you have "grown" when you can charge more per hour for your services? Or does growth mean having a larger organization? Do you want both? If you plan to become larger, how big do you want to be?

# Time Management

Time management is the secret to achieving your goals, and there are many popular time-management techniques. If you're not already using one of them, do some research—find a book, tape, or scheduling system that appeals to you, and put it to work! Here's an added benefit: In the early months of operating your home business, you may often be struck by a pit-of-the-stomach anxiety that urgently cries, "Right now, you're not earning any money!" On one level, this is probably healthy. But on another, it can produce panic or even paralysis. I believe consistent time management reduces "new entrepreneur panic" because it puts you in control.

To me, the main characteristics of time management are

- Doing regular planning
- Listing tasks (or subtasks)
- Prioritizing them
- Following through
- Rewarding yourself for achievement

## Setting priorities

Many systems for prioritizing employ some variant of the "ABC Priority System" described by Alan Lakein in his 1973 classic, *How to Get Control of Your Time and Your Life.* Once you have listed the tasks that need doing, you assign an A to those that have high value in terms of your long-range goals, B to those that have medium value, and C to those with low value. Then you do the As first, saving the Bs and Cs for later.

But why bring in your long-range goals? Why not assign an A to those tasks that are urgent or important today? One reason for managing your time is so that you don't spend it "putting out fires." For example, to avoid paying a penalty on an overdue bill, you may find yourself canceling an appointment with a potential client so you can deliver the late payment to your creditor's office. That's "time out of control"—and it can damage or destroy your business.

## Following through and rewarding yourself

Good time management systems have many techniques for overcoming procrastination and getting started on the As—breaking big tasks into smaller tasks, working on a task for a short period of time, analyzing your motives, trying to match some phase of the task to your current mood, doing more detailed planning, and combining pleasant tasks with difficult ones. They also advise you to reward yourself for priorities accomplished—a practice I strongly endorse. If you've gotten this far in this book, you deserve at least a weekend in the mountains. Develop a series of big and little rewards that mean something special to you. Hey, we're all human!

## Avoiding interruptions at home

According to home-business gurus Paul and Sarah Edwards, "one or two out of ten people" have trouble running businesses from their homes because of family and household demands and interruptions. My gut-level feeling is that 10–20 percent is a very low estimate, so be on the alert for your own solutions to these problems.

*Isolating your office.* If you can isolate your office in a separate room or section of the house, that's great. If not, establish a symbolic isolation—some signal that lets the rest of the family know you are at work and not to be disturbed. This could be drawing a curtain, putting up a sign, even the way you dress—whatever carries the message that you are now open for business.

*Phone interruptions.* An early problem will be friends and relatives who will call to chat, knowing you are at home. Stop this practice from the start by saying something like, "Sorry, I can't talk. I'm at work right now. Could you call back after five?"

*Child care.* If you have small children at home, you may need to arrange for child care during certain periods of the day in order to do work that requires heavy concentration. Some work is almost impossible to do piecemeal. Consider the hourly cost of child care versus what you can bill for productive time, and you'll see the value of getting help.

# Your Management Style

There is no ideal management style, but it's wise to know what your style is. Often an authoritarian, *micro-management* style in which the owner has a say in every business decision makes a small business successful. But it's the very thing that hampers the business when it starts to grow. Successful entrepreneurs face such issues squarely—sometimes changing their styles, sometimes changing their management structure so that problem areas are handled by others. Here are some questions that will help you identify your management style—

- As the business owner, you must make final decisions. But how do you arrive at those decisions? Do you invite others to participate?

- Do you focus primarily on products or relationships?

- Do you focus primarily on processes or outcomes?

- Do you like joint ventures or do you prefer to work alone?

- When you work with other professionals, do you team, or do you want to be in charge?

# Staying Current
# with Knowledge and Skills

My friend, Polly Pattison, of Westminster, California, an internationally known trainer in newsletter design, had reached the top of her field when the desktop publishing revolution hit. Instead of resisting new developments, she jumped in with both feet, even writing a book on the subject. Learning about computers and helping to guide their impact on design gave a whole new impetus to her career.

We all learn in our own way—whether it's through reading, audio and video tapes, meetings and seminars, conversations with colleagues, or experimenting on our own. Whatever works for you, it's vital that you continue learning—not only to keep up with the competition but to stay creatively alive. Grow your business by growing your own knowledge and skills!

## Keeping up with computer developments

If you're a desktop publisher, accept the fact that since computers are essential to your work, *you must be informed!* Subscribe to one or more general publications relating to your Mac or PC and to one or more desktop publishing publications. Go to seminars. Visit computer stores. Attend software demonstrations.

Desktop publishers and writers, to some extent, should also allow regular time in their administrative schedules to learn new computer software and hardware. In the computer age, this is an unavoidable cost of doing business.

Desktop publisher Wayne Kaplan of Huntington Beach, California (profiled in chapter six), says he learns new versions of software programs while he is still working for his clients on the old version. Kaplan's approach to learning new programs impressed me. Perhaps it's because he's a former computer trainer that he accepts this ongoing task. I usually struggle with new software and resent having to take time to learn it. "Anywhere from one to six months after the new version is released, I probably will be ready to start using it productively," Kaplan says.

# Your Morale

## Job-related stress

Aside from the stress of having to find new clients and new jobs, which is just part of being an entrepreneur, home-based writers and desktop publishers often experience stress because jobs come in bunches. There's nothing to do one day, and too much the next—and with one or two workers, it's tough to even out the flow. Advanced scheduling and personal time management can solve the majority of these problems. When confronted with several As to do, for example, many people start on Cs because the As just seem too overwhelming. This strategy will, of course, compound rather than solve the problem.

When deadlines stack up, you can reduce stress by taking a moment to examine the situation, asking, "What really must be done now and what might be delayed?" When I was selling printing, our production manager occasionally asked me to "try to get us a little more time on this job." At first I hated making such calls, fearing that my clients would be annoyed, but I was surprised to find that often they had no problem with a moderate delay. People frequently say they want something as soon as possible when the job is not really urgent. If you find yourself routinely asking for extra time, however, take a look at the production estimates you're giving your clients. Telling them what they want to hear makes you look good when estimating but bad at delivery time.

*Get help.* In a real work-flow crisis, having trusted colleagues you can call on for help is a solution, even though subcontracting the job may take most of your profit. For an entrepreneur with a "can-do" attitude, the important thing is to get the job done. And, who knows? When your colleague gets overloaded, he or she may send a job your way.

## Loneliness

Feeling lonely a few months into your new business? Isolation is a problem that many home-based entrepreneurs complain about— especially when they're used to being surrounded by fellow workers. As you adapt to working at home, this feeling will probably decrease, but don't ignore it. Arrange what Paul and Sarah Edwards describe as "people breaks." This could be a trip to a vendor or a client's office, instead of using a delivery service. It could be lunch with a friend or business colleague. Even a phone call will help when you're feeling disconnected from the world. I often receive such calls from home-based business friends (and I make them, too). But be sure your colleague has time for the ego-reviving chat you have in mind.

## Rekindling motivation

When your motivation drops, as it will from time to time, make a list of the benefits of running a home business—or keep one handy to review. There will be days when you will wonder why you ever started your business, when you long for the security of a full-time job, when you want to escape from the continuing search for new clients or from vendors demanding payment while cash is just not flowing. It shouldn't take you long to come up with arguments to counter these negative feelings. Remind yourself how important it is to be in command of your own destiny and how good it feels to be away from office politics. A trick I use is one I picked up from the motivation expert, Anthony Robbins. Robbins tells of feeling overwhelmed and discouraged by business demands, then jumping into his home spa during business hours and returning phone calls as the bubbles massaged away his troubles. I've tried it, and he's right. It works!

# Retirement Planning and Investing

*Running a One-Person Business* by Whitmyer, Rasberry, and Phillips (1989), an otherwise exemplary book, advises new entrepreneurs that, "On the whole, the idea of retirement should probably seem ridiculous to you. Salaried people retire to do the things they have always dreamed of. . . . But you are already doing what you dream of."

Sorry, but I couldn't disagree more! And I can't believe these authors ever cared for an infirm, destitute relative. Guess what? We don't always get to spend our old age doing "the things we dream of," and we need to prepare for what may be ahead.

Perhaps you don't want to hear this now—as you're starting your business. Sure, it's nice to know you can't be forced to retire. It's nice to be able to say, "I love what I'm doing, and I'll do it as long as I can." But one day you *will* want to slow down. Or health problems will slow you down. Or your spouse will want to move to Arizona. And even though the government gives small business owners tax incentives to save for retirement, many creative entrepreneurs pay no attention.

"Well, what about selling my business?" you ask. "Won't that be a source of funds?" Unfortunately, as creative workers, our businesses are not as saleable as a store, repair shop, or medical practice—though this is may be less true for desktop publishers.

## Start investing

Don't let your final years be less than rosy. Take pro-active measures now. Unfortunately, there's no automatic retirement deduction. We have to set one up. And with no generous "employer contribution," we have to pay it all. Furthermore, there rarely is a large sum left over to invest each month when we finish balancing the books. Instead, we must do as financial planners advise: Pay yourself first. In other words, invest a fixed portion of your income every month *before* you pay your bills—no matter how small the amount. Look into government Keogh and IRA plans. Look into stocks, mutual funds, bonds, real estate. Or perhaps you can continue adding to a plan you are already in.

Don't wait until a few years before retirement to deal with this. When it comes to investing, time is money's best friend, and you cannot catch up ten or twenty years from now with where you would have been if you had started today.

# The Impact of Your Business on Your Family

Early in this book, we discussed the cooperation you must have from those you live with in order to open and operate a home business. But even when you have strong cooperation at home, it's important to stay alert for the impact—both positive and negative—of your business on your family. Common problems are access to the phone, parking, or certain parts of the house; sound control; visitors; even your own hours and accessibility. If a problem is developing, don't let it fester. Catch it early by discussing it and seeking a solution.

## Business vs. personal time

One of the key advantages of a home-based business—your ability to integrate your business and personal life—can sometimes become one of its key disadvantages. If you tend to get deeply involved in your work, your home-based business can take over your personal life. You will never "go home." You will never stop thinking about business. Basically, you will never leave the office. Added to this, if you tend to let deadlines turn into crises, your business crises may start to dominate the entire household.

I realize that deeply ingrained work traits cannot be changed with pat advice, but I urge you to think about the damage that can result to relationships and to young lives if all the needs and priorities of the family become subservient to THE BUSINESS. For an ounce of prevention, set aside inviolable "family time" and "personal time" every week. Sports? Hobbies? Entertainment? Talking? Walking? Whatever it is, spend time with the family and create an escape valve for yourself.

## Chip off the old block

There's another kind of influence a home business can have on your family—and that's the example you set. Not long out of college, my son has started his own home-based computer consulting business, billing more per hour than I do. And my daughter is earning money at home as a college student, designing flyers for local bands. Seeing me enjoy my home-based business—financial worries and all—must have had some impact, even though I'm not sure they're ready to be self-employed. Watch out! If you have kids, nieces, nephews, or young friends, the same thing may happen to you.

## Working Toward a Business Plan

### BUSINESS SUCCESS WORKSHEET NINETEEN

Concept: *Manage yourself first.*

*Use goal-setting and time-management techniques to keep your performance sharp. Know your management style. Continue learning. Find ways to deal with stress, loneliness, and motivation. Plan and invest for retirement. Make time for your family and yourself.*

- **Goal setting**

  Do you have a system for setting long- and short-range goals? Do you use it? What are your goals for business growth?

- **Time management**

  Do you use a time-management system? How do you plan your day and prioritize tasks? How do you reward yourself? How do you avoid interruptions at home? Have you given thought to isolating your office? Screening calls? Child care during key projects?

- **Your management style**

  Do you tend to be authoritarian or participatory? Are you more interested in products or relationships? Processes or outcomes? Do you like joint ventures with other professionals?

- **Staying current with knowledge and skills**

  How do you learn best? Do you regularly pursue new ideas and information in your field? Desktop publishers: How do you keep up on computers? Do you set aside time to learn new software?

- **Stress, loneliness, and motivation**

  How will you recognize and handle stress on the job? Loneliness? How will you keep your motivation strong?

- **Retirement planning and investing**

  How do you feel about retirement? Do you have a retirement plan? Do you invest for retirement on a regular basis?

- **The impact of your business on your family**

  How will you know if your business is causing problems for family members? Do you regularly spend quality time with your family? Do you make personal time for yourself?

# Writing Your Strategic Business Plan

Many writers and desktop publishers open and operate their businesses without a written business plan, but no one opens a business without a mental plan. Without a plan you wouldn't know what to sell or whom to sell it to—let alone what to charge. A written business plan is a normal requirement for a business loan, and no doubt that's why many entrepreneurs develop one. (Good thing, too, because producing them sometimes provides employment for writers and desktop publishers.) The reality is, however, that in a creative start-up like yours, you will probably not be applying for an initial business loan. So why write a business plan?

No one should have to tell writers and desktop publishers the value of writing something down. Writing forces you to think it through, clarify it, put it in order, eliminate conflicts and contradictions. What make it strategic, in normal business terminology, are your strategies for success, based on an analysis of the market and your business's strengths and weaknesses—along with your tactics and timing for implementing each strategy. You have already done this planning as you used the Business Success Worksheets throughout this book.

But at another level, what makes your business plan strategic is your strategy for *using it* as a working document. For establishing a timetable and adjusting it to keep it realistic. For taking out what doesn't work and adding new elements that do. It's your strategy for believing in the plan, living by it, and updating it on a regular basis—every six months for the first two years and annually thereafter. This plan is for *you*—not for your mentor, your spouse, your former boss, a loan officer, or a teacher who will give you a good grade. It should be your most useful business tool.

That said, I want to stress that a business plan is not too fluid or too personal to share. It's written and clearly organized so that you can share it and get feedback on it—especially from your mentor and any other trusted colleagues. As Napoleon Hill pointed out decades ago in his classic business success book, *Think and Grow Rich* (1937), sharing your ideas and plans with what he calls your "Master Mind group" sharpens your focus and increases your commitment.

## What should a business plan contain?

There is no set pattern or length for a written business plan, but there is general agreement on the topics it should cover. I like this seven-part formulation.

1. *The executive summary.* Though often written last, this comes first for the convenience of busy readers. Keep it under three pages. It contains your mission statement and a brief description of your business—what services you will perform for what clients. This has been covered in chapters one, two, and three, and further refined throughout the book.

2. *The management plan.* This section covers personnel—your resumé and those of any other key staff. Explain important areas of responsibility. If appropriate, include one or more associates who can do writing or desktop design (whichever you don't do) to increase your business opportunities. If resumés are lengthy, summarize them and include the full documents in an appendix. If additional training is a key part of your plan, explain it here. This section also covers your basic management systems. (See chapters one, two, four, and ten.)

3. *The organizational plan.* This section covers business structure—the way your business is licensed and organized. It also
includes your office set-up—including major equipment and
software—as well as maintenance plans and plans for obtaining
outside services. Finally, it should include your timetable for getting your business started and the initial phases you expect to
go through. (See chapters one, four, five, six, and ten.)

4. *The service and product plan.* What services and products do you
plan to sell? Describe them here, pointing out special features
and discussing pricing. (See chapters three, seven, and nine.)

5. *The marketing plan.* This section summarizes the results of
your marketing research. What is the demand for your services and the outlook for the future? What is your
competition? What are your strengths and weaknesses in
entering the market? How do you plan to get the business
you're seeking. Describe your procedures for marketing and
selling. (See chapters seven and eight.)

6. *The financial plan.* This key part of your business plan includes
the following—

A balance sheet showing your business's assets and liabilities

An analysis of your start-up costs and your anticipated sources
of funds

Anticipated monthly sales and expense figures for at least the
first year

Monthly profit-and-loss statements for at least the first year

A monthly cash flow statement for the first year, showing
whether you will have enough cash on hand to meet expenses
and how cash will be utilized

Your personal financial statement, showing all your personal
assets and liabilities as well as your net worth

(See chapters one, seven, eight, nine, and ten.)

7. *The forecasting plan.* Here you explain your plans for keeping
your business on course. On what do you base your forecast
of anticipated sales and expenses? Do you have contingency

plans? When will you review and revise your Strategic Business Plan? (See chapters one, seven, nine, and ten.)

## What format to use

A business plan can be as brief as twenty-five or thirty pages, but it can run much longer. Business plan software is available, which should be especially helpful as you develop the financial section of your business plan.

Here are two programs, both available from many software vendors in either Mac or PC versions. One source is MacWarehouse, (800) 255–6227, for Mac software, and MicroWarehouse, (800) 367–7080, for PC software. Street prices are $75 to $80.

*BizPlanBuilder*, published by JIAN Tools for Sales, provides a structured framework to use with your word processor and spreadsheet. Prompts ask questions and make suggestions.

*Business Plan Toolkit* from Palo Alto Software was rated 4½ mice by *MacUser*. It provides a prompted text writer that takes you step-by-step with your own words. Compatible with many popular spreadsheet programs, it also helps you estimate cash flow, profit and loss, and other financials.

Books are also devoted to this subject (see Bibliography), providing suggested formats for your plan. Again, they're especially useful for presenting your financial data. The plan should have a cover page and a table of contents. Detailed resumés and reports (such as a marketing survey) are often included in an appendix.

---

### Robert C. Brenner

*Brenner Information Group, San Diego, California*

#### Riding the Wave of "Change"

In his 1970 classic, *Future Shock,* Alvin Toffler compares staying abreast of social and technological change with riding the crest of a wave. Writer/desktop publisher/book publisher and spare-time futurist Robert C. Brenner handles that task like a veteran surfer. In so doing, he sets an example for writers and desktop publishers who are establishing new businesses during a time of massive change in communications.

Today such concepts as "information superhighway," "electronic publishing," "on-line," "interactive," and "virtual reality" suggest a communications world we can barely imagine. Yet it is one many of us will be required to deal with if we are to stay competitive. No matter what happens, writing and dseign services will still be needed.

What can Brenner teach us?

From a kid who drew his own comic books—using the reverse sides of cereal boxes as covers and sewing them together with yarn—Brenner grew up dreaming of being a writer. But instead, out of money in the 1960s, he enlisted in the Navy. He got married and, after earning a degree in electrical engineering, was commissioned an officer. Later, he earned graduate degrees in systems management and electrical engineering.

Then in 1981, while serving as an engineering duty officer in San Diego, Brenner took leave and spent $700 on a three-day seminar that would change his life.

"The seminar was designed by Buckminster Fuller," he recalls. "It taught me how to bring the left and right sides of my brain to the same operating level. After that, things went crazy. I found the only barriers to my success were those I imagined and created."

Still an aspiring writer and entrepreneur, Brenner began writing church newsletters and volunteer articles to gain experience. Soon he was being paid for his work. In 1983, he proposed a series of books on troubleshooting computers to a major publisher and eventually wrote seven computer books for Howard W. Sams/McMillan. He also started several businesses, including a technical writing business in his home.

In 1984, Brenner retired from the Navy and worked for a seminar presentation company supporting the Department of Defense, then for TRW as a senior staff engineer, where he rose to technical marketing manager, flying 143,000 miles one year and working with many large U.S. defense companies. When he proposed a commercial application for a TRW research product, however, he was rebuffed. "They wanted to remain in defense," he explains, "so I became independent again in 1987. The next day I bought a Mac II, PageMaker software, and a LaserWriter NTX."

Intrigued with microcomputers and their potential for self-publishing, Brenner again started on the ground floor, designing business cards and flyers. "I knew the only way to master desktop publishing was to get in the trenches," he says, "so I forced myself to learn, working fourteen-hour days."

Soon he was writing and designing manuals for clients, and by 1990, he self-published his first book, *The Silent Speech of Politicians,* written by a psychologist colleague. Brenner lost money on the venture, which he now calls "a good book with poor design."

"I've experienced almost every pitfall in desktop publishing," he admits, "but I've learned from them." One mistake was moving into a suite of offices to create a "company image." When the costly lease was up, he moved back into his San Diego home—just months before the major recession hit California.

From the beginning, Brenner collected information about the emerging marketplace for desktop publishing. Today he monitors some 120 publications a month with the aid of his wife, who is a banker, and his grown children, who work with him in related ventures. In 1990, as requests came from clients for various desktop publishing jobs, Brenner realized he "didn't have a clue" what to charge, and he began doing research on pricing. What he discovered was that few owner-operators in the industry seemed to have a clear idea of costs and pricing—and the concept for his book, *Pricing Guide for Desktop Publishing Services,* was born.

"It took all of 1991," Brenner recalls. He compiled a list of almost 15,000 desktop publishers from Yellow Pages, trade magazine ads, and other sources. He wrote a tutorial on cost, pricing strategies, and estimating for the new book. Then he invited some 500 shops nationwide to complete a questionnaire on pricing and an astonishing 50 percent complied! He interviewed an additional 128 desktop publishers, analyzed the data with the help of a statistician, and published the first edition of the *Pricing Guide* in January, 1992. Industry reaction was positive.

For the second edition, Brenner queried almost 15,000 desktop publishers with a more detailed survey and received replies from nearly 1,500—a statistically significant response. This has led him to prepare special reports comparing the practices of men and women in the business and articles for several desktop publishing-related trade publications. One intriguing study found that a "significant number" of desktop publishers gross more than $90,000 a year in a home office.

As an industry authority, Brenner has begun speaking to organizations and offering consulting services to new desktop publishers. Sometimes he consults over coffee at Denny's or McDonald's "to reduce anxiety for a frightened entrepreneur." Sometimes it's via modem with clients as far away as Argentina and Japan. He's also considering 900 numbers as a medium for selling information.

"I see people in our country traumatized by downsizing in the workplace," he says, "and *I'm* saying 'How do I want to have fun working and make money today?' There are so many ways to make money in a home office!"

Amplifying his views, Brenner explains, "The workplace paradigm is changing and power is shifting from money to knowledge—driven by microelectronics. The old hierarchal corporate structure is changing forever. Information now flows horizontally and vertically so fast that you no longer need the middle level. New jobs are being born every day, but they are totally different jobs involving the processing and movement of information. I see opportunities like never before in history for those who know how to move information."

# Bibliography

## Books

### Business books

Attard, Janet. *The Home Office and Small Business Answer Book: Solutions to the Most Frequently-Asked Questions about Starting and Running Home Offices and Small Businesses.* New York: Henry Holt & Co., 1993. Like a long talk with a good mentor.

Blake, Gary, and Robert W. Bly. *How to Promote Your Own Business.* New York: (Plume) New American Library-Dutton, 1983. Practical advice with lots of examples. Includes a chapter on marketing with newsletters, one on trade shows and expositions, plus many promotional ideas.

Bly, Robert W. *Targeted Public Relations: How to Get Thousands of Dollars of Free Publicity for Your Product, Service, Organization, or Idea.* New York: Henry Holt & Co., 1993. Useful techniques for promoting your services.

Boyan, Lee. *Successful Cold Calling.* New York: Amacom, A Division of American Management Association, 1983. A useful and thoughtful book on a difficult subject.

Brabec, Barbara. *Homemade Money: The Definitive Guide to Success in A Homebased Business.* Cincinnati: F&W Publications, Inc., Betterway Books, 1992. Workbook approach to starting a home-based business. Includes instructions for writing a business plan. Provides an A-Z glossary of business terms, advice on personal and business management, and an extensive resource directory.

Breen, George Edward, and A.B. Blankenship. *Do-It-Yourself Marketing Research.* New York: McGraw, 1991. Guides you through the arcane mysteries of marketing research with clear writing and instructive examples. Suggests low-cost methods.

Davidson, Jeffrey P. *Marketing for the Home-Based Business.* Holbrook: Bob Adams, Inc., 1990. (260 Center St., Holbrook, MA 02343.) Includes launch plan for a home business, ideas for creating an image, descriptions of marketing tools, marketing with newsletters, telephone marketing, hiring parttime help. Offers detailed listing of home business organizations, magazines and periodicals, and marketing directories.

Edwards, Paul and Sarah. *Making It on Your Own: Surviving and Thriving on the Ups and Downs of Being Your Own Boss.* Los Angeles: Jeremy P. Tarcher, Inc., 1991. A supportive emotional road map for new entrepreneurs.

Edwards, Paul and Sarah. *Working from Home: Everything You Need to Know about Living and Working under the Same Roof.* Los Angeles: Jeremy P. Tarcher, Inc., 1990. The "bible" of our industry. While part of this book is devoted to identifying work you can do from home, many sections apply to those who already know what they want to do. Emphasis is on the human side of business. The Edwardses also write a column for *Home Office Computing* and conduct a CompuServe forum and a radio program on home business. Watch for their show in your area.

Floyd, Elaine. *Marketing with Newsletters: How to Boost Sales, Add Members, Raise Donations & Further Your Cause with A Promotional Newsletter.* New Orleans: EF Communications, 1991. (5721 Magazine St., Suite 170, New Orleans, LA 70115.) Covers newsletters from planning to production and includes new, electronic "newsletters" as well. Good bibliography.

Hill, Napoleon. *Think and Grow Rich.* New York: Fawcett, 1989. A classic, first published in 1937. It still offers inspiring, practical advice to new entrepreneurs.

Kamoroff,Bernard. *Small-Time Operator: How to Start Your Own Small Business, Keep Your Books, Pay Your Taxes, and Stay out of Trouble*, 18th Edition. Laytonville: Bell Springs Publishing, 1993. (Box 640 Bell Springs Rd., Laytonville, CA 95454.) A good introduction to starting and running a small business, with emphasis on financial records and planning. Advice on setting up your accounts.

Levinson, Jay Conrad. *Guerrilla Marketing: How to Make Big Profits from Your Small Business.* Boston: Houghton Mifflin Co., 1985. Excellent, accessible overview from the small business perspective. Emphasizes effective, low-cost techniques.

Levinson, Jay Conrad. *Guerrilla Marketing Attack: New Strategies, Tactics, and Weapons for Winning Big Profits for Your Small Business.*

Boston: Houghton Mifflin Co., 1989. Levinson puts his ideas to work with many specific programs. Explodes thirty-three marketing myths.

Levinson, Jay Conrad. *Guerrilla Marketing Weapons: 100 Affordable Marketing Methods for Maximizing Profits from Your Small Business*. New York: (Plume) New American Library-Dutton, 1990. Levinson fires off even more specific techniques under ten "weapons groups." A solid idea builder.

Levinson, Jay Conrad. *Guerrilla Marketing Excellence: The Fifty Golden Rules for Small Business Success*. Boston: Houghton Mifflin Co., 1993. More good ideas.

Lulow, Kalia. *The Freelancer's Business Book*. New York: Ballantine Books, 1984. Practical start-up advice for all freelancers. Writing a business plan. Negotiating with clients.

Phillips, Michael, and Salli Rasberry. *Marketing without Advertising: Creative Strategies for Small Business Success*. Berkeley: Nolo Press, 1989. A good overview. Offers forms, questionnaires, and specific help in designing and implementing your marketing plan.

Urquhart, James R., III. *The IRS, Independent Contractors and You*. Irvine: Fidelity Publishing, 1993. (2061 Business Center Drive, No. 112, Irvine, Ca 92715.) Tax attorney who give seminars nationwide on use of independent contractors explains how to avoid pitfalls, discusses common law factors that define an independent contractor, and provides model agreement and IRS forms.

Whitmyer, Claude, Salli Rasberry, and Michael Phillips. *Running A One-Person Business*. Berkeley: Ten Speed Press, 1989. Covers the basics, including legal, financial, and human factors. Includes profiles of eight one-person business successes. Appendix is a tight summary of steps in starting a business.

## Books on writing a business plan

Abrams, Rhonda. *Successful Business Plan*, 2nd Edition. Emeryville: Publisher's Group West, 1993. (4065 Hollis Street, Emeryville, CA 94608.)

Gumpert, David. *How to Create A Really Successful Business Plan*. Lanham, Md: National Book Network, 1990.

McKeever, Mike. *Write A Business Plan*. Berkeley: Nolo Press, 1992.

## Booklets on writing a business plan

*The Business Plan for Home-Based Businesses* has sections on preparing the financial aspects of a business plan. *Business Plan for Small Service Firms* contains worksheets for cash flow and income projections. Both are available from the Small Business Administration, 409 3rd St. SW, Washington, DC 20476; (800) U–ASK–SBA (827–5722), or through your local SBA office.

## Time management, organization

Hobbs, Charles R. *Time Power: The Revolutionary Time Management System Than Can Change Your Professional and Personal Life*. New York: HarperCollins, 1988. Emphasis is on prioritizing, unifying, and taking action. Hobbs' organization does seminars and sells tapes and is tied in with the popular Day-Timer scheduling system.

Kanarek, Lisa. *Organizing Your Home Office for Success*. New York: Plume, 1993. Practical, easy-to-use tips for home-based entrepreneurs.

Lakein, Alan. *How to Get Control of Your Time and Your Life*. New York: New American Library-Dutton, 1989. A classic first published in 1973. You'll find many of Lakein's ideas in other books on time management.

## The business of writing

Bly, Robert W. *Secrets of A Freelance Writer: How to Make $85,000 A Year*. New York: Henry Holt and Co., 1988. A guru of the freelance writing business, Bly focuses on writing for business and government, with advice on setting fees and ideas for adding to your writing income through self-publishing, training, and consulting.

Bower, Donald E., and James Lee Young, eds.*The Professional Writers Guide*. Aurora: The National Writers Association, 1990. (1450 S. Havana, Suite 620, Aurora, CO 80012.) Primarily for traditional writers, this book may be useful to business writers for its advice on billing rates and copyright.

Burack, Sylvia K., ed. *The Writer's Handbook*. Boston: The Writer, Inc., published annually. Articles by distinguished professionals, advice on the creative process, information on writing techniques. Directory of over 3,000 current markets, including magazines and publishers. Listings of literary agents, writers' organizations, contests, and awards.

Garvey, Mark, ed. *Writer's Market: Where & How to Sell What You Write.* Cincinnati: Writer's Digest Books, published annually. Contains 4,000 mostly traditional markets for writers—invaluable if you're submitting to editors and publishers. If not, front of book contains helpful information on research, new freelance opportunities, contracts, copyright, setting prices, and other topics.

Holtz, Herman. *How to Start and Run A Writing & Editing Business.* New York: John Wiley & Sons, Inc., 1992. Offers advice on penetrating business and government markets and serving individuals. Covers writing and marketing special reports. Suggests good work habits and techniques. Discusses research via electronic databases. Good coverage of copyright issues and writers' organizations.

Schultz, Dodi, ed. *Tools of the Writer's Trade: Successful Writers Tell All about the Equipment and Services They Find the Best.* New York: HarperCollins Publishers, 1990. Over 300 pages of concise tips on working as a writer contributed by members of The American Society of Journalists and Authors. Annotated lists of professional writers' organizations and mail order sources of writers' supplies and services.

Sorenson, George. *Writing for the Corporate Market: How to Make Big Money Freelancing for Business.* Denver: Mid-List Press, 1990. (P.O. Box 20292, Denver, CO 80220.) Covers major types of business writing and strategies for obtaining business.

Writer's Digest Books. *The Writer's Essential Desk Reference.* Cincinnati: Writer's Digest Books, 1991. Useful information for writers on finances, taxes, law, writers groups, conferences, workshops, and instruction, research techniques, working with others, book publishing, and sales. Special section on writing and selling in Canada.

## The business of desktop publishing

Brenner, Robert C. *Pricing Guide for Desktop Publishing Services.* San Diego: Brenner Information Group, 1993. (9282 Samantha Ct., San Diego, CA 92129.) Covered in detail in Chapter Nine.

Crawford, Tad, and Eva Doman Bruck. *Business and Legal Forms for Graphic Designers.* New York: Allworth Communications, 1990. (10 E. 23rd St., New York, NY 10010.) Includes numerous business forms with advice on using them, plus wording for letters, agreements, and contracts. Blank forms for reproduction in tear-out section.

Kramer, Felix, and Maggie Lovaas. *Desktop Publishing Success: How to Start and Run A Desktop Publishing Business.* Homewood: Business One Irwin, 1991. (1818 Ridge Rd., Homewood, IL 60430–9924.) A thorough overview of planning, starting, and running a desktop publishing business. Includes subcontracting, charging, and strategies for surviving in a technologically uncertain future. Successful desktop publishers are profiled.

Neff, Jack. *Designer's Guide to Making Money with Your Desktop Computer.* Cincinnati: North Light Books, 1992. Lively, illustrated start-up guide. Covers marketing, writing your business plan, setting fees, choosing a collaborator, and more. Includes profiles of successful professionals.

Williams, Thomas A. *How to Make $100,000 A Year in Desktop Publishing.* Crozet: Betterway Publications, Inc., 1990. (P.O. Box 219, Crozet, VA 22932.) The title is misleading. What is covered is a wide range of local independent publishing opportunities (tourism guides, membership directories, local histories, etc.) and ways to produce and sell information by mail. Provides a few sample business forms.

Fleishman, Michael. *Starting Your Small Graphic Design Studio: 21 Case Studies, Along with Step-by-Step Guidelines and Worksheets, Show How It Can Happen for You!* Cincinnati: North Light Books, 1993. Case histories lead you through the traditional steps of starting a business. Heavily illustrated. Many forms and checklists. Not very computer savvy.

# Media guides

These standards guides to U.S. media are available in many libraries.

Bacon's Information. *Bacon's Newspaper-Magazine Directory; Bacon's Radio/Television/Cable Directory; Bacon's Business/Financial Directory; Bacon's Media Calendar Directory;* and *Bacon's International Media Directory* (Western Europe). Chicago: Bacon's Information, published annually. 332 S. Michigan Ave., Suite 900, Chicago, CA 60604, (800) 621–0561, fax (312) 922–9008.) Bacon's also offers a national clipping service and a press release distribution service.

Gale Research Inc., *Gale Directory of Publications and Broadcast Media.* Detroit: Gale Research Inc., published annually.

# Periodicals

If any of these periodicals interests you, write for a sample copy.

## Business periodicals

*Creative Business,* 275 Newbury St., Boston, MA 02116–9643. Six bimonthly issues and four special reports a year, $59. Covers practical aspects of running a small creative business. Information based on real-life experiences of graphic designers, illustrators, and copywriters around the country.

*Entrepreneur.* Subscription Dept., P.O. Box 50368, Boulder CO 80321–0368. Monthly, $19.97. *Entrepreneur* covers all aspects of small business, including home-based business.

*Home Office Computing*, P.O. Box 51344, Boulder, CO 80321–1344. Monthly, $16.97. Success stories, new products, tax and legal issues for home entrepreneurs, office design, monthly column by home-office experts Paul and Sarah Edwards. A valuable resource.

*Succeeding in Small Business,* The Applegate Group, P.O. Box 637, Sun Valley, CA 91353–0637. Quarterly, $20. Small business authority Jane Applegate, whose syndicated newspaper column and radio show on small business have aided countless new entrepreneurs, publishes this newsletter full of tips and techniques.

## Periodicals for professional writers

*Freelance Writers Report*, Cassell Network of Writers, Maple Ridge Rd., North Sandwich, NH 03259. The network represents several freelance writers associations (see Organizations for Professional Writers) and publishes a monthly national newsletter available to nonmembers for $39 a year. Price includes a listing in the network writers' data bank.

*The Working Communicator*, Ragan Communications, 212 W. Superior St., Suite 200, Chicago, IL 60610. Monthly eight-page newsletter plus four free books, $89. Aimed primarily at corporate communicators, with new ideas, trends, and techniques. Useful for sharpening your skills and serving your clients.

*Writers Connection*, 1601 Saratoga-Sunnyvale Rd., Suite 180, Cupertino, CA 95014. Monthly newsletter for working writers, $18. Covers many genres. Includes freelance business column and market news.

*Writer's Digest*, Subscription Dept. P.O. Box 2124, Harlan, IA 51593–2313. Monthly, $21. One of the oldest and best writer's magazines. Covers all aspects, but places more emphasis on traditional markets. Lists writers' conferences and market news.

*The Writer*, 120 Boylston St., Boston, MA 02116–4615. Monthly, $27. Emphasis on traditional markets and techniques. Lists writers' conferences and market news.

## Periodicals for desktop publishers

*Board Report for Graphic Artists*, Circulation Dept., P.O. Box 4416, Denver, CO 80204–9922. Ninety-six dollars covers monthly subscription to Board Report newsletter, providing news and ideas for both in-house and freelance designers, as well as monthly *Designer's Compendium*, showing sample jobs and how they were created—plus monthly *Trademark Trends* newsletter, reviewing current creative logos being registered at U.S. Trademark Office.

*Business Publishing*, Circulation Dept., P.O. Box 5019, Brentwood, TN 37024–9846. Monthly, free to qualified professionals. Aimed directly at desktop publishers, with techniques, new products, trends. The November 1992 issue included a round-up of U.S. college degree and certificate programs in desktop publishing.

*Color Publishing*, Circulation Dept., P.O. Box 3093, Tulsa, OK 74101–9617. Bimonthly, $19.90. Coverage of high-end desktop publishing issues, technology, and techniques. May be free to qualified professionals.

*Communication Arts Magazine*, Subscription Dept., P.O. Box 10300, Palo Alto, CA 94303–9979. Four issues and four annuals each year, $50. Respected voice of the American graphic design industry, lately adding emphasis on electronic publishing.

*Computer Artist*, Subscription Service Center, P.O. Box 2649, Tulsa, OK 74101–9632. Monthly, $24.95. Solutions to problems, techniques, artist profiles, product news. May be free to qualified professionals.

*How, The Bottomline Design Magazine*, P.O. Box 12575, Cincinnati, OH 45212–9927. Six issues a year, $37. Reports on trends and techniques in graphic design. Views design as a business. Strong electronic emphasis.

*InHouse Graphics*, United Publications Group, 11300 Rockville Pike, Suite 1100, Rockville, MD 20852–3030. Monthly twelve-page newsletter, $117. Jammed with good ideas and trends for in-house publications. Aimed at your clients—corporate communicators (with corporate budgets).

*National Association of Desktop Publishers Journal*, 462 Old Boston St., Topsfield, MA 01983–9900. Monthly, $48. Free to members (see organizations for desktop publishers).

*The Page*, The Cobb Group, 9420 Bunsen Parkway, Suite 300, Louisville, KY 40220. Monthly, $69. Sixteen-page magazine serves as a visual guide to desktop publishing. Excellent articles on techniques, uses of color, design concepts, making maximum use of popular software. Mac and PC versions are available.

*Publish: The Art and Technology of Electronic Publishing*, Subscription Dept., P.O. Box 5039, Brentwood, TN 37024–9816. Monthly, $23.95. Heavy emphasis on techniques and tools for both Mac and PC environments. Features a monthly design makeover.

*Publishing and Production Executive*, 401 N. Broad St., Philadelphia, PA 19108. Monthly, free to qualified professionals. Aimed more at your customers and vendors than at you, but full of electronic publishing industry news.

*Seybold Report on Desktop Publishing*, P.O. Box 500, Media, PA 19063–9744, Monthly, $225. This costly newsletter maintains its lead in reporting on the desktop publishing industry with product reviews, news and analysis, and practical advice. Offers a free inspection copy.

*Step-by-Step Electronic Design*, P.O. Box 1901, Peoria, IL 61656–9941. Sixteen-page full-color monthly newsletter, $48. Shares techniques used to produce real-world desktop publishing projects. Subscription to both *Step-by-Step Electronic Design* newsletter and *Step-by-Step Graphics* magazine (six issues a year) is $90.

# Audiovisual Resources

Piscopo, Maria. *How to Get Paid What You Are Worth,* Newport Beach: Turner Video Communications, 1993. P.O. Box 8252, Newport Beach, CA 92658. Videotape by author, lecturer, and creative services consultant Maria Piscopo. (See Chapter Eight).

Other titles by Piscopo in this series are *How to Find and Keep New Clients, How to Create More Time and Less Stress,* and *How to Get Clients to Call You.* $29.95 each or $99.95 for all four videos.

# Source Directory

## Sources for specialized books

**Graphic Artist's Book Club,** P.O. Box 12526, Cincinnati, OH 45212–0526; (513) 531–8250; fax (513) 531–4744. Monthly flyers are sent to members listing books on graphic design techniques, desktop publishing, running a graphic arts business, legal advice.

**Polly Pattison,** 5092 Kingscross Rd., Westminster, CA 92683; (714) 894–8143. Nationally known trainer in newsletter design carries books on all aspects of designing and producing newsletters. Call or write for a listing.

**Tools of the Trade: Books for Communicators,** 3148–B Duke St., Alexandria, VA 22314–4523; (703) 823–1919; (800) 827–8665; fax (703) 823–8948. Publishes a 64-page catalog of books on desktop technology, editing, graphics and design, indexing, multimedia, newsletters, production, publishing, reference, typography, and writing. A great source for both writers and desktop publishers.

**The Writers' Computer Store,** 11317 Santa Monica Blvd., Los Angeles, CA 90025–3118; (310) 479–7774; (800) 272–8927. Publishes a 24-page catalog of books, software, and videos of interest to writers. Special emphasis on the film and television industries.

**Writer's Digest Book Club,** 1507 Dana Ave., Cincinnati, OH 45207; (513) 531–8250. Monthly flyers are sent to members listing books on the craft and business of writing, as well as books on time management and organization.

## Insurance Resources

**National Association for the Self-Employed,** 2121 Precinct Line Rd., Hurst, TX 75054; (800) 827–9990. This organization specializes in health insurance, along with purchasing and travel benefits.

**National Association of Socially Responsible Organizations,** 1925 K St., Suite 310, Washington, DC 20006; (800) 638–8113. Provides "alternatives to the health care crisis for nonprofits, small businesses, and the self-employed."

# On-line Resources

**American Online,** 8619 Westwood Center Dr., Vienna, VA 22182–2285; (800) 827–6364. Services include electronic mail, conferencing, software, computing support, interactive magazines and newspapers, and online classes.

**CompuServe,** P.O. Box 20212, Columbus, OH 43320; (800) 368–3343. One of the oldest and largest on-line information services, CompuServe offers most of the features listed above. Among its many other services are a Working from Home Forum, an Entrepreneurs Forum, a Desktop Publishers Forum, and several forums for writers.

Many other on-line services can be accessed from home-based Macs and PCs, including the worldwide Internet, designed originally for government and large technical organizations. Many on-line services specialize in specific types of information. America Online and CompuServe are both good places to hone your skills before broadening your on-line outreach.

# Other Resources

**Advertising Specialties.** A wide range of custom imprinted gifts and novelties is available from retail stores and by mail. Check your Business-to-Business Yellow Pages under advertising specialists, or look in sales and trade journals for mail order offerings that interest you and request their catalogs.

**Copyright.** For a free Copyright Information Kit or registrations forms, contact the Copyright Office, Library of Congress, Washington, DC 20559; (202) 479–0700. The office will answer specific questions, but will not provide legal advice.

**Sales Training.** John Klymshyn, of Palmdale, California, originator of the Klymshyn method for telemarketing, is cited in Chapter eight. He can be reached at (805) 265–8550.

**Service Core of Retired Executives Association** (SCORE), 409 3rd St. SW, Suite 5900, Washington, DC 20476; (202) 205–6759. SCORE, a service of the Small Business Administration (SBA), is made up of some

12,500 volunteer members nationwide—retired businesspersons who give seminars to entrepreneurs and provide free assistance to small businesses. Check with your local SBA office or Chamber of Commerce.

**Small Business Administration,** 409 3rd St. SW, Washington, DC 20476; (800) U–ASK–SBA. Personnel locator: (202) 205–6600. See current U.S. Government Manual, usually available at libraries, for the address and phone number of the SBA field office in your region, or check the phone book.

**Tax Information.** *Business Use of Your Home,* Internal Revenue Service Publication 587, may be obtained by calling (800) TAX–FORM. Specific questions about home office tax regulations can be answered by the IRS's tax information hot line, (800) TAX–1040.

**Telephone Services.** Telephone companies nationwide are strong supporters of the work-at-home movement and many provide special services for home-based entrepreneurs. Pacific Bell, for example, has a Home Office Information Line, (800) 281–8811, and publishes *The Complete Work-At-Home Companion,* available free. Check with your local phone company.

**Time Management.** Excellent pocket and desk calendar systems are available from Day-timers, Inc., One Day-Timer Plaza, Allentown, PA 18195–1551.

**Tradmarks and Service Marks.** For information on registering a trademark nationally, contact the office of Public Affairs, Patent and Trademark Office, Washington, D.C. 20231; (703) 305–8341. Offices are located at 2011 Crystal Drive, Arlington, VA 22202. The U.S. Government Printing Office, 732 North Capitol NW, Washington, D.C. 20401, sells a book for $2.00 on applying for trademarks. For information on registering a trademark or service mark in your state, contact your state department of commerce. To search for a trademark, check *The Trademark Register,* a federal periodical, or call on a trademark research firm such as Thomason and Thomason of North Quincy, Massachusetts, (800) 872–8833, or Trademark Research Center of New York, (212) 228–4084 or (800) 872–6275. Trademark is an online database produced by Thomason and Thomason and is available through CompuServe.

# Organizations

Each organization has a different emphasis and offers different services to members. Write or call for information.

## For home-based entrepreneurs

American Home Business Association, P.O. Box 995, Darien, CT 06820–0995; (203) 655–4380.

Mothers' Home Business Network, P.O. Box 423, East Meadow, NY 11554; (516) 997–7394.

National Association for the Cottage Industry, P.O. Box 14850, Chicago, IL 60614; (312) 472–8116.

National Association of Home-Based Businesses, P.O. Box 30220, Baltimore, MD 21270; (410) 363–3698

## For professional writers

American Medical Writers Association, 9650 Rockville Pike, Bethesda, MD 20816; (301) 493–0003.

American Society of Indexers, P.O. Box 386, Port Aransas, TX 78373; (512) 749–4052; fax: (512) 749–6634.

American Society of Journalists and Authors, Suite 302, 1501 Broadway, New York, NY 10036; (212) 997–00947.

Associated Business Writers of America, Suite 620, 1450 S. Havana, Aurora, CO 80012; (303) 751–7844.

Association of Great Lakes Outdoor Writers, 301 Cross, Sullivan, IN 47882–1419; phone/fax: (812) 268–6232.

Aviation/Space Writers Association, 17 S. High St., Suite 1200, Columbus, OH 43215; (614) 221–1900.

Cassell Network of Writers, Maple Ridge Rd., North Sandwich, NH 03259; (800) 351–9278.

Computer Press Association, 3661 W. Fourth Ave., #8, Vancouver, BC V6R 1P2, Canada; (604) 732–4280.

Editorial Freelancers Association, P.O. Box 2051, Madison Square Station, New York, NY 10159; (212) 677–3357.

Freelance Editorial Association, P.O. Box 835, Cambridge, MA 02238; (617) 729–9253.

Garden Writers Association of America, 10210 Leatherleaf Ct., Manassas, VA 22111; (703) 257–1032.

Independent Writers of Southern California, P.O. Box 34279, Los Angeles, CA 90034; (310) 558–4090.

International Food, Wine and Travel Writers Association, P.O. Box 13110, Long Beach, CA 90803; (310) 433–5969; fax: (310) 438–6384.

The International Women's Writing Guild, P.O. Box 810, Gracie Station, New York, NY 10028; (212) 737–7536.

Midwest Travel Writers Association, P.O. Box 3535, Omaha, NE 68103; (402) 571–4097.

Midwest Writers Association, 2315 Brown Ave., Evanston, IL 60201.

National Association of Science Writers, P.O. Box 294, Greenlawn, NY 11740; (516) 757–5664.

National Writers Association, 1450 S. Havana Suite 620, Aurora, CO 80012; (303) 751–7844.

National Writers Union, 873 Broadway, Suite 203, New York, NY 10003; (212) 254–0279.

New York Business Press Editors, 68–38 Yellowstone Blvd., Forest Hills, NY 11375; phone/fax: (718) 275–8396.

North American Ski Journalists Association, P.O. Box 5334, Takoma Park, MD 20913; (301) 864–6428.

Outdoor Writers Association of America, 2017 Cato Ave., Suite 101, State College, PA 16801; (814) 234–1011.

Philadelphia Writers Organization, P.O. Box 42497, Philadelphia, PA 19101; (215) 649–8918.

Society of American Travel Writers, 1155 Connecticut Ave. NW, #500, Washington, DC 20036; (202) 429–6639.

Society of Professional Journalists, 16 S. Jackson, Greencastle, IN 46135; (317) 653–3333.

Travel Journalists Guild, P.O. Box 10643, Chicago, IL 60610; (312) 664–9279.

Washington Independent Writers, 220 Woodward Blvd., 733 15th St. NW, Washington, DC 20005; (202) 347–4973; fax: (202) 628–0298.

Writers Connection, 1601 Saratoga-Sunnyvale Rd., Suite 180, Cupertino, CA 95014; (408) 973–0227.

# For desktop publishers

American Center for Design (formerly Society of Typographic Artists), 233 E. Ontario, Suite 500, Chicago, IL 60611; (312) 787–2018.

Association for Information and Image Management, 1100 Wayne Ave., Suite 1100, Silver Springs, MD 20910; (301) 587–8202.

Association of Imaging Service Bureaus, 5601 Roanne Way, Suite 605, Greensboro, NC 27409; (800) 844–AISB (2472).

National Association of Desktop Publishers, 462 Old Boston St., Topsfield, MA 01983; (800) 874–4113; fax: (508) 997–6117.

National Association of Printers and Lithographers, 780 Palisades Ave., Teaneck NJ 07666; (201) 342–0700; fax: (201) 692–0286.

National Association of Quick Printers, 401 N. Michigan Ave., Chicago, Ill 60611; (312) 644–6610; fax: (312) 321–6869.

Printing Industries of America, 100 Daingerfield Rd., Arlington, VA 22314; (703) 519–8158; fax: (703) 548–3227.

Society of Illustrators, 128 E. 63rd St., New York, NY 10021; (212) 838–2560.

Typographers International Association, 2233 Wisconsin Ave. NW, Washington, DC 20007; (202) 965–3400.

Ventura Publishing User Groups and CorelDRAW! User Groups. For information about local meetings and national conferences, contact Michael Bellefeuille, User Group Coordination, Corel Corporation, 1600 Carling, Ottawa, Ontario, K1Z 8R7 Canada; (613) 728–0826.

# For both writers and desktop publishers

International Association of Business Communicators, One Hallidie Plaza, Suite 600, San Francisco, CA 94102; (415) 433–3400; fax: (415) 362–8762.

Public Relations Society of America, 33 Irving Pl, 3rd Floor, New York, NY 10003–2376; (212) 995–2230; fax: (212) 995–0797.

Society for Technical Communication, 901 N. Stuart St., Arlington, VA 22203; (703) 522–4114.

Women in Communications, Inc., 2101 Wilson Blvd., Suite 417, Arlington, VA 22201; (703) 528–4200; fax: (703) 528–4205.

# Index

# About the Author

Lucy V. Parker is a fulltime writer and desktop publisher working out of her home in Orange, Ca. Her previous experience was in higher education public relations and publications and in commercial printing. A graduate of Northwestern University's Medill School of Journalism, Lucy has taught graphic design at California State University, Fullerton, and Chapman University in Orange, Ca, and often lectures on writing, graphic design, and newsletters. She is active in the Independent Writers of Southern California, the International Association of Business Communicators, and Women in Communications, Inc.

OTHER TITLES IN GLOBE PEQUOT'S

# Home-based Business Series

*How to Open and Operate a Bed & Breakfast Home*
Third Edition
by Jan Stankus - $14.95

*How to Open and Operate a Home-based Catering Business*
by Denise Vivaldo - $14.95

*How to Open and Operate a Home-based Landscaping Business*
by Owen E. Dell

*How to Open and Operate a Home-based Photography Business*
by Kenn Oberrecht

*How to Open and Operate a Home-based Secretarial Services Business*
by Jan Melnik

To order any of these titles with MASTERCARD or VISA, call toll free 1–800–243–0495; in Connecticut call 1–800–962–0973. Globe Pequot offers free shipping on orders of three or more books. There will be a $3.00 shipping charge per book when only one or two books are ordered. Connecticut residents add sales tax.

Please request a complimentary copy of Globe Pequot's book catalogue. We publish quality books on recreation, travel, nature, business, gardening, cooking, crafts, and more.

Prices and availability subject to change.